D1617074

Galula in Algeria

Galula in Algeria

*Counterinsurgency
Practice versus Theory*

GRÉGOR MATHIAS

**Translated by Neal Durando
Foreword by David H. Ucko**

Praeger Security International

 PRAEGER

AN IMPRINT OF ABC-CLIO, LLC
Santa Barbara, California • Denver, Colorado • Oxford, England

Library of Congress Cataloging-in-Publication Data

Mathias, Grigor, 1971–
   [David Galula et la contre-insurrection en Algerie. English]
   Galula in Algeria : counterinsurgency practice versus theory / Gregor Mathias ; translated by Neal Durando ; foreword by David H. Ucko.
        p. cm.
   Includes bibliographical references and index.
   "This work is the English translation of Gregor Mathias's David Galula et la contre-insurrection en Algerie: la theorie a l'epreuve des faits au Djebel Aïssa Mimoun, SHD, Vincennes, 2010 with the addition of a fifth part dealing with Galula's life between 1958 and 1962"—Preface.
   ISBN 978-0-313-39575-8 (hardcopy : alk. paper) — ISBN 978-0-313-39576-5 (ebook)   1. Galula, David, 1919–1967.   2. Algeria—History—Revolution, 1954–1962.   3. Algeria—History—Revolution, 1954–1962—Mass media and the revolution.   4. Counterinsurgency—Algeria.   I. Title.
   DT295.3.G378M38   2011
   965.0464—dc22   2011023369

ISBN: 978-0-313-39575-8
EISBN: 978-0-313-39576-5

15 14 13 12 11   1 2 3 4 5

This book is also available on the World Wide Web as an eBook.
Visit www.abc-clio.com for details.

Praeger
An Imprint of ABC-CLIO, LLC

ABC-CLIO, LLC
130 Cremona Drive, P.O. Box 1911
Santa Barbara, California 93116-1911

This book is printed on acid-free paper ∞

Manufactured in the United States of America

It is certainly easier to launch an insurgency than it is to repress it.
—David Galula, *Counterinsurgency Warfare: Theory and
Practice* FM 3–24.22, *Tactics in Counterinsurgency,*
U.S. Army Training and Doctrine Command,
April 2009, chapter 2, "Foundations of
Insurgency," pp. 2–139

In the fight between a fly and a lion, the fly cannot deliver a knock-out blow and the lion cannot fly. It is the same war for both camps in terms of space and time, yet there are two distinct warfares—the revolutionary's and, shall we say, the counterrevolutionary's.
—Mao, quoted by Galula in *Counterinsurgency
Warfare: Theory and Practice*, "Introduction"

Contents

Foreword

Mark Twain apparently quipped that while the past does not repeat itself, it certainly rhymes. So, 30 years after it had left the jungles of Vietnam and forgot all about insurgency, the U.S. military again faced the same problem, though in Iraq this time, following its invasion of the country in 2003. Counterinsurgency had been under-researched if not deliberately neglected between these two wars, so it was only natural that when it came to studying and learning about this concept many officers and scholars would turn to the 1950s and 1960s for advice. For better and for worse, insights were drawn from Vietnam and made to apply to the war in Iraq, though notable attention was also given to other countries' experiences with these types of campaigns: the British in Malaysia; the French in Algeria.

This intellectual rediscovery of counterinsurgency elevated an unlikely group of experts mostly forgotten since their heyday of the 1960s. Foremost among this group stood David Galula, a French military officer whose combat experience in Algeria and writings on counterinsurgency were viewed as particularly instructive to understanding the challenges of modern counterinsurgency. When doctrine writers from the U.S. Army and Marine Corps got together to write their new counterinsurgency doctrine in 2006, Galula's influence was evident, not least because his *Counterinsurgency Warfare: Theory and Practice* was one of three works cited in the field manual's final preface.

To those in the U.S. military seeking to gain a better understanding of counterinsurgency, Galula offered an accessible guide to the difficulties and dilemmas typical of these campaigns. From his experience in Algeria

he derived and illustrated various counterinsurgency principles that have
not only been found to apply elsewhere, but were now picked up on and
reiterated in the most recent doctrine. These touch upon the importance
of achieving a nuanced political understanding of the campaign, operating under unified command, using intelligence to guide operations, isolating insurgents from the population, using the minimum amount of force
necessary to achieve security, and assuring and maintaining the perceived
legitimacy of the counterinsurgency effort in the eyes of the populace.
Galula's writings offered a clear illustration of how these time-tested principles could be implemented based on his own experience in Algeria.

Counterinsurgency Warfare soon earned the reputation of a classic in the
field, though it would be fair to say that far more people had heard of the
book than actually studied it; indeed, it is another of Mark Twain's say-
ings that a classic is a "book which people praise and don't read." Far less
attention still has been paid to Galula's own life and *practical* record as a
counterinsurgent, of which little is known besides that which he himself
shared in his books. The result of this curious neglect has been a tendency
toward hagiography in much of the writing on Galula, underpinned by a
fundamental uncertainty of how this maverick officer himself handled
the problem of insurgency in his day.

This is where Grégor Mathias steps in, providing us with a carefully
researched, densely packed and in many ways unique account of Galula's
own practical experience with counterinsurgency. The picture that emerges
is of a remarkable and intellectually hungry French officer, a polyglot, a
traveler, explorer, and keen learner. His most formative experience with
counterinsurgency was his command of a French company in the Djebel
Aïssa Mimoun subdistrict of Kabylia, Algeria, in 1956–57; though as
Mathias makes clear, much of what he later taught derived equally from
his time as a military attaché in China during the civil war; as a member
of the UN commission in Greece during its civil war; and from his visits
the Philippines, where he observed ongoing counterinsurgencies without
himself participating.

It is said that it is a curse to live in interesting times, yet Galula appears
to have taken this fate in his stride. Indeed, his international exposure
and encounters not only help explain his fine grasp of political violence,
but also provide a fascinating narrative intertwined with major historical events. Still, perhaps this book's greatest service to counterinsurgency
scholars today is to provide a more comprehensive account of how Galula
fared when seeking to put into practice the very theory for which he is now
so famous.

It soon emerges that even for Galula, it was far easier to derive principles from ongoing campaigns than to make sure they were properly
implemented. Indeed, Mathias's account reveals a company commander
grappling with many of the same dilemmas facing today's military

leaders—in Afghanistan, Iraq, and elsewhere. While Galula was compara-
tively successful as a commander, his time in Algeria clearly shows the
limited ability of an outside force to exert legitimate influence and pressure on a local population. It also shows the difficulty of honoring the
principle of civil-military unity of command when there are tangible dif-
ferences in priority and approach between these two sets of actors. Like
many commanders today, Galula struggled with troop shortages, wres-
tled with a domestic press unconvinced of his operational gains, and out-
right stumbled in the delicate transition from French to Algerian control
and governance. Not all of Galula's setbacks can be placed at his own
doormat: after all, a company commander can only wield so much control. Even so, perhaps one of the more interesting insights in Mathias's account regards the difficulties of determining success in counterinsurgency
campaigns and the related tendency, one certainly shared by Galula, for
unwarranted optimism in the face of short-term gains.

If Galula's own record mirrors many of the frustrations felt by today's
commanders, does he nonetheless merit the reputation and influence that
he has now earned posthumously? Certainly. His writing offers one of the
most lucid and accessible treaties on counterinsurgency, helpful to any
student and practitioner seeking to understand the difficult dilemmas
common to these campaigns. His principles, while difficult to implement,
nonetheless provide a foundation upon which to base action. That Galula's
own record as a counterinsurgent is more mixed should not surprise, but
rather act as a helpful reminder that this form of warfare is never easy,
but rather "messy and slow, like eating soup with a knife."[1] Arguably, it is
precisely because Galula struggled with the same challenges that we see
today that makes his record and his writings so relevant.

For this reason, Mathias's account is also a helpful corrective to some of
the overblown and under-researched portrayals of Galula in recent years.
Neither Galula's writings, nor his experience in Algeria, were ever going
to provide us with the right answers, but rather help us ask the right questions. As Mathias persuasively shows in this book, there is no master key
to these types of operations, and Galula's principles provide no checklist
for success. This is something the French counterinsurgency expert would
no doubt have agreed with: counterinsurgency, he noted, "may be sound
in theory but dangerous when applied rigidly to a specific case."[2]

All of this—Galula's mixed record and his tentativeness in proposing
his concept—should instill a much-needed measure of humility about

---

[1] T. E. Lawrence, *Seven Pillars of Wisdom* (Ware, Herfordshire: Wordworth, 1997),
p. 182.

[2] David Galula, *Contre-insurrection: théorie et pratique* (New York: Praeger, 1964;
re-published Paris: Economica, 2008), p. 56.

what is possible in counterinsurgency operations, and through military intervention writ large. For this very reason, it is incumbent on those militaries with expeditionary ambitions to study the history of their intellectual forefathers, to learn from their experiences, and try not to repeat their mistakes.

David H. Ucko, Ph.D.[3]

[3] David H. Ucko is assistant professor at the College for International Security Affairs, National Defense University. He is the author of *The New Counterinsurgency Era: Transforming the U.S. Military for Modern Wars* (Washington, DC: Georgetown University Press, 2009) and the co-editor of *Reintegrating Armed Groups After Conflict: Politics, Violence and Transition* (New York: Routledge, 2009).

Preface

During the Algerian War, in 1956–57, Captain Galula was ordered to pacify the subdistrict Djebel Aïssa Mimoun. Galula's pacification operations in Kabylia were completely forgotten until rediscovered by U.S. general Petraeus. Petraeus and Lieutenant Colonel Nagl consider him "the Clausewitz of counterinsurgency" and speak of his book, *Counterinsurgency Warfare*, as "the greatest book written on unconventional warfare." In any case this work served as the basis for the new counterguerilla doctrine represented by U.S. Field Manual 3-24, published in December 2006 by Petraeus and Nagl. Petraeus subsequently encouraged officers serving in Iraq and Afghanistan to read it. Since January 2007, he has successfully applied Galula's ideas in Iraq and, since October 2008, at U.S. Central Command in the Middle East. General McChrystal, American and NATO force commander in Afghanistan from June 2009 to June 2010, was inspired explicitly by "the lessons taught by Lyautey and Galula on the subject of counterinsurgency" in his fight against the Taliban.[1] Major Philippe de Montenon's 2008 French translation of Galula's theoretical work demonstrates the French army's interest in the stored experiences of one of their own. The greatest tribute comes from General Ollivier,[2] commander of the Centre de Doctrine et d'Emploi des Forces (CDEF), who told a journalist: "We reread David Galula, Roger Trinquier, and Lawrence of Arabia," the principal counterinsurgency thinkers.

Even if Galula's counterinsurgency theory has reached the informed public the implementation of it in Algeria is much less known. *Pacification in Algeria* had not yet been translated into French, even though it was more frequently read in the American army than his theoretical work,

Counterinsurgency Warfare. Galula's operations described in the English-language work *Pacification in Algeria*[3] need to be made known to French speakers just as English speakers must be made aware of the French administrative and military archival records of Galula's area of operations. Moreover, Galula's is still the only analysis available, as no other objective analysis of operations in Djebel Aïssa Mimoun exists. If Galula is recognized as an excellent theoretician, it should be worthwhile considering whether he was also a good practitioner when evaluating his own operations, with respect to sources other than those he cites.[4] Therefore, it is worth analyzing exactly how Galula's actions were undertaken in his sector over the long and short term. This book was undertaken to fill the gap in the record of what happened on the ground at Djebel Aïssa Mimoun by going to the archives of the *Section administrative spécialisée* (SAS), the unit history of Galula's regiment, and reactions in the press about pacification in Kabylia.

In his preface to *Contre-insurrection*, Galula's translator, de Montenon, called for more French participation in the debate surrounding the implications of French experience fighting the *Armée de liberation nationale* (ALN) in Algeria.[5] This work is intended as a contribution to the debate about Galula's counterinsurgency methods in Algeria.

To understand Galula's operations, it is necessary to retrace the atypical career of this officer before his time in Algeria and to explain the administrative, geographical, human, and security contexts of Djebel Aïssa Mimoun, especially as he was not alone in wanting to resolve the population's problems. In his theoretical work, *Counterinsurgency Warfare*, Galula describes a sequence of eight operations necessary to pacify insurgent activity within a region. This study takes up the eight steps and compares them to methods used by Galula at Djebel Aïssa Mimoun that are described in his account *Pacification in Algeria*, his journalism, as well as in the SAS archives and unit histories.[6] Galula also pays a great deal of attention to the media, the importance of whose influence on the French and Algerian population he knew well. It is worthwhile analyzing the manner in which Galula tries to wrong foot the media or use it to his advantage. Galula's time in the Djebel Aïssa Mimoun sector lasted a little over a year. Studying the evolution of the sector after his departure reveals how long the effects of his operations lasted.

AUTHOR'S NOTE

For the English-speaking public, Algerian geographical place-names are translated to conform with *Pacification in Algeria*. In some cases they are spelled differently in French and in official documents.

Acknowledgments

To Lieutenant Colonel Noulens, whose support from the beginning of this study of Galula facilitated my access to the archives of the SHD.

To Neal Durando, who understood the importance of this work in the understanding of counterinsurgency and for his translation and help in publishing it in the United States.

To the 2009 staff ride participants of Etat-Major Force 2 (Nantes) under the command of Lieutenant General Marengo and Colonel du Vignaux, whose teaching and questions have contributed to my thinking about Galula.

Abbreviations

ACM: *actions civilo-militaires,* civil-military cooperation.

ALN: *Armée de libération nationale,* acronym for the armed rebellion fighting for the independence of Algeria.

AMG: *assistance médicale gratuite,* free medical assistance rendered to the populace by the SAS and regular army units.

ANOM: *Archives nationale d'Outre-mer d'Aix-en-Provence,* National Overseas Archives. Territorial archives of the former French empire.

BCA: *bataillon de chasseurs alpins,* mountain troops battalion.

BIC: *bataillon d'infanterie colonial,* battalion specialized in deployment within the French colonial empire.

CDEF: *Centre de Doctrine et d'Emploi des Forces,* French doctrine command.

CHPT: *compagnie de haut-parleurs et de tracts,* PSYOPs company specializing in broadcasting and publishing, equipped with loudspeakers.

CHSP: *Centre d'histoire de Sciences Politiques,* political and administrative archives of high-level officialdom.

CIMIC: Civil-military cooperation.

CMISOM: *Centre militaire de spécialisation et d'information sur l'Outre-mer,* military center for overseas information dealing with the former colonial empire during the 1960s.

CORDS: Civil Operation and Revolutionary Development Support, U.S. pacification program implemented during the Vietnam War.

CRH: *compte-rendu hebdomadaire,* twice- or thrice-weekly report (C.RH.2 and C.RH.3 respectively) written by the *sous-préfecture* SAS officer.

CSP: *Comité de salut public,* Committee for Public Welfare. Civil and military move-ment that, having assumed control of Algeria from the Fourth Republic, contrib-uted to De Gaulle's return and the creation of the Fifth Republic.

DBFA: *Demi-brigade de fusiliers de l'air,* demi-brigade, air force air assault infantry.

DIA: *Division d'infanterie alpine,* alpine infantry division.

DIC: *Division d'infanterie coloniale,* division specialized in deployment within the French colonial empire.

DOM: *Département d'Outre-Mer,* administrative offices of French overseas terri-tories.

DOP: *détachement opérationnel de protection,* intelligence unit specialized in inter-rogation.

DP: *division parachutiste,* airborne division.

DST: *Direction de la surveillance du Territoire,* a police force charged with surveil-lance and territorial security. The French equivalent of the CIA.

ENA: *Ecole nationale d'administration,* public policy and administrative school for high-level French civil servants.

FLN: *Front de libération nationale,* political branch of the Algerian independence movement.

GAD: *groupe d'autodéfense,* community defense organizations recruited from Mus-lim villagers set up and armed by the SAS

GMPR (later GMS): *groupe mobile de protection rurale,* Muslims recruited and trained by the army to operate in groups of about 100 to conduct static defense, cordons, and other operations. Equivalent to the U.S. National Guard.

HLL: *hors-la-loi,* military abbreviation for Algerian rebels (outlaws).

IEP: *Institut d'études politiques,* Institute of Political Studies.

JMO: *Journaux des marches et d'opérations,* unit histories. Daily log of a military unit's operations and a record of friendly and enemy casualties.

MIT: Massachusetts Institute of Technology, Cambridge, Massachussetts.

OAS: *Organisation de l'armée secrète,* terrorist organization including both civilians and the French military, created to oppose De Gaulle's Algerian independence policy.

ONU: *Organisation des Nations unies,* United Nations.

OPA: *Organisation politico-administrative,* political cadre of the FLN recruited among villagers. Responsible for collecting "revolutionary taxes," aiding and pro-visioning the rebels of the ALN, collecting intelligence, and spotting and eliminat-ing French sympathizers.

OTAN: *Organisation du Traité de l'Atlantique Nord,* NATO.

RAM: *régiment d'artillerie de montagne,* mountain artillery regiment.

RAMa: *régiment d'artillerie de marine,* French colonial artillery unit. Also deployed in independent African states in defense agreements with France.

RCA: *régiment de chasseurs d'Afrique,* French colonial armored unit.

REC: *régiment étranger de cavalerie,* French Foreign Legion armored regiment.

REP: *régiment étranger de parachutistes,* parachute regiment of the French Foreign Legion.

RFO: *Radio télévision française d'Outre-Mer,* French Overseas Network broadcasting.

RIC: *régiment d'infanterie coloniale,* French colonial infantry.

RIMa: *régiment d'infanterie de marine,* new name adopted in 1958 for the colonial infantry.

RTS: *régiment de tirailleurs sénégalais,* light infantry unit recruited mostly in Senegal.

SAP: *secours agricoles de prévoyance,* agricultural planning assistance organization.

SAS: *Section administrative spécialisée,* military teams living in Algerian villages, conducting pacification (constructing schools and roads and dispensing medical care), and collecting intelligence.

SAU: *Section administrative urbaine,* military teams living in Algerian slums serving the unemployed, helping the poor, building houses, and collecting intelligence.

SFOM: *Société française d'histoire de l'Outre-Mer,* French historical association founded in 1913, specialized in studying French territories and colonies in Africa, Asia, and Oceania. It publishes *Outre-mers, revue d'histoire.*

SHD: *Service historique de la Défense,* Defense Historical Service. Central French archive overseen by the army where all military documents are held.

SNP: *sans nom patronymique,* no last name. Many Algerian Muslim families had no last name to report to the census. The army and the SAS marked their identity cards with this acronym.

UNSCOB: United Nations Special Committee on the Balkans, created during the Greek Civil War.

CHAPTER 1

David Galula and the Djebel Aïssa Mimoun Subdistrict

DAVID GALULA, MAN OF ACTION AND "CLEAR-EYED OBSERVER"[1]

Before joining the fight in Algeria, Captain David Galula, was an experienced warrior and observer of asymmetrical combat. He graduated from St. Cyr at the moment of the Franco-British partnership (1939–40), with an above-average standing, 212th of 580 on leaving the military academy.[2] He chose to serve in the Sixth Moroccan colonial light infantry regiment. In September 1941, Galula, along with 95 other Jewish officers, was summarily thrown out of the officer corps as required by the Vichy anti-Jewish laws of October 3, 1940, April 11 and June 2, 1941.[3] Galula nevertheless remained under the protection of the military, serving as a spy for the Army of North Africa at Tangier from 1941 to 1943, according to information provided by Galula's widow, Ruth Morgan, and assembled from a cousin's account reported by Ann Marlowe.[4]

It is highly likely that Galula found himself either working the army's intelligence service under Colonel Rivet or in the intelligence network GILBERT. The latter was created by General Groussard, who had commanded in St. Cyr the Franco-British partnership class and served in the colonial infantry, two characteristics which he shared with Galula.[5] With the support of General Huntzinger, minister of war, he installed his network inside the Vichy regime and separate from the reconstituted French army. GILBERT operated in mainland France and in Africa and was responsible for preparing for revenge against Germany by conducting intelligence operations, training military cadres, and setting up secret arms depots. Groussard met personally with Winston Churchill to provide intelligence to British services.[6]

North Africa figured importantly for GILBERT. Groussard[7] hoped for a termination of the armistice by French authorities, after which units operating in North Africa would revolt against the Germans, supported by British landings. There was nevertheless the problem of the presence of many Axis spies who would have aired any plans of an Allied landing. Groussard's network, in which Galula played a role, exposed, monitored, neutralized, and arrested Axis spies in Morocco while protecting British and American ones. The network also was involved in preparing the Allied landing in North Africa and to consider a response in case of an invasion by Axis troops.[8] The German consulate in Tangier, as well as the one in Casablanca, was crucial in aiding propaganda, sabotage, and keeping watch on French Morocco.[9] It is likely that Galula was employed in monitoring the consulate at Tangier, neutralizing its agents, and feeding them false information. Far from idealizing the role played by a spy, Groussard describes an intelligence officer's work: "Obscure, thankless work . . . it requires an ordered, methodical, and prudent character as well as discretion and courage. . . . It also requires a focused personality, modesty, and a willingness to accept sacrifice of which few men are capable." It is therefore understandable that there were few active officers who volunteered. Until November 1942, Groussard complained of the passivity of armistice-army officers in North Africa.[10] Galula's service record shows he was officially reinstated to the army on July 9, 1943, nine months after the Allied landings in North Africa. What had Galula been doing during this period? It is quite possible, according to the novelist Seymour Topping who had known Galula while a journalist in China, that he served as a liaison officer to the U.S. Army during the North African landings in 1942, which would have allowed him to improve his knowledge of English.[11]

Galula was officially reinstated into the First Army by General Giraud in July 1943. In October 1944, he participated in the liberation of Europe, distinguishing himself on Elba by taking 50 German prisoners, among them 2 officers.[12] The U.S. Army newspaper *Stars and Stripes* of June 24, 1944, characterized the invasion of Elba as "the toughest of all the Mediterranean invasions."[13] As a communications and intelligence officer of the 1/21st Colonial Infantry Regiment (RIC) he fought during the encirclement and liberation of Belfort in November 1944. In upper Alsace, he took part in the liberation of the city of Mulhouse, fighting at Cité Sainte Barbe (Wittenheim) in January 1945.

Within the 9th Colonial Infantry Division (DIC), the 1/21st RIC took part in the occupation of Germany. Although French forces were expecting conventional warfare within German territory, they also feared asymmetrical conflict with Werewolf units. These paramilitary units made up of Hitler Youth and veterans dressed as civilians, were thought to be ready to conduct behind-the-lines sabotage of military vehicles, poisoning wells and food, and harassing or attacking Allied troops. The units received clear instructions on countermeasures.[14] The 1/21st RIC took a part of the city of Karlsruhe, where it ran into barricades, snipers, and small antitank teams with automatic weapons. South of Karlsruhe, the 1/21st RIC was faced with an enemy applying the principles of conventional warfare: at Mersch, it came up against a line of barbed wire over watched by block-houses, the so-called West Wall, a less-elaborate German version of the Maginot Line. The unit took the town of Rastatt, defended by snipers.[15] The 1/21st RIC was then ordered to take the narrow Kinzig Valley, which the Germans defended village by village, before refusing combat to escape encirclement. General de Lattre remembered this fight speaking of "the difficulties in moving up the Kinzig Valley."[16] Neustadt was the last town taken by the 1/21st RIC in April 1945. The different commanders of the 1/21st RIC wrote of Galula, saying "he showed himself in combat as an experienced and driven platoon leader" (1944) and that he was an "active and intelligent" officer (1945).[17] Within the units of the 9th DIC participating in the same campaigns as the 1/21st RIC, was the 24th Senegalese Light Infantry Regiment (RTS), of whose second company of the first battalion was commanded by Lieutenant Colonel Guillermaz, a sinologist, reporting to the intelligence section of the French embassy in China since 1937, who observed the Sino-Japanese War. Guillermaz explained that he returned to Europe "to obtain the names of officers from the colonial units qualified for our intelligence service in China and two officers to study Chinese."[18] One could well imagine that Galula's qualities as an officer and his experience as an intelligence agent in Tangier made him the best candidate for this mission. Recruited to Guillermaz's team, Galula left for China with Captains Bourgeois and Léouzon, and Major Raymond.[19]

From 1945, Galula found himself posted to countries in the grip of guerrilla warfare. In his writings he refers to his experience as an observer of counterinsurgency methods.[20] Posted to Calcutta, he spent two months learning Mandarin Chinese. He was subsequently named military attaché to Beijing from 1945 to 1949, at the moment the Chinese communists were taking power. The type of intelligence work undertaken by Galula at Beijing was probably the same sort done by Guillermaz at Nanjing—that is, analyzing press releases and the journalism of the belligerents, studying orders of battle, operations, communist documents, and gathering information by talking with U.S. correspondents and British and American diplomats. French intelligence in China had objectives other than studying the conflict between Chinese nationalists and communists. Rather, it had been ordered to find out whether the Chinese communists would take control of the border with Indochina and when.[21] From interviews conducted by Marlowe[22] with Morgan, we know that Galula spent time at Beijing with the journalist Topping, who had served as an officer in World War II and who covered the Chinese Civil War from 1946 to 1949 and then the French Indochina War for the Associated Press. Topping would go on to be a foreign correspondent for the *New York Times* for more than 32 years in Moscow and Hong Kong. He was also an editor, professor at the Columbia University School of Journalism, and author of *Fatal Crossing: A Novel of Vietnam* and *Journey between Two Chinas* as well as being an administrator of the Pulitzer Prize. According to Marlowe, Topping wrote of Galula in *Peking Letter: A Novel of China's Civil War,* under the pseudonym J. Leone, whom he describes as "a military attaché at the French consulate," whose presence corresponds exactly with Galula's.[23] Galula is described as "cynical and worldly, a connoisseur of fine food and wine," according to Marlowe. The book also portrays him as incredulous of the nationalists' pronouncements of victory over the communists and as holding a cynical view of the Chinese conflict: "civil war is a game played between generals and politicians."[24] This vision of war as a game is actually found in Galula's writing.[25]

By this time, Galula had mastered Mandarin. Guillermaz remarks in 1947 that "he speaks Mandarin fluently and interprets written texts well." Galula's perfect knowledge of Mandarin doubtlessly owes to the courses he took at the missionary language school situated near the diplomatic quarter.[26] Having a very open mind, "he knew the geography, history, and customs of this country extremely well." Galula studied the customs and attitudes of the Chinese population with which he was in contact.[27] Knowledge of the language and customs would serve him well; in April 1947, while traveling alone by jeep, he was captured in the Shanxi region and detained for a week receiving good treatment from communist troops. In *Counterinsurgency Warfare,* Galula explains[28] that his detention allowed him to discuss politics, strategy and tactics, and to observe the treatment of prisoners by political commissars, the communist military leadership, of whom General Ch'en Keng was "one of the best communist generals" according to Guillermaz. He claims that Galula reported on the military situation in Shanxi province based on his observations and interviews with political and military leaders in Mao's communist army. This report is reproduced without citation in General Chassin's book, *La conquête de la Chine par Mao Tsé* (*Mao's Conquest of China*).[29] Chassin, a theoretician of the French school of revolutionary warfare, is considered "one of the most important and interesting military authors" by Professor F. Géré.[30] An air force general, Chassin commanded the expeditionary air force in Indochina (1951–53) and was commander in chief of the territorial air defense from 1953 to 1956. He founded and directed the French *Air Force Review.* He has given us his work, *Histoire militaire de la Deuxième guerre mondiale,* which was recognized by the Académie Française, and two works on Mao's rise to power. He also wrote several articles on revolutionary warfare, among them "The Ideological Role of the Army"[31] and "Toward the Encirclement of the West."[32]

It is easy to identify Galula as the author of the report cited by Chassin as he describes the author of the report as "a French observer of communist operations in the south of Shanxi in 1947." The nationality, date, and geographical location (Shanxi in Chassin's book; Xinjiang, in the southwest of Shanxi in Galula's) correspond exactly with the time and place of Galula's capture. The report is a summary of battles, tallying losses (dead, wounded, and captured) suffered by the nationalists and the communists: "The capture of Houma cost the Reds two hundred killed and wounded, but brought them eighteen hundred prisoners, including a brigadier general. The capture of the town of Sinkiang cost them four wounded, and they took six hundred prisoners. . . . The capture of Kuwo, defended by two Nationalist regiments and attacked by three Red regiments, yielded the Communists two thousand prisoners—the entire garrison." He gives a number of indications of the nationalists' weak morale: "the Nationalists do not bother to destroy their weapons before they surrender. . . . The lack of fighting spirit shown by the common soldier demonstrates the degree to which the Nationalist army has disintegrated. . . . Their troops do not want to fight."[33] In *Counterinsurgency Warfare,* Galula places more emphasis on the treatment of the thousands of nationalist prisoners taken by the communists, which rounds out the report reproduced by Chassin. As a political commissar explains to Galula: "We leave them the choice between joining the communist forces; settling in communist territory, where they will receive a patch of land to cultivate; go home; or return to the Nationalist army." In the prison camp of 200 officers that he visited as an uninvited guest of the communist Chinese, "the author asked a group of prisoners in Chinese whether anyone among them had already been captured by the communists. Three Nationalist officers admitted that this was the second time they had been captured." Galula explains that, at the same time, another French military attaché visited a communist prison camp at Hangzhou and confirmed that most of the inmates were previously released nationalists who were now mistrusted by their own side.[34]

The conclusions Galula drew from this experience differ on comparing his 1947 report with the one found in his 1964 book. In 1947, he emphasized the transformation of nationalist prisoners into excellent communist fighters: "After Communist indoctrination and political instruction, the ex-Nationalist soldier, typically passive and disheartened until then, becomes an enthusiastic and aggressive fighting man."[35] In hindsight, Galula only mentions in passing in his 1964 book *Counterinsurgency Warfare* that "the Communists had achieved the trick of having the nationalists themselves watching their own men!"[36] In the 1947 report, Galula explains the communists' victories as owing to well-organized headquarters. "The Communist plan clearly shows not only the sound logic of its conception, but a perfect unity of views in the Communist high command, since it calls for the close coordination between the theaters of operation commanded by General Ho Lung and by General Liu Po-ch'eng. This is in marked contrast to the Nationalists, who have always found it extremely difficult to get their generals to cooperate, and even more so to get them to do it on their own initiative."[37] This aspect does not appear in *Counterinsurgency Warfare*, rather, Galula continues with the 1947 operations to illustrate the idea that, in revolutionary warfare, when the insurgent puts pressure on one region, the counterinsurgent cannot shrink from the pressure in attacking another region. He cites this example, "the Chinese Nationalists launched an offensive against Yen'an, the Communist capital," that he developed in a previous chapter of his book.[38] Chassin's book sheds some light on Galula's remarks. In 1947, the nationalists launched several offensives in Northern China to "cut apart communist zones," fortified Manchuria, and conducted operations on the Liaoning Peninsula and at Rèhé Sheng. Chassin added that the nationalist offensive in Yan'an mounted "with their best troops," intended to be a decisive success in taking the communist capital. Chassin continued, "The battle only influenced the evolution of operations in allowing the Reds to conduct a timely maneuver putting the attacking forces in a delicate position. To maintain liaison between the Yan'an and Shandong regions" the communists launched a diversionary operation to fix a maximum of nationalist forces in a strategic trap in the Northeastern provinces supporting Chiang Kai-shek consisting of five offensives in Manchuria and one in Jehol.[39] Following Chassin's line of thinking, these operations conducted by nationalist troops, three or four times more numerous in Manchuria and Jehol, were an error but not that of Yan'an, which was only a symbolic goal for the nationalists. Galula, therefore, uses an inappropriate example to support his idea.

To construct his theory, one can well imagine that Galula consulted Chassin's book. We even find two identical facts cited in both books. The sentence about the communist situation in China, August 1945, is practically the same: the facts concerning the area controlled by each side, the number of inhabitants, the size of the armies and militias are all the same; only the territory controlled by the communists is different.[40] Galula describes communist policy toward farmers in their zone as "strict control of rents and interest rates," which is information also found in Chassin's book which is in turn taken from General Stilwell's book.[41] In *Counterinsurgency Warfare*, Galula doesn't cite Chassin even though he cites four other sources in this study of China.[42] It does seem surprising that Galula doesn't reuse Chassin's analyses in the chapters dealing with "Chiang Kai-shek's Counterrevolutionary Warfare" or about Mao, "The Military Principles of the Liberation Army" or his conclusion on "The Reasons for Mao's Triumph" which would have handily completed his analysis of counterinsurgency.[43] This suggests that Galula used Chassin's work very superficially, preferring instead to rely more heavily on his

personal experience at the risk of de-emphasizing other essential information.

Chassin is not Galula's sole source on Mao's strategy. Marlowe[44] shows
us that he also read the writing of Captain Samuel B. Griffith closely. As
Mao's theory and strategy had still to be translated in the 1950s, Galula
studied them in English, by means of Griffith's translation of Mao published in the *Marine Corps Journal* in 1947.[45] Author of a philosophy thesis
in 1960 on Sun Tzu (the sixth-century strategist), Griffith next translated
The Art of War,[46] which had a huge influence on Mao's strategic thinking. Galula knew Griffith well as they had met in northern China where
Griffith commanded a Marine regiment at the end of World War II.

Galula explains clearly that a would-be counterinsurgent "will not find
in Mao and in other revolutionary theorists the answers to his problems,"[47]
and doesn't hesitate to quote him several times. In the introduction he paradoxically quotes Mao which emphasizes the need to study "the laws of
war and of revolutionary warfare."[48] He begins by evoking the struggle
between guerrillas and counterguerillas, which he compares to a chess
game of infinite combinations. "The campaigns and battles which the
enemy brings against us and those we bring against the enemy resemble
the taking of pawns and our bases of support resemble the squares on the
board."[49] Galula also takes up Mao's thoughts about the importance of
the guerrilla's rear-area bases. "Combat without a rear-area base is nothing more than itinerant banditry: [the guerilla is] incapable of maintaining
a link to the population, he cannot flourish and is condemned to defeat."[50]
Chassin reproduces extracts from Mao's *Problems of Strategy in China's Revolutionary War* quoting exactly: "[We] oppose the purely military view-
point and the ways of roving rebels, and recognize that the Red Army is
a propagandist and organizer of the Chinese Revolution. We are against
banditry and for strict political discipline."[51] It may be noted that the quote
was considerably shortened and transformed by Galula to evoke guerrilla
warfare. There are also similarities between Galula's thought and Mao's
tactics described in numbered steps[52] for the geographical advantages for
the guerrilla.[53]

This initial experience in China seems to have counted for a lot in developing Galula's counterinsurgency doctrine. The first three chapters of
Counterinsurgency Warfare are based primarily on his Chinese experience
and describe the general traits of revolutionary warfare, the victory conditions of insurrection, and insurgent doctrine. His conclusion emphasizes a
Chinese geopolitical vision.

In China, Galula did not confine his attentions to Mao's strategic
thought; he broadened his knowledge of the country and its people. Following Galula's lead, Guillermaz travelled with him twice by jeep. In May
1947, they traveled through the northwestern provinces to Lanzhou, Sin-
ing, and Tsinghai, then completely under the control of Muslim nationalists, finally reaching the border of Tibet and the start of the Silk Road. They

met different military governors and the Panchen Lama, the second most important religious figure in Tibet, a rival to the Dalai Lama. In January 1949, when the communists threatened Nanjing, they went to the headquarters of a nationalist division at Ts'ai Shih and an army headquarters at Tang Tu to study the defenses.[54] Guillermaz appreciated Galula's initiative and resourcefulness, praising the young officer as "a brilliant, quick-witted officer. Conscientious and hardworking, a knowledgeable and engaged observer."[55] The various reports sent by the intelligence section of Guillermaz to Paris and Saigon (to General Salan) were the product of teamwork. Guillermaz, in reviewing the merits and qualities of his team explained, "Captain Galula displayed a fertile, quick mind in discussions and interpretations of events."[56]

After his time as a military attaché in China, Galula became part of the UN commission in Greece from 1949 to 1950. He was an UNSCOB observer on the border between Macedonia and Thrace, where he supported the operations of Greek forces against the communist guerillas at Mount Gramos. The guerillas had taken refuge in this mountain chain, whose summits reached 2,500 meters (8,200 feet). The guerilla fighters, numbering about 12,000, controlled three inaccessible valleys surrounded by alpine forests on the Bulgarian border. After an initial failure in 1948, the army seized Mount Gramos in August 1949 and put and end to the civil war.[57] In *Counterinsurgency Warfare*, Galula explains the causes for the Greek communists' defeat as owing to organizational errors, unfavorable geography, and the withdrawal of support from bordering communist countries.[58] During a counterinsurgency seminar in the United States, Galula advanced a further explanation: "During the Greek Civil War, the communists organized commando-type operations rather than more ordinary guerrilla actions. Infiltrating the terrain and operating behind the Greek lines was easy, but they failed to implant themselves, lacking the population's support. When they did contact the population, they were reported and arrested."[59] As a UN observer, Galula facilitated the delicate relations between UN observers and the Bulgarian authorities, allied with the communist insurgency in Greece. Owing to his language skills, he was appreciated by foreign delegations to the UN, notably the Chinese "by their own admission," according to the report of the commander of the French military mission to UNSCOB in 1949.

After the communists took power in China, Guillermaz became chief of post to the British concession in Hong Kong. But the post was underfunded and understaffed, although it was "a good position for observing Chinese affairs." He requested a transfer and suggested Galula as a replacement.[60] Galula's Chinese career owes a great debt to General Guillermaz, with whom Galula maintained correspondence between 1954 and 1956.[61] Guillermaz later became advisor to the French delegation at the Geneva conference on the future of Vietnam in 1954. In 1958, he founded and directed the Center for Documentation and Research on Contemporary

China at the Ecole des Hautes Etudes en Sciences Sociales. He wrote several reference books on China, including *A History of the Chinese Communist Party*.[62]

From 1951 to 1956, Galula was a military attaché in China at Hong Kong, where he was reported to be "a reliable expert on Far East questions." His inquiring mind was noted by his superiors. "He didn't hesitate to leave the confined atmosphere of western military advisors in Hong Kong," and kept company with Europeans as well as Chinese to gather information about the situation in China.[63] Fascinated by the Chinese people, in 1964 Galula went so far as to write a book (under the pseudonym of Jean Caran) called *Les moustaches du tigre*[64] (The Tiger's Whiskers) in which he describes the mindset of the Chinese and European population of Hong Kong with a great deal of humor. By his description of the travels of the Chinese in Hong Kong, he demonstrates the application of communist terror on the mainland and the consequence of the Korean War on Hong Kong- and Maoist-Chinese society. Over the course of several humorous anecdotes, he describes the Chinese mindset, religious beliefs, and relations between Hong Kong and the Chinese diaspora, love of gambling and trade, and the British surveillance of the Chinese community in Hong Kong. The publisher, Flammarion, described the author in 1964 as "one of the most penetrating observers of contemporary China," and explained that it was written under a pseudonym "because the author deals with serious matters."

Galula's mission necessitated that he associate with American journalists on a daily basis, which allowed him to gather information and attend the Canal Road Press Club, just as his predecessor had done.[65] Galula rubbed elbows with journalists like Henry Luce and Joseph Alsop. Luce, a journalist at *Time* magazine,[66] was also the founder of *Fortune* and *Life*. Whereas Alsop was a journalist at the *New York Herald Tribune*, and later, at the *Saturday Evening Post* and *Newsweek*. Later these two influential journalists would visit his subdistrict in Kabylia and write about him. Galula was very familiar with American journalists and had a network that contributed to his reputation in the United States.

From Hong Kong, he visited the Philippines twice to study the communist Huk rebellion. In Hong Kong he met and conversed with French, British, and American officers, such as General Salan and the American general Landsdale, returning from Indochina, Malaysia, and the Philippines, where they had been fighting communist guerillas.[67] His position allowed him to meet many people involved in counterguerilla operations, yet this did not mean his view was comprehensive. In the novel he wrote under the name of Caran, Galula explained that Hong Kong was a rest and recreation spot and stopover, just as Japan was for the ships of the American Seventh Fleet operating off the Korean coast since 1952.[68] During the Korean War the Americans undertook two major counterguerilla operations, RAT KILLER (December 1951 to March 1952) and TRAMPLE

(December 1953 to June 1954); Galula makes no mention of them in contrast to the other counterinsurgency theoretician, Roger Trinquier, who was fighting in Indochina during this time.[69]

Meeting these other officers who had experimented with counterinsurgency methods allowed him to gather information on guerilla warfare which he would later use in his doctrine, even at risk of misinterpretation (as was the case with China). Lieutenant Colonel M. David,[70] doctor of history, specialist in the anticommunist militias in Indochina, raises another of Galula's misinterpretations, this time concerning the French operation ATLANTE launched in central Indochina while the battle of Diên Biên Phu was being fought in the northwest of the country.[71] Galula used this example to illustrate the idea that in revolutionary warfare, when the insurgent puts pressure on one region, the counterinsurgent cannot shrink from the pressure in attacking another region. David said, "The French command never thought of operation ATLANTE as a diversion to relieve the pressure on the garrison on Diên Biên Phu. ATLANTE, to the contrary, had been prepared beforehand and took place according to plan, in spite of the battle at Diên Biên Phu."[72] The objective of ATLANTE was to place the pacification of the south in the hands of the young Vietnamese army within the framework of Vietnamization of the war and to protect the region's rice supply.[73]

When Galula arrived as an officer in Algeria, he already had solid conventional warfare experience behind him, having fought at Elba, Belfort, Alsace, and in Germany. He had observed two guerilla wars on the ground, in China and Greece. He had served as a World War II intelligence officer, later as a military attaché in China, and his superiors considered him a good observer. He knew how to get noticed in reports and how to play on his charisma with foreigners and superiors. He focused on new forms of guerilla warfare in Asia (Burma, China, and Indochina) and counterguerilla intervention (Indochina, Malaysia, Philippines) through meetings, travel, and reading. A good linguist in English and Mandarin, he knew how to adapt to foreign attitudes and cultures perfectly. Finally, he knew the people and mindset of the Maghreb, having been born in Sfax, Tunisia, and with his parents living in Morocco. He had spent his childhood in Marrakech and later commanded Moroccans in a colonial infantry regiment. Better preparation for company command in the Algeria War is difficult to imagine.

CAPTAIN GALULA'S SUBDISTRICT AND HIS RELATION WITH THE SAS

Galula was given command of a company at Djebel Aïssa Mimoun.[74] The town is situated in Kabylia on the slopes of a mountain (*djebel*) which reaches 801 meters (2,627 feet) and is located five kilometers (three miles) to the north-east of Tizi Ouzou. On Djebel Aïssa Mimoun, the villages of Bou Souar and Igonane Ameur are one kilometer (a little more than half a mile) apart as the crow flies but the terrain is so rugged that it takes 45 minutes to travel between them, owing to the ravine that lies between. The zone that was Galula's subdistrict is bordered by the wadis Stita and Sebaou, and by the Tizi-Ouzou-Tikobain road. According to Galula's figures, the population numbered around 15,000.[75] However, SAS reports of Djebel Aïssa Mimoun claim there were less than half of that number. The subdistrict of Djebel Aïssa Mimoun was closer to 7,000 inhabitants,[76] while the battalion's entire area of operations approached 12,000.[77] The population was poor in the north around Tahanouts, extremely poor in the center, and relatively well-off around Akaoudj. The forests of Mizrana and Yakouren (in the Azazga region) were traditional refuges for the ALN.

The companies of the 45th BIC (colonial infantry battalion) were responsible for the sector. Galula's company's subdistrict consisted of the villages Igonane Ameur, Bou Souar, Ighouna, and Grand Remblai. To the north and east, the Tahanouts region was under fourth company's responsibility and, to the west, Akaoudj fell under the second company. The SAS archives give us an overview of all the aspects of pacification in the three subdistricts, for the SAS headquarters for Aïssa Mimoun was at Grand Remblai.

In *Pacification in Algeria 1956–1958*, Galula accurately describes the condition of the armed forces operating in Aïssa Mimoun. He also mentions Lieutenant Bauer, the commander of the Djebel Aïssa Mimoun SAS: "Lieutenant Bauer had recently replaced Lieutenant Villon. . . . A Foreign Legion cavalry officer, he had specialized in native affairs in Morocco. He applied for a transfer to a Legion unit in Algeria after Morocco became independent, but was instead assigned to an SAS job. He was very bitter about it. He had lost any illusion about the Muslims in Morocco, where he had seen them turning suddenly from genuine friendliness to murderous savagery on the eve of independence."[78] "Bauer" is a pseudonym, as with all officers named in the book, adopted here to speak of Lieutenant Pfirrmann, an officer from Alsace. He replaced Lieutenant Colomb Clerc ("Villon") in the post from October 1955 to September 1956. Clerc served as an artilleryman before becoming an SAS officer. Following an ambush near a village, he was ordered to evacuate the populace so that the village could be destroyed. Clerc warned the villagers to evacuate, but the commanding general reversed his decision without warning and the village was left intact. Having lost his credibility with the population along with his motivation, he asked for a transfer to his original regiment based on the Tunisian border.[79] Pfirrmann still remembers him: "My predecessor didn't speak the language. He didn't have what it took to be an SAS officer."[80] Pfirrmann replaced him at the end of September 1956 and he commanded the SAS until April 1957.[81] He described, in report after report, the manner in which he perceived the evolution of SAS pacification in the area of operations of the 45th BIC, including Galula's subdistrict.

Pacification was the responsibility of the head of the SAS, who was an officer detached from Algerian Affairs, dealing with two or three villages. He was the local representative of the prefecture as well as the military district, with the responsibility of reporting his activity in the *sous-préfecture*. The SAS archives of Djebel Aïssa Mimoun[82] are exceptionally well preserved with all the reports from 1956 to 1957 present, averaging three reports per month. Such regularity is fairly rare, as during this period bimonthly reports are the norm with the SAS. Finally, the archives are almost entirely complete,[83] a rarity for the SAS. The only defect in the documents is the quality of the ink, which is sometimes only barely legible. But the quantity of reports allows us to fill in some of the missing information. Three times a month, the SAS officer from Djebel Aïssa Mimoun wrote an 11-point report called a C.RH.3 (*compte-rendu hebdomadaire*): (1) Operations; (2) Patrols; (3) Harassment; (4) Arrests; (5) Schools; (6) Medical Assistance; (7) Relief Efforts; (8) SAS Officer Outreach; (9) Agricultural Planning (SAP, *secours agricoles de prévoyance*); (10) Inspections; and (11) Miscellaneous. This last category gave the SAS officer an opportunity to express his general opinion of the situation, especially when expressing any grievances, with total honesty. In November 1956, a new report format was adopted. The report, called "C.RH.2" reduced the number of categories to (1) Operations with political impact; (2) Schools (this category only included changes in staffing, student and staff morale, as well as other school needs); (3) Medical assistance including the number of doctors, dispensaries, outcomes of care, and progress in eliminating disease; (4) Inspections and persons of interest; and (5) Political situation. In the weekly reports from the SAS archives on Djebel Aïssa Mimoun we also find remarks from the director of the mixed community (equivalent to a subprefect), which is fairly rare for this sort of record. The SAS archives are complete from 1958 to 1960, allowing us long-term perspective on Galula's operations in his subdistrict.

The richness of civil and military information in the record reflects the scope of the mission given to the SAS, the current equivalent in the French army to *actions civilo-militaires* (ACM) or in NATO parlance civil-military cooperation (CIMIC). The SAS, the special administrative sections, were created by the governor general of Algeria Jacques Soustelle[84] modeled on the Moroccan Bureau of Indigenous Affairs of Lyautey. Its mission was to maintain contact with the population and collect the intelligence necessary for successful operations. The absence of officers familiar with the population was keenly felt in 1955 and the vestigial local administration had been swept away by the insurgency. Soustelle implemented the SAS to administer the villages in Algeria to combat the economic misery and political inequality that were the root causes of the insurgency. With their civilian personnel and Muslim auxiliary troops, they were the administrative intermediaries responsible for development of their districts. They rebuilt schools burnt by the ALN—or created them *ex nihilo*—and enrolled both boys and girls. They cared for the sick by establishing free medical assistance. They conducted censuses to establish welfare services and organized elections for municipal officials. They improved agriculture and husbandry, built roads and bridges, dug wells, provided for sanitation in the villages, and built houses for people who had been resettled. They built work camps for unemployed men and distributed benefits and family allowances. They improved living conditions for women, setting up meeting places and workrooms for them, and taught hygiene. Within the population, SAS officers were responsible for resolving conflicts (*chicayas*) between inhabitants, rendering them de facto judges. In military terms, SAS officers dismantled the efforts of the *organization politico-administrative* (OPA) of the FLN and collected intelligence on the ALN. They protected the villages with their auxiliaries (*moghaznis*), by patrolling, setting day and night ambushes, as well as desert operations. They controlled supply and movement of the population to keep them from any contact with the rebels. SAS officers were even able to arm village self-defense militias and rally members of the ALN to the French side. In some cases they were able to take over the responsibility of an entire sector from the army once the level of insurgent activity had been significantly reduced. Galula summarizes an SAS officer's mission like this: "To confine soldiers to purely military functions while urgent and vital tasks have to be done . . . would be senseless. The soldier must then be prepared to become a propagandist, a social worker, a civil engineer, a schoolteacher, a nurse, a boy scout."[85]

Galula realized the importance of the SAS in the sector and discussed its creation and mission on page 24 of *Pacification in Algeria* and attributes the following mission to them: "Static forces, permanently assigned to an area, where they would deploy in a grid, track the rebels in their own area, and work on the population in liaison with the SAS." However, pacification wasn't their only responsibility according to Galula: "The company commander in his subdistrict, being directly in contact with the population, had the key job in the war. Echelons above him could always issue orders. He was the man who had to translate them into concrete action. And in the absence of sensible orders from above, he had to make his own if he wanted to achieve anything. For the SAS officer was absolutely unable to operate as long as the area was not reasonably safe, and to make it safe required at least the control of the population, and preferably the cooperation of the population. In other words, the SAS officer was effective only when the basic problem was solved."[86] Galula noted that there was competition between the missions of the SAS officer and the subdistrict company. The company had certain advantages over the SAS officer in the force it could employ, while the SAS officer's only force was that of persuasion. Galula neglected to clarify, however, that the company should shed its repressive role, after which it was to be taken in by the populace who would forget past grievances committed in the area by other units. It is true that under Galula's orders, his company established good relations with the residents. Under conditions where the rebellion was on the defensive in Djebel Aïssa Mimoun and shunning all contact, the company could devote itself to pacification work. To the contrary, where the rebellion was strong and aggressive, the company spent most of its time protecting itself and trying to come into contact with the rebels. It had neither the time nor the energy to devote to the population. Thanks to the geographical location of the SAS post and the zones of rebel activity, effective, coordinated action between the SAS and Galula's company was easy. Indeed, the SAS did not have a permanent presence throughout the subdistrict, although platoons from Galula's company did and could therefore serve as an efficient link for SAS operations.

The SAS at Djebel Aïssa Mimoun played an essential role in the pacification of Galula's subdistrict. The problems stemmed from the difference of status between the SAS and the regular military in the sector. One might ask, as Galula did, whether the SAS should have been subordinate to Galula or whether it should have been entirely independent of his unit. On paper, the SAS officer was subordinate to the sector commander. In practice, he was commanded by the civil administration of the *sous-préfecture*. The competing military and civilian hierarchies caused many problems for SAS officers. An SAS officer could accept the authority of the subdistrict commander or he could try to remain totally independent. The SAS also could interpret its mission as falling under the control of the subdistrict commander or even as having complete operational liberty.[87] Galula doesn't equivocate. The subdistrict SAS should be subordinated for the following reasons: "Doing this kind of work on the population in depth with an elite of Native Affairs Officers who had done nothing else during their entire career was one thing. But 600 new SAS officers could not become experts overnight. Their action would have to be closely supervised. SAS officers, besides, could not operate unless a reasonable degree of security was provided by the Army."[88] The limits of this line of reasoning owe to the fact that the SAS at Djebel Aïssa Mimoun was led by a former Native Affairs Officer who couldn't be influenced in the same way as a young, inexperienced SAS officer. When Galula took command of the third company of the 45th BIC in August 1956, Pfirrmann arrived about a month later. "Lt. Bauer [Pfirrmann] was a disciplined, conscientious, and able officer. We worked together very well after he realized that I had other goals in mind than distributing candies to local children."[89] It would seem Galula discussed his strategy at length with Pfirrmann and gradually won him over. Today, Pfirrmann remembers the time: "We spoke together discretely to avoid compromising the SAS or the army. He told me stories about his time in China as a military attaché." The subject of subordination of the SAS with respect to Galula's company seems to deserve some revision. Galula and Pfirrmann's views were rather close even if "they weren't 100% in agreement." We can say more about the shared pragmatism and mutual support between Galula and the SAS officer: "When Galula had an idea he would ask my opinion. When the SAS needed resources Galula secured them. It worked out well." With respect to chain of command problems, Pfirrmann remembers that they were both subordinates in their respective hierarchies, but at the same time they both enjoyed a large degree of freedom of action. "Galula never deviated from his colonel's orders. Myself, I was under the orders of the subprefect. Everyone did his job. He [Galula] was not the sector commander. We were constantly told that the SAS was under the orders of the civil and military area command."[90] This vision does not correspond to the position taken by Galula, who said that coordination and subordination of the civil structure of the SAS to the military allowed a greater economy of force. Galula applied this method with greater success over the short time Lieutenant Brousse, Pfirrmann's replacement, was on leave. The tone of the SAS officer's reports changes with respect to the subdistrict commander; there is a complete convergence of opinion on community representation and child policies (November 26 and 29, 1956). In practice, however, the civil and military structure of the SAS operated in conjunction with companies in the subdistrict, with each authority engaged in turf wars.

INSECURITY AT DJEBEL AÏSSA MIMOUN: "IT WASN'T EXACTLY HELL!"

Galula describes rebel forces at Djebel Aïssa Mimoun, which were located in the ALN district Wilaya 3, Zone 3 (Tizi-Ouzou). The local ALN leader Oudiaï recruited in the villages of Bou Souar and Igonane Ameur. "With a minimum of executions here and there, he established his power over the populace. . . . Oudiaï rapidly attracted to his groups volunteers from the other villages and was soon officially recognized by the FLN as the boss of his *douar*." Oudiaï's unit consisted of 25 men, divided into two platoons, each led by a sergeant. With no other targets, Oudiaï ambushed civilian cars on nearby roads. At Khelouyene, where the populace showed little support, Oudiaï forced them to destroy the only school at Aïssa Mimoun, constructed in 1950, attended by two classes of 60 students. The patrol sent to investigate the demolition was itself ambushed at Ighouna. In retaliation, the inhabitants of Ighouna were forced to leave the village and were resettled at Igonane Ameur. Oudiaï named an FLN chief in each village and hamlet, who in turn selected two lieutenants. Cells of the OPA indentified suspects: people hostile to the movement, skeptics who lacked confidence in the future victory, people who refused to pay the FLN's taxes. The OPA collected the FLN tax (500 to 50,000 francs per month according to the wealth of the individual) which sometimes reached as much as 900,000 francs per month, or "the equivalent of a day's aid to the populace." The OPA's propaganda targeted the *djemaa* (the village council of elders). The OPA also organized popular support of the rebellion in terms of lookouts, lodging, food, and supplies. It organized a parallel government,[91] made all the easier by the absence of any other in the villages and supplanted the judiciary of the *cadi* (Muslim judges) of Tizi-Ouzou.[92]

But in terms of military affairs, the ALN did not pose a great danger, as Galula wrote in an article published in the journal *Contacts* in April 1957.[93] "Only the remnants of bands, incapable of action, remain." Four nightly ambushes in his subdistrict are without result after three months. It was a sign that "thanks to their reduced numbers . . . their complete elimination could only be achieved with the cooperation of the populace." According to Pfirrman's recollection, the "work of the SAS at Djebel Aïssa Mimoun was easier than in other regions. It wasn't exactly hell! Being [stationed] close to Tizi-Ouzou seemed to be worth something. [We] were too close for a dangerous rebel presence [to develop]." SAS archives for April 20, 1957 seem to support Pfirrmann's claims; two attacks against rural policemen (Aïssa Mimoun and at Tala Gaya) are mentioned. Galula gives his explanation: "French power in Djebel Aïssa Mimoun on the eve the rebellion was embodied in a *garde-champêtre* (rural policeman).[94] These attacks were far from harmless, as this was a means employed by the FLN to eliminate local Muslim government and isolate the administration from any source of local information. Galula confirms this conclusion in his insurgency doctrine: "The aims are to isolate the counterinsurgent from the masses . . . and to obtain as a minimum its passive complicity. . . . This is done by killing . . . some of the low-ranking government officials who work most closely with the populace."[95] The administrator of the mixed community of Mizrana, belonging to Djebel Aïssa Mimoun, showed the effects of local governance by the ALN in a report to the SAS commander: "In my opinion Djebel Aïssa Mimoun has long remained in the dark. I trust you to turn on the lights bit by bit" (October 28, 1956).

The insurgency remained active in the sector as shown by the wounding of Pfirrmann's predecessor, Clerc, while on operation in July 1956. Two disturbances at Igonane Ameur were reported in August 1956. The SAS seems to have underestimated the strength of the FLN, as it established a self-defense militia at Akaoudj (the neighboring subdistrict to Galula's) which turned into a fiasco. Four men deserted with their shotguns issued just eight days before[96] and three others responsible for guiding a patrol also fled. Nevertheless, the SAS increased patrolling. According to the record, between four and eight were mounted every two to four days, all without result. As the SAS officer bitterly reports on September 24, 1956, "Racing the clock leads to superficial results." The territory of Djebel Aïssa Mimoun cannot be considered severely dangerous, in spite of the rebel presence that manifested itself in harassment. But ALN control of the populace resulted in desertion of men trusted by the SAS and the army. The situation did not stop the SAS from doing its work. It hired construction workers (100–120) according to requests from the AMG and local constituents. In 1956, the situation was much worse for many SAS officers who were attacked with increasing frequency. The populace refused any contact. No construction could be organized owing to insecurity. Certain SAS posts were threatened with attack. Djebel Aïssa Mimoun was a world away from these troubles.

CHAPTER 2

The Eight Steps of Counterinsurgency at Djebel Aïssa Mimoun

On arriving in Algeria, Galula was confronted with an absence of instructions and counterguerilla doctrine. One of his chapter titles in *Pacification in Algeria* explicitly evokes the situation: "No counterinsurgency doctrine."[1] Every guideline insisted on the necessity of winning and pacifying the populace. "But exactly how?" he writes. "The sad truth was that, in spite of all our past experience, we had no single, official doctrine for counterinsurgency warfare. Instead, there were various schools of thought, all unofficial, some highly vociferous." Over the same period another officer, Captain Argoud, also noted in his report number 266/EMS of September 25, 1956, to General d'Elissagaray, "it has been found that there are no organized methods anywhere and, with rare exceptions, all are nearly ineffective." This is only partly explained by the absence of doctrine. In spite of "numerous official directives issued at every echelon, not one addressed the problems as a whole. Most often they did not go beyond vague generalities. Mostly they went untried." Additionally, Argoud found "an anarchy of procedure from one sector to another or even in the same sector over time."[2] As we shall see later, this officer's report, reproduced in the novel of the young draftee officer J. J. Servan Schreiber, will have an indirect influence on Galula's thinking. In the absence of any doctrine, Galula conceives of the eight steps of counterinsurgency, which he describes in his theoretical work.[3] We will look at each step and study the manner in which Galula applied them in his subdistrict.

FIRST STEP: "CONCENTRATION OF SUFFICIENT FORCE"

In his book, *Counterinsurgency Warfare*, Galula explains, "the destruction of guerilla forces . . . is, obviously, highly desirable. . . . This operation is not an end in itself, for guerillas, like the heads of the legendary hydra, have the special ability to grow again. . . . The real purpose of the first operation, then, is to prepare the stage for the further development of the counterinsurgent action."[4] Galula rightly insists that the implantation of small units in contact with the populace is one of the conditions for developing operations, saying, "small detachments of troops cannot be installed in villages so long as the insurgent is able to gather superior force and to overpower a detachment in a surprise attack."[5] Indeed, when the rebellion was too powerful, the sometimes-isolated SAS willingly abandoned its civilian mission to focus on the military mission, simply to protect itself from attacks and harassment. Once the security situation had been restored after major operations or after a tighter *quadrillage* of units had been established, the army or the SAS could spend time addressing the needs of the populace.

In the journal *Contacts*, Galula proudly writes of the high troop density in Kabylia and the presence of an experimental zone to test new methods.[6] In 1957, there were about six battalions in Kabylia, as well as a counter-guerilla unit patrolling the region[7] and 77 SAS officers to serve administrative needs.[8] In 1956, a pacification plan was developed to rally the populace within the test area, the mixed community of Tigzirt, that at first also included Djebel Aïssa Mimoun. The rally operation was mounted by the DST (*Direction de la Sûreté du Territoire*) in cooperation with the army. Galula explains the objective:[9] "It was based on the idea that pacification would be achieved if we could gradually compromise the population in the eyes of the rebels." The idea was expressed in the formula: *il faut mouiller la population* (let's soften them up). The army had planned the operation since August 1956, laying out a detailed 13-point plan: (1) Hiring men for public works directly benefitting their village; (2) Hiring men for public works in the interest of the administration and the army; (3) Hiring men to work on strictly defensive installations (defense walls and watchtowers); (4) Paid requisition of muleteers to support civil and military authorities; (5) Requisitions of muleteers to convoy supplies; (6) Unpaid requisition of muleteers to patrol across the villages; Mules carried radio sets and batteries; (7) Requisition of muleteers for a night exercise; (8) Kabyles keeping watch with soldiers in the post protecting the village; (9) Kabyle guides for night patrols; (10) Kabyle participation in armed night patrols; (11) Weapons withdrawn after each sortie; (12) Weapons left with Kabyles at night under a guard's supervision; and

(13) Official distribution of weapons to the populace. The final phase was known under the codename BLUEBIRD.

This last phase in the process goes unmentioned in C. Lacoste-Dujardin's book *Operation BLUEBIRD*. Galula only applies the program up to point 11 in Igonane Ameur. "The last three points were implemented after I had established a platoon in the village itself." He noted that in point 8, two of the eight Kabyles protested participating in the watch and joined the ALN the next day. Galula was critical of the process. "The program didn't accomplish what it set out to do. It was insufficient to convince the populace to change sides."

Moreover the DST based the entire operation on the recruitment of one Kabyle, who after admitting to being an FLN officer, was asked to develop contacts among local sympathizers of the FLN. The general government also called on the anthropologist J. Servier to study the ethnological layout and to identify pro-French villages and tribes. Lacoste-Dujardin, who was an ethnographer trained in a school critical of Servier's methods, would have favored traditional, time-proven approaches in spite of recent economic, social, and political changes. Because of these two mistakes, the FLN quickly subverted the operation to its own ends. Yet the information provided by the head of the Tirmitine SAS, Lieutenant Burthey, showed that the Kabyle leaders in the joint operation weren't reliable. The gendarmerie, the intelligence section at Tizi-Ouzou, and the headquarters of the 27th *Division d'infanterie alpine* (DIA) had been warned by Burthey in vain.[10]

On September 17, Prefect Vignon and General Gouraud attended a ceremony organized at Agouni Gouhrane under the auspices of the 15th BCA arming the 293 men of the self-defense militias, of whom 80 Iflisseni and 5,000 Kabyles were gathered. Three hundred weapons were issued. The inhabitants of Igonane Ameur received their weapons. On returning to Igonane Ameur, Galula disarmed them "as I had been ordered to do. Neither the French authorities nor the population had been fooled by the show." The weapons were not left to the militias, as suggested by Lacoste-Dujardin's study. Only selected *groupes d'autodéfense* (GAD) from Iflissen kept their weapons. Galula saw positive aspects in this operation that allowed his command to establish contact with the populace, to bend them to his will, without the ALN or OPA being able to do anything about it. Galula noted how the atmosphere at Igonane Ameur had changed.

The defense militias that had been infiltrated by the FLN joined the rebellion and turned their weapons on the French. On October 1, 1956, a platoon from the 15th BCA was led into an ambush by a militia unit. The French suffered two killed and six wounded. The region was secured and a 10-battalion sweep operation was mounted lasting from October 9 to 11, 1956. The rebels suffered about 100 killed while the French had 16 killed. Only 141 of the 300 issued weapons were recaptured.[11] Galula suggested reasons for the operation's failure: "The theory that the population would join our side once it felt protected from the threat of rebel bands had proved wrong. The idea that we could forcibly implicate the population on our side had not worked. It was clear to me that the major stumbling block was the OPA. We would make no progress as long as we had not purged the villages of the insurgent political cells."[12] For Galula the authorities had their priorities backward: instead of dismantling the OPA, they tried to rally the people first allowing the FLN to infiltrate the GAD militias causing the failure of the joint operation.

SECOND STEP: "ASSIGN SUFFICIENT TROOPS TO OPPOSE THE INSURGENT'S COMEBACK AND INSTALL THESE TROOPS IN EACH VILLAGE"

In *Counterinsurgency Warfare*, Galula writes, "The purpose in deploying static units is to establish a grid of troops so that the population and the counterinsurgent political teams are reasonably well protected, and so that the troops can participate in civic action at the lowest level."[13] Still, military authorities were faced with the problem of their units' vulnerability to guerilla attack. Should units be broken up to occupy terrain at the risk of becoming more vulnerable to attack or should they be gathered to give them a numerical advantage in combat? Command seemed to have chosen concentration of force. The concentration of manpower had been criticized at the time by Argoud in a report reproduced by Servan Schreiber minus the first sentence. "What has been left out in the orders . . . has been responsible for a high percentage of losses. Influenced by these losses, an inferiority complex has developed which has driven command to increase minimum authorized force levels for patrolling and force protection." Argoud blamed the situation on the hierarchy. "Command at every echelon adapted poorly to the unique conditions [of this war]." Servan Schreiber popularized the idea with the following: "Imagine asking generals to chop up their magnificently organized, armored, powerful units . . . signs of high importance, into so many slices of salami and scatter them about the countryside. It was pure insanity."[14] In Galula's subdistrict, the two battalion commanders allowed the dispersion of units he requested but always put military requirements first and always with respect to success fighting the ALN. However, opposition to this dispersion actually came from the zone commander of Kabylia, Gouraud, who temporarily slowed the dispersion of Galula's units, as we shall see later. General Noguès, sent to inspect deployment in different subdistricts and to remedy the shortfall of manpower, was also hostile to the dispersion. "With your forces spread out as they are, you have lost all military value. Your posts are utterly useless, their strength is too small to allow any serious sortie against the guerrillas."[15] Galula complained several times of the fact, "We were living among ourselves at Grand Remblai [where the SAS and Galula's company had been posted] isolated from the population. . . . I was too far from my two main villages,"[16] which posed real problems for working on the populace. The battalion commander assented to the deployment of a platoon to Igonane Ameur, one of the two larger villages in Galula's subdistrict in mid-September 1956. The village was a ten-minute walk from Grand Remblai and was the perfect spot for setting ambushes. In November 1956, after having dismantled the Bou Souar OPA cell, Galula requested permission to deploy a platoon in the village to keep the ALN from pressuring the villagers to form a new OPA cell. Only one platoon was left to protect the SAS. The battalion commander and the SAS approved the decision. At the end of November 1956, the two largest villages of the subdistrict were watched by the first platoon at Bou Souar and the second platoon at Igonane Ameur.[17] With the goal of pacifying the region and not "wasting energy in futile military operations," he asked for the expansion of his subdistrict. The modification of Galula's subdistrict, made by taking over responsibility for some of the subdistrict of the fourth company, was made with the support of the SAS. Indeed, a few weeks before, SAS officer Pfirrmann complained October 18, 1956,[18] at the sous-préfecture that "the battalion's deployment was very dispersed in the region and that the platoon at Tala Ilane [belonging to the fourth company] could only patrol with difficulty and accordingly had less-than-satisfactory results." That Pfirrmann's argument supports Galula's request for the extension of his subdistrict is surprising, as it could just as well have been a critique of Galula's tactic of dispersed units. While the units' dispersion allowed them to monitor the populace, it made them less effective in counterguerilla operations, as Galula himself admitted.[19] Finally, Pfirrmann's request had to be taken under further advisement as, the day after his report, a patrol from the fourth company was ambushed by Soltani's ALN band (October 22, 1956).[20] Galula saw his subdistrict absorb the fourth company's responsibility for the villages of Khelouyene, Aït Braham, Iril Ou Abba, and Tala Ou Abba. The small detachment from the fourth company left Tala Ilane and was replaced by the third platoon from Galula's company. Galula wanted to continue his strategy of controlling the population with one embedded unit. He asked that a small detachment from Tala Ilane be moved to Aït Braham, where the situation seemed more promising for contact with the populace. This time, Gouraud opposed the new deployment. "He thought that my company was too dispersed to be militarily effective." But a month later, Gouraud granted the request, after a meeting at Bou Souar.[21] In November 1956, Galula considered embedded deployments in the villages to be nearly finished.[22] "Tactical and logistic exigencies would not allow us to embed in all the villages, which were numerous and dispersed. But the largest ones were occupied." In spite of the danger of dispersing the platoons, dividing them into smaller details, rendering them more vulnerable to attack from even a weakened rebel force,

Galula decided to continue occupying territory. In January 1957, with the villages under control, Galula further extended his military presence. With the four main villages having already been occupied by four platoons and unable to expect reinforcement, he "ignored the table of organization and reduced the strength of the platoons to between twenty and twenty-five men according to the size and situation of the village. In order to save more personnel, I moved my command post and all that went with it to Tala Ilane."

As the units were very dispersed and more vulnerable to ambushes, he had to develop tactics against them. In the event of ambush, the closest unit established a defensive line while other nearby units converged on the ambush site. He trained his men in this type of maneuver. To supplement the static units working on the population, he suggested the creation of a 20-man command composed of four volunteers from each company to track the ALN throughout the subdistrict. This was a novel initiative anticipating the future use of special operations troops;[23] however, from 1955, the Action Commandos had been set up by General Massu, "in elite units which had served in Indochina whose leaders were well aware of counterguerilla tactics."[24] Once *harka* units had been set up (Muslim auxiliaries recruited and commanded by the army), he employed them, dressed as civilians, in roving two- or three-day patrols and to mount ambushes. In September 1957, Galula's subdistrict extended to the south and took in two new villages, Timizar Laghbar and Tala Atmane, consisting of 3,000 additional inhabitants. He was obliged to reduce the detachments occupying Timizar, a heavily populated village where the OPA was very active, even further. He requested reinforcements and was promised a *Groupe mobile de protection rurale* (GMPR), a mobile rural police, which he never received.[25] The village could not be occupied by Galula's units.

In fact, at Djebel Aïssa Mimoun, Galula practiced the ink-spot strategy invented by Marshall Gallieni in Tonkin from 1892 to 1896 and developed by Marshall Lyautey in his article "Du rôle colonial de l'armée" (The Army's Role in the Colonies) in the journal *Revue des Deux mondes.* The ink spot refers to the idea of creating military posts that are gradually extended with economic and social development (markets, clinics, schools) and the establishment of local government, control of the populace, elimination of adversaries, and arming supporters before moving on to another region.[26] Galula also uses the expression ink spot four times in his writing.[27]

It may also be noted that Galula's tactics were inspired by Colonel Nemo. This revolutionary warfare specialist commanded a battalion in Indochina, served as a staff officer in the Pleiku highlands (1946–48) and as a commander in the southern zone and at Haiphong (1952–55). He authored a number of articles on revolutionary warfare. In his January 1956 article, "L'infanterie dans guerre de surface," Nemo advocates use of *quadrillage,* use of "blocking teams . . . to hold fixed combat outposts and assault teams charged with mobile missions."[28] In another article by Nemo "La guerre dans la foule"[29] published May 1956, he describes a similar tactic in which he outlines the necessity of having two units with different objectives in the same sector: "military forces responsible for in-sector missions and those responsible for force-on-force confrontation with the enemy." Nemo's thinking could be mistaken for the tactics Galula applies a few months later at Djebel Aïssa Mimoun.

THIRD STEP: "CONTACT WITH AND CONTROL OF THE POPULATION"

In *Counterinsurgency Warfare,* Galula lists three objectives for this phase: "To re-establish the counterinsurgent's authority over the population; to isolate the population as much as possible, by physical means, from the guerrillas; to gather the necessary intelligence leading to the next step." These objectives require that the population not be treated as an enemy by the counterinsurgent and that it benefits from "actions which are directly of use to it." In this phase, control and protection of the population are established by the counterinsurgent.[30] When Galula took command of the third company, "there was no contact with the populace." The necessity of winning people to the loyalist side in a guerrilla war seemed to have come from his experience observing guerrillas in China and Greece, as well as Hong Kong, where he studied them and antiguerrilla warfare in Indochina, Malaysia, and the Philippines. "There was no doubt in my mind that support from the population was the key to the whole problem for us as well as for the rebels."[31] Galula also reproduces one of his conversations with a lieutenant colonel in Kabylia, a veteran of Indochina, who underscored the same idea. "He had no precise idea of what to do in our situation in Algeria except that [we shouldn't refight the French-Indochina War]. He knew we had to win over the population, discouraged firmly any show of indiscriminate hostility toward Kabyles on the part of his units, always had his pockets full of candy for the kids, and a ready smile for the adults whom he treated with courtesy."[32] This conversation only reinforced the case for the importance of winning the hearts and minds of the population. We can break down rule number three advocated by Galula. If steps A and B aren't explicitly delimited by Galula in *Counterinsurgency Warfare,* they are clearly apparent in *Pacification in Algeria.*

A. Trusting the Population: J.-J. Servan Schreiber and "Captain Marcus," Galula's Inspiration

In the sort of asymmetric conflict that was the Algerian War, where the population was manipulated, exploited, and used as a screen by the guerillas, the objective for the forces of order is to distinguish the rebel from the inhabitant and "to isolate the rebel from the population." Galula explained the strategy to his company: "Our job, precisely, is to stop this support. [The people's for the FLN.] If we lump together population and rebels–and this is what the FLN want us to do—we are sure to keep the population supporting them. If we distinguish between people and rebels, then we have a chance. One cannot catch a fly with vinegar. My rules are: outwardly you must treat every civilian as a friend; inwardly you must consider him as a rebel ally until you have positive proof to the contrary."[33]

Galula's thought may seem original; however, it is laid out in a very similar way in the work of Servan Schreiber,[34] cofounder of *l'Express* with Giroud. After returning from his Algerian service, he wrote down his thoughts about the Algerian War in the form of a novel under the name of Captain Julienne. He then served at the DBFA under Colonel Barberot and General de la Bollardière at Rivet in the Blidan Atlas mountains south of Algiers and tried to establish a unit of false-flag operators (administratively attached to the 20th Dragoons). The scene is a meal over which officers discuss their views of the Algerian War, notably the problem that the government has distinguishing rebels from civilians. Julienne explains: "And that father, brother, or son who dies by our guns will inevitably make them hate us. I suggest that it is a poor practice to kill people who might be innocent. Julienne was wrong, and he would find it out pretty quick. The fellagha are not, more's the pity, beings apart, marked with a cross on the forehead. The fellaghas are anybody, anywhere. To get a real one, you have to round up—or to kill—four or five, at least." Captain Martin replies to Julienne: "Either you consider a priori that every Arab, in the country, in the street, in a passing truck, is innocent until proved guilty—and allow me to tell you that if that's your attitude you'll get your men bumped off . . . or you do your job right, that is, put the fellagha in his place and protect your men as best you can. In any case there's only one way: treat every Arab as a suspect, a possible fellagha, a potential terrorist." Servan Schreiber reformulated Julienne's position, that of avoiding the killing of innocents and keeping the army from provoking hostility when it came into contact with the population. Julienne and Martin have the following exchange: "You consider a priori that every Arab . . . is innocent until proved guilty." Servan Schreiber also drew inspiration from Martin's rejoinder: "Consider every Arab a suspect." Bringing the two propositions together, we have the oath of the *commandos noirs* (false flag operators) in the following: "I will regard every Moslem as a friend, rather than a suspect, without proof to the contrary."[35] Galula simply repeated the oath in Servan Schreiber's book, changing the wording slightly: "Outwardly you must treat every civilian as a friend; inwardly you must consider him as a rebel ally until you have positive proof to the contrary." The author of *Lieutenant in Algeria* was not unknown to Galula. Indeed, the company Galula assumed command of returned from an operation in Rivet and Bilda,[36] which was also the basis for Servan Schreiber's unit. On the other hand, the Algérois region was much more difficult than Djebel Aïssa Mimoun.

In his novel Servan Schreiber also reproduces a report on the army's failures in Algeria written by Captain Marcus, commander of a detachment of *harkis* and a squadron of Dragoons.[37] This unknown Marcus did indeed exist, as did all the characters in his novel, and went by the name of Argoud. He commanded the 3rd *Régiment de chasseurs d'Afrique* (RCA) in the neighboring sector of Rivet, south of Arba. He trained a *harki* unit to hunt the ALN.[38] He also wrote several articles on revolutionary warfare.[39] Later, Colonel Argoud would become chief of staff for Massu, the corps commander at Algiers, where he would draw on his experiences to develop a pacification doctrine in 1959.[40]

Marcus's original report can be found in the memoirs of Argoud.[41] Report number 266/EMS of September 25, 1956 begins by describing the course of his regiment, of which Servan Schreiber merely changes the numbers: "Over three months the regiment traveled eight thousand kilometers in the Algérois and Constantinois, participated in operations in fourteen communes, worked with more than twenty different units." If Servan Schreiber published a large part of Argoud's report, Argoud published only excerpts. Missing from his excerpts are the reflections from the beginning of the report concerning the links between the population and the rebels and the army's attitude toward the population. The excerpts reproduced by Servan Schreiber, "Without the population's active cooperation, the problem faced by the forces of order was insoluble. Incapable of distinguishing rebels from peaceful citizens, they were constrained by the lack of information to blind repression. . . . Every citizen treated like a fellagha was replaced by ten real ones. . . . The army must primarily seek the support of the population, to earn its trust. To win the support of the population, to earn its trust, it must first become familiar with it and seek human contact as much as possible." Argoud on the other hand denounced the "unacceptable excesses of [the army] in its attitude toward the population: this attitude oscillates between the most egregious weakness and the most guilty lashing out." He continues, "Operations hardly deal with the populace, or at least everything happens as if they hardly cared . . . instead of taking care of the population which was the heart of the matter, the army furiously hunted the rebels, which were only a secondary aspect." Galula's article in *Contacts* raises the same criticism of the army as Argoud: the failure to adapt its units to the mission, the lack of firmness or overreaction. "Between comprehensive action and complete overreaction, there was a wide margin where humanity and common sense can be deployed while remaining within the spirit of our institutions." Galula would later theorize on the necessity of the army working on the populace. "And so intricate is the interplay between the political and the military actions that they cannot be tidily separated; on the contrary, every military move has to be weighed with regard to its political effects and vice versa."[42]

B. Address the Needs of the Population

To reconnect with the people, the SAS was charged with responding to their needs by setting up schools, constructions (roads and forts), and organizing medical visits. According to SAS reports, schools were opened in October 1956 in Galula's sector. There were 28 students at Igonane Ameur, 14 at Tala Ilane and 10 at Akaoudj in the neighboring sector.[43] Two construction sites were set up to build a *bordj* (fort) for the SAS and a landing strip, which allowed the hiring of 100 to 120 workers six days a week, eight hours a day. The SAS also distributed food to the needy. The report of October 15, 1956, detailed exactly what this aid consisted of: 280 kilograms of wheat, 280 kilograms of semolina (617 pounds, each) and five meters (16 feet) of cloth. Medical visits, *assistance medicale gratuite* (AMG), were organized in the five villages of the SAS. As for the units, the SAS indicated that, at Akaoudj, the second company, which was building shacks in the village, was assisted by the population, who was "happy to help out with the construction" (October 8, 1956). In the sub-district next to Galula's, where the population seemed to have a favorable attitude toward the French, we must nevertheless qualify this with the fact that it was from this same village which four members of the defense militia had deserted 20 days before.

The statistics from the medical visits were well kept by the SAS. In Galula's subdistrict, from October 1 to 25, 1956, AMG reports the following numbers: 153 men, 23 women, 301 children cared for, or a total of 477 people. The most frequent infections treated were eye problems (196 cases), sprains (85 cases), digestive disorders (60 cases), lung disorders (35 cases), and trachomas (30 cases). Galula explained how the AMG worked in *Lettre d'informations:* each post had an infirmary with a medic and assistant. The battalion doctor made rounds once a week in each commune to care for the more difficult cases beyond the medics' abilities. "About 400 to 500 villagers and farmers were cared for each week by the AMG, most of them women."[44] This last figure is exaggerated. In reality, about 500 people were treated each month. In January 1957, the total number of people treated by the AMG in the whole district was 744, the majority of them children (January 3, 1957).

Addressing the needs of the population requires steady allocation of financial resources. Any interruption of funding necessarily had an impact on hiring the populace and its attitude toward the counterinsurgent. Galula doesn't mention this point, as he didn't manage the population's daily needs and, therefore, didn't always see the effect. The SAS officer, responsible for daily material and financial questions, saw such effects immediately and complained of them to the *sous-préfecture*. "The decrease

in the number of workers employed at construction sites is unwelcome
at a time when, after several months of effort, the population was coming to work in good faith. . . . It would be preferable, in the future, to employ fewer workers to avoid resorting to massive layoffs" (October 11,
1956). "Your disappointment with the downsizing of the workforce is
noted. Don't lose your temper! A reduction isn't the same as elimination. . . . The reduction should be applied gradually, spread out in time
so that it doesn't cause a significant disruption, especially politically."
The report of November 15, 1956 shows that the number of workers employed dropped to 30 and, after a few days this dropped to 3 or 4. Three
days later, after the SAS officer's complaint, the numbers were back up
to 100 workers at the site. In the area of education, facilities were the
problem (lessons at Tahanouts were held under a tent) and school supplies, which the poor village children lacked (November 29, 1956).

Due to the size of the territory and the small number of SAS officers,
the companies in the Djebel Aïssa Mimoun area took an active part in taking care of the population, as explained in the SAS report of April 25 and
May 25, 1957: "In this SAS area of six communes, where the companies
take an active part in daily administration (meetings of delegates, keeping minutes for want of a secretary, holding meetings to set up a work
program, involvement in 7 schools with 630 students) . . . the task of the
SAS is more and more complicated once the valuable help rendered by
the companies decreases."[45] It is notable that, of seven schools, five were
in Galula's subdistrict whose number of students doesn't add up to the
total he gives, that is 1100 students among five schools.[46] Rather, it was
630 students among seven schools. The difference can be explained by
the fact that Galula's figures came later. In August 1957, there were
640 students, but in November 1957, the number climbs sharply to
922 students. If the numbers given are dated to the beginning of the
school year, September 1958, they are plausible in view of the rise in attendance. Galula provides some information on teachers in his *Lettre
d'Informations:* "They are wood turners, plumbers, farmers. Only one was
a substitute teacher in civilian life." The record of the number of children in school is even more spectacular as, before 1954, only 60 boys were
enrolled.[47]

C. Control the Populace

Above all, for Galula this step consists of isolating the rebellion from
popular support. "Finally, the rebels knew that their guerrilla forces
would be lost if we ever succeeded in isolating them from the population."[48] Even if at first the rebels enjoyed spontaneous popular support,
they didn't hesitate to resort to terror on the slightest suspicion of losing the population's loyalty. So the army had to control the population
which meant conducting censuses to know exactly who belonged in the

villages and to be able to spot outsiders. Every citizen was registered and received an unalterable ID card. Family record books were also instituted and the head of the family was charged with reporting any change. Apart from getting to know the population, Galula saw other benefits of the census: it allowed him to know the exact makeup of the populace. The family heads were implicated to the French side by being made responsible for reporting changes. Finally, in *Counterinsurgency Warfare,* Galula writes that the census checked against the names of known rebels allowed identification of the clans and families supporting the insurgents.[49]

Apparently this census-based strategy seems coherent but the problem lay with organizing its undertaking in a Muslim country where the collection of public records faced numerous cultural obstacles that made the job more difficult than expected. Lack of surnames (abbreviated SNP, *sans nom patronymique* or "no surname") and the similarity of first names (Abdelkader, Mohamed, Mouloud, Fatima) were only the first problems in establishing public records. Moreover, Muslims accounted for time differently, rarely marking dates of birth exactly and according to the changes in season or by agricultural events (the year when hail destroyed the crops, the year of the locusts or the drought) or by religious holidays.[50] Finally, while photo IDs for men were not a problem, they raised real problems when it came to photographing women who had to be asked to unveil by male photographers. Such a situation was sure to offend a head of the family. At least in Kabyle country, where Galula found himself, this wasn't a problem as women went unveiled unlike in Arabic-speaking regions. With an illiterate population, signatures are little more than a cross, requiring replacement by a more reliable system of fingerprinting. Mistrust of the state and its representatives caused constant underreporting, not only of incomes but also of births.[51] It is surprising that Galula does not mention these problems when describing conducting the census of Igonane Ameur,[52] which is also confirmed in the unit history of Galula's company.[53] He recorded the name, age, and sex of every inhabitant as well as the addresses of everyone living in the area and of those living in mainland France. He drew up a record of supplementary information for men above 15 years of age and added it to the family record book. Galula didn't seem to fear that the FLN might destroy the papers; as such an action might have provoked the discontent of a populace sure to suffer further inconvenience and annoying paperwork to satisfy the army and the SAS.

Galula divided each village into sectors and assigned a team to deal with identifying the inhabitants. Organizing this way allowed his soldiers to get to know the villagers and to spot intruders. The army also had to control the movement of inhabitants in such a way that they had no contact with outsiders. Galula's method for doing this was inspired by the Chinese communists. He declared "nobody could leave the village for more than twenty-four hours without a pass; nobody could receive a stranger to the village without permission. The rules were announced to the population at a meeting. . . . Passes and permissions were not refused unless we had some definite reason. . . . The system inhibited the FLN agents in the village and gave the inhabitants a valid alibi for refusing work as messengers or suppliers to the guerillas."[54] In his account of his operations at Djebel Aïssa Mimoun, Galula brings up another advantage of this system of controlling movement: it forced villagers to apply for a pass at a company office, which gave the lieutenant an opportunity to question them and obtain information in confidence.[55] The SAS also looked after administrative documents for the people. Galula arranged it with Pfirrmann, the SAS officer, "that each Kabyle in his subdistrict see him first." As he put it, bureaucratic pressure was also a means of obtaining information. Galula, writing in his article in *Contacts*, November 1956,[56] that point three, controlling the population, "has been fully realized in the villages of Igonane Ameur and Bou Souar which I've controlled and watched for a long time and is being implemented in the village I've just occupied. . . . Movement has been watched to the extent that repeated contact with people living outside the village has been virtually eliminated." Galula provided for a system of fines to enforce his rules. He recognized two flaws. He complained of the absence of a summary code of infractions and fines and asked himself: Should an offender's sheep be confiscated, slaughtered, and distributed to the poor or should other methods be used, like beatings, a simple lecture, or a work detail? He feared that the population wouldn't see the difference of treatment between units and therefore would not accept the punishment. The second flaw was the fact that it was impossible to control the population completely by censoring the mail. Nor was it possible to control it in the markets of Tizi-Ouzou, where the influence of the rebellion was strong.

After gaining control of the population, the next objective becomes rallying or pacifying. Writing in *Contacts*, Galula defined what he meant by pacification: for him it was a matter of detecting "the minority who supports us then using it to destroy the hostile minority and to take control of the neutral majority." Wanting to pacify a sector is condensed in steps four, five, and six, described in *Counterinsurgency Warfare*.

FOURTH STEP: "DESTROY THE LOCAL INSURGENT POLITICAL ORGANIZATIONS"

In *Counterinsurgency Warfare*, Galula explains, "The necessity for eradicating the insurgent political agents from the population is evident. The question is how to do it rapidly and efficiently, with a minimum of errors and bitterness."[57] Destroying the local organization of the FLN is the essential objective of this step. "It was clear to me that the major stumbling block was the OPA. We would make no progress as long as we had not purged the villages of the insurgent political cells. This was the problem I had to solve."[58]

To weaken the insurgents' local political organization (OPA), the SAS undertook actions that clearly benefited the population to win its heart and mind and to detach it gradually from the rebellion. The work sites, the AMG medical visits, and school enrollments included in the strategy all seemed to bear fruit: information flowing into the SAS. "Several reports indicate the presence of the Oudiaï band at Tazmalt [Galula's sector]."[59] The operation launched the night of October 2–3, however, was unable to exploit the intelligence. About this undertaking, SAS officer Pfirrmann reported the arrest of five people at Tahanouts (second company): they were collecting funds for the FLN, stopping people from smoking and from selling goods to soldiers (report October 4, 1956). For Pfirrmann, these facts, "show how the villages are still worked over, in spite of our presence, and explain the fear that locals show at all times." The ALN seemed to circulate with complete freedom and benefitted from the active support of the OPA. However, the amount of information from one case and the arrest of an OPA member showed that the situation seemed to be turning in favor of the French.

By civil action, the SAS showed the population a return of French authority, while at the same time showing that they could take care of the population's problems. The FLN could not remain indifferent, as both its influence and operations came into question. On putting the emphasis on schools, the SAS went in the direction desired by the Kabyle population. School taught the children to read, which later allowed young Kabyles to go to the city to find work and to support the village, even though agricultural resources could feed the entire population. This is why the education policy was so successful in Kabylia.

Galula's action figures importantly among the explanations for this success, as he was able to overcome the population's reticence. When he asked that boys from 8 to 14 be sent to school, he was told that the children had to look after the herds or help cultivate farmland. Galula assented to one-child families keeping their child at home but others had to send their children to school. In the hope of making women his allies, Galula tried to empower them from the earliest age: he ordered that girls aged 8 to 13 (marrying age) go to school in the afternoon. He ignored the parents' complaints and opened two classes for girls.[60] A fourth school was opened at Djebel Aïssa Mimoun, a third in Galula's sector: at Agouni Taga, 28 students were registered (October 15, 1956); three days later, a report indicates the number went up to 56. The unit history of the third company, 45th BIC, announced that on October 17, 1956, 61 students were enrolled at this school, among them 15 girls.[61]

The FLN, which had destroyed the only school at Djebel Aïssa Mimoun, saw its influence counteracted by SAS educational policy, which had brought enrollments up to higher levels than before the insurrection began. The FLN responded, via the OPA, by menacing the parents and students, attacking school children, and circulating slogans urging a boycott of the school. The response was awkward, as it went against the interests of the people: the flow of intelligence to the SAS shows that the population was turning against the FLN. The intelligence bulletin of October 19, 1956[62] explained that the inhabitants of Bou Souar asked that their children going to school be protected. They even asked that the SAS force children to attend: "21 children from Bou Souar only wanted to go to school, but the parents wouldn't allow it. They were threatened by the rebels."

Having seen an increase in enrollment "in astonishing proportions at Tala Ilane (31 students, up from 15) and at Igonane Ameur (88 students rather than 28, among them 36 girls)," Pfirrmann provides another explanation in his reported dated October 22, 1956. "This strange fact seems to confirm the intelligence, recent and vague, according to which the outlaws would change methods and encourage workers, Kabyles, to send their children to school in droves." He continues: "[This put] us in the embarrassing situation of having to turn away some of the children, with our school yet unrepaired and our teachers who have not yet arrived. The propaganda line would be the following: the French have hyped up the beginning of the school year, but they are incapable of dealing with the students who come." This analysis, absent from Galula's book, is interesting as it shows how the OPA, over the span of a few days, went from fighting against enrollment to supporting it. At first children were prevented from attending school, which proved unpopular and difficult to carry out. The OPA changed strategy and encouraged all parents to send their children to school to upset the attendance policy.[63] The OPA justified its contradictory instructions and intensified its propaganda. Because of the FLN's tactics in Djebel Aïssa Mimoun, contrary to other SAS sectors, it is impossible to use school enrollments as an indicator of progress in pacification or the effectiveness of Galula's strategy. However, the FLN's position also indirectly shows they lacked the means to impose a school boycott on parents. In November 1956, enrollments at Igonane Ameur in Galula's sector reached 103 students (49 of them girls)!

This report based on information gathered by the SAS officer showed that the OPA made maximum use of propaganda in all areas to counter the French army's success. A successful operation conducted by the French army in Azazga was spun by the OPA in the following way: "The dead we named were not rebels, but patsies whom we placed with weapons in their hands after the fact" [taken from a conversation with a citizen of Tikobain]. To strengthen the morale of the FLN's supporters, the OPA explained that the withdrawal of reactivated troops "affected nearly half of French forces in Algeria. . . . Even if they were replaced from reserves, how long would the soldiers continue to fight?" [From conversations with citizens of Akaoudj]. Pfirrmann concludes in his report, "This goes to show that the population was subjected to incessant propaganda. How could it be otherwise when we saw that at Djebel Aïssa Mimoun . . . a band of fifteen men set an ambush not far from Tahanouts, supposedly one of the more secure villages with a capable self-defense militia."

A method used by the OPA to show its strength to the authorities and impose its will on the population were high-visibility symbolic actions, such as prohibiting smoking and calling for strikes. Calls for strikes and boycotts of all sorts of activity throughout Algeria to celebrate the anniversary of the FLN's uprising on All Saints' Day 1954 was of course undertaken by the OPA at Djebel Aïssa Mimoun. Galula cites the following facts:[64] "[At Igonane Ameur], No children had come to school, the streets were empty, all the villagers were staying home, and even at the fountain no women had appeared. I went to Bou Souar and found the same situation." The same tone is struck in the SAS report of October 30, 1956:[65] "On October 28, a day when Tizi Ouzou was on strike, nobody came to the office, while just the day before, there had been many. A sure sign of the effects of propaganda." The extent of the strike at Djebel Aïssa Mimoun would become known in the SAS report of November 5, 1956. "On November 1, in many villages, the people did not go out to work in the fields. Several local cafés and stores supported the strike. K., a suspected informer (wrongly or not) was found dead, shot in the chest about thirty times."

To avoid losing all credibility with the population in the face of the OPA's propaganda, Galula tried to find a defense to show his determination against the OPA. The unit history of the 3/45th BIC[66] explains that on November 1, "The population of Agoni Taga, Oumbil, and Igonane Ameur had been warned that if work did not resume they would be confined to their villages for fifteen days." In the other large village of the subdistrict, the unit history records, "The people of Bou Souar claim to have stayed in the village to elect a headman and delegates. If these posts aren't filled, they should suffer the same penalty as Igonane Ameur." We learn by Galula's 1963[67] account that the men of Bou Souar were taken to Igonane Ameur to clean the helicopter landing zone. On November 2, 1956, the strike continued in his subdistrict. In his 1963 account, he wrote that he asked the *djemaa* (council of village elders) of Igonane Ameur the name of the person who passed on the call to strike. Receiving no response, he confined them to their homes until he was given the name. Only women and children were authorized to go out for an hour to the well and to go to school. Soldiers visited the homes to verify that the children were being correctly fed and, if not, to bring them to the dispensary to be fed and given milk.

Confronted with a simultaneous resistance from these two main villages, Galula saw a sharp improvement in the situation. A villager from Bou Souar denounced his nephew and his cousin at Oudiaï as OPA chiefs and named 50 FLN sympathizers in the village. The unit history confirms that on November 3 an operation based on this information was mounted at Bou Souar. "Eleven out of 14 suspects were arrested at Bou Souar, including two who had been wanted for three months, and a rebel leader." SAS officer Pfirrmann reports on November 5, "the November 3 operation mounted by the 3rd company 45th BIC, after receiving intelligence, resulted in the arrest of the OPA political network at Bou Souar, six people." The residents of Igonane Ameur, after five days of sequestration to their homes, also denounced the OPA chief of Bou Souar. In the SAS report of November 8, 1956, Pfirrmann tells us, "the end of restricted movement in the *douar* was welcomed by the population," indirectly confirming that Galula's method was employed. Pfirrmann's report notes Galula's reaction in vague terms, "A psychological operation began on November 2 at Akaoudj, Tala Ilane, and Igonane Ameur."

The OPA's response seems to have been well-prepared in advance, as Galula implies in *Pacification in Algeria*. The SAS commander was warned of the coming tactic during a meeting held on October 31. Pfirrmann mentions the meeting twice in his reports (November 1 and 5, 1956). On November 8, Pfirrmann explains that he sent a detailed report on psychological operations at Igonane Ameur. Unfortunately, the report is missing from both the SAS and *sous-préfecture* archives. In his writing, Galula also claims to have been aware of a rise in FLN activity and the only instructions he had dealt with patrols and checkpoints, as confirmed in the unit history (the posts at Agouni Taga and Igonane Ameur were reinforced October 31). From October 28, Djebel Aïssa Mimoun began to show the first signs of the oncoming strike. Galula had the time to develop a strategy and have it prepared for the October 31 meeting. Galula had anticipated the problem and was prepared for a psychological battle with the OPA over Igonane Ameur. By chance, the reckoning came at Bou Souar rather than Igonane Ameur. The confrontation led to Galula's successful dismantling of the OPA at Bou Souar and Igonane Ameur. The SAS at Djebel Aïssa Mimoun was kept informed, "Those arrested at Bou Souar are beginning to provide interesting intelligence" (November 12, 1956). To hold on to the village, Pfirrmann explained that a platoon sent from battalion would set up there. This took place on November 15, 1956, "It is therefore reasonable to hope for a change of atmosphere in this village in the near future."

Galula's action and that of the SAS seemed to be bearing fruit. The OPA and the ALN reacted by murder and attacks on two pro-French Muslims, a *moghazni* and the brother of a police officer. Pfirrmann was on leave, temporarily relieved by Brousse who thought, "to stop the political and administrative restructuring in the *douar* [by the SAS and the army], rebels would increasingly resort to terrorism" (November 19, 1956). Having improved security, the policy of designating the members of delegations and communes continued. Brousse's fresh perspective as interim SAS commander was optimistic, "The political situation seems to be evolving quite favorably, especially in the western part of the *douar*" (November 26, 1956). There were other successes against the OPA. East of the subdistrict, a platoon from Galula's company based at Tala Ilane took care of Khelouyene and Aït Braham. The lieutenant, the post commander, recruited 12 veterans and former professional soldiers as sources of information. Invited to a meal, with the help of a few drinks, they named suspects to the post commander. They were 16, 2 in each village or hamlet. The rebels' organizational structure was reconstructed and completed with reports coming from 4 others. The OPA leaders were arrested at Aït Braham.[68]

Even if SAS reports no longer speak of the OPA, it shouldn't be thought that it had completely disappeared. Other, more discrete, OPA members recovered. Galula recognized that owing to the positive attitude of the village of Igonane Ameur with respect to the army, he did not completely purge the village, unlike the others. The remaining OPA restricted their activities to levying taxes, as mentioned indirectly in the SAS report, "During an operation January 23, 1957 at Tazemalt, a notebook with the names and amount of tax paid to the rebels by the residents was found" (January 24, 1957). In February, the names of suspected tax collectors and those furnishing supplies to the rebels were given at Aït Braham (February 4, 1957).[69] Galula also explains that in March 1957, a man from Igonane Ameur was caught carrying 32,000 francs and was unable to justify having such a sum.

The OPA showed itself mainly through propaganda against the forces of order. In Indochina the Vietminh proceeded in the same manner. In "La Guerre dans la foule," Nemo describes the Indochina War as "a revolutionary war in which psychological factors and passions combined with purely military ones." He explains, "The Vietminh fully mobilized the population, giving it mystique and by solidly organizing it by influencing public opinion with incessant propaganda."[70] For Galula the solution was to turn the guerillas' own methods against them: counterinsurgency was to employ both psychological and military means. Mastery of information was an important point for Galula, as was emphasized in 2008 by U.S. general Petraeus in his preface to Galula's theoretical work. Galula complains, in an article in *Contacts*,[71] of the inadequacy of the company to conduct counterpropaganda operations. "Where are my political officer, my propaganda team, my intelligence section, my police? Where are my reams of paper, my mimeograph, my projector, my film, my pots of paste and paint?" He also notes the absence of trained personnel and equipment to conduct counterpropaganda through leaflets, posters, speaker trucks, movies, and even newspapers. He continues noting the absence of a systematic approach or, more exactly, a clear method to use "propaganda in all its forms, such as public meetings and individual discussions." He considered the twice-monthly reporting to the Psychological

Operations sections insufficient. There were too few reports at too long
an interval. Galula wanted to replace them with reports putting the Algerian situation in international context (every 15 days), fact sheets on
the current situation in Algeria (weekly) and local news sheets (daily).
Nemo thought the most effective methods used in Indochina were
"crudely printed leaflets and especially rumors circulated in public . . . the
themes were local subjects easily understandable by everyone . . . grand
ideas were expressed in terms of local turf wars." Galula goes the same
way when he complains of not having the means to conduct basic propaganda such as reams of paper or a mimeograph. Moreover, among
the fact sheets provided by civil-military affairs, Galula asked for "mention of current events which had import on local affairs."

Soldiers trained in counterpropaganda did indeed exist at the time.
Psyops officers did work in speaker truck and leaflet companies (CHPT).
This is one of the initiatives taken by the revolutionary warfare theorists.[72] In *Pacification in Algeria*,[73] Galula describes their material and operations performed in his subdistrict. CHPT officers were equipped with
recording material, cinema projectors, cameras, and photo labs. The psyops officer suggested images and propaganda films and entertainment,
locally recorded music, while loudspeakers broadcast speeches and general facts about the local situation. They had material to print propaganda
leaflets. Galula criticized the results thus, "if the photos taken of villagers were a success, the films shown at the cinema proved a total failure.
Cartoons, the olive economy in Kabyle villages, fighting in the Vosges in
1944–45 [where many soldiers of Algerian origin fought] provoked no
interest." He criticized the fact that the CHPT teams had no budget to
procure better quality films and better cameras. As for the detailed instructions to organize meetings proposed by psyops officers, former
prisoners of the Vietminh, Galula found them ridiculous. He explained
that this method worked in Indochina, for "the French officers were prisoners, isolated from their normal environment, while Kabyle civilians
were not prisoners and were living in their normal environment."[74]

Tacking propaganda methods onto completely different environments
could only lead to failed psychological operations. Galula's experience
as a military attaché at Beijing and at Hong-Kong, where he could analyze
the communist guerillas' methods, made him suspicious of the methods
adopted by officers who had fought against guerilla influence in Indochina. Yet we can say that Galula did not entirely reject all of their opinions,
as he showed in the first paragraph of his article in *Contacts*. He evokes
the principles of sociological warfare as he saw the conflict in Algeria as
centered on the populace. *Contacts* rejected this nonofficial expression in
the introduction to the article. This expression was lifted from Nemo, author of "La Guerre dans la foule" in *Revue de la Défense nationale* published
in 1956, seven months before sending his article to *Contacts*. The similarities between Nemo and Galula don't end there. Nemo wrote, "wanting

to find simple solutions for complex problems; this is neither political, nor military—it must be total," and he notes, "political action and military force are complimentary. Counterrevolutionary warfare must be applied at all levels."[75] Galula adds little in writing, "And so intricate is the interplay between the political and the military actions that they cannot be tidily separated."[76] There is, however, a slight nuance to the words of Nemo. For Galula "the concepts' simplicity and their implementation is a prerequisite for any counterinsurgency doctrine." Galula thought that a simple counterinsurgency mode of action could be offered. He also joined Nemo in his vision of total counterinsurgency, describing the actors in it. "The counterinsurgent personnel who implement this strategy—and they are a widely mixed group of politicians, civil servants, economists, social workers, soldiers—yet with enough precision to channel their efforts in a single direction."[77]

Clearly Galula was inspired by Nemo's thinking on the lessons learned in Indochina and adapted them for Algeria. He ends his article in *Contacts*, explaining that this was his contribution to "the conduct of sociological warfare." Galula based his tactical recommendation for counterinsurgency operations at Djebel Aïssa Mimoun on Nemo's description of the Vietminh: fight the ALN, embed platoons in the villages, and control the populace by observation and systematic propaganda.

In the *Contacts* article of November 1956, Galula also thought it would be possible to employ instructors, soldiers detailed from the unit to teach, to "plant a few political seeds in the minds of the young. It would be necessary for them to have specially-prepared instruction sheets." The use of instructors also shows up in the SAS report of November 29, 1956. "According to the intelligence gained from interrogation of suspects and by school monitors, it seems that rebel propaganda has failed to reach the children. The opportunity is there for the taking. The commander of the subdistrict agreed to try the following: team sports and theatre for the children. An organizer would be found among the soldiers. I think that with 15,000 or 20,000 francs for equipment could get us started." It seemed that the initiative came from Brousse, the interim SAS officer, and that Galula found the idea interesting. But was it applied? Galula's writing seems to cast doubt: he says that the children were apolitical and weren't mobilized, as were those of the Vietnamese and Chinese communists. "It was tempting to take advantage of the rebels' oversight. I could not, however, bring myself to do it. This war was already bad enough for children to be involved in."[78] However, if intelligence was inadvertently given by the children, it was included in the reports.

In his account of his activities in Algeria, Galula writes of how he informed the public. He selected news stories from the newspapers and news of local events for the populace. One of his lieutenants communicated them to the *djemaa* or at public meetings. But the propaganda work was too much for a lieutenant. He realized, "collective propaganda was inefficient as it was transmitted by word-of-mouth as people were reluctant to express their thoughts publicly." He described how he changed his methods in *Contacts*: each military team was responsible for a village neighborhood and did the job "with a notebook in which the propaganda theme of the day was recorded, along with the names of people to speak to, the duration of the contact, and the subject's reactions." Analyzing the notebooks allowed him to draw conclusions about the populace's state of mind. Galula refused to see propaganda as brain washing responsible for spreading lies. He saw it, rather, as a way to make the army's successes known to the populace. "What good were our successes if they were unknown by the population or only known in an abstract manner?"[79]

Among the original methods used by Galula, a notable one was whitewashing the houses in the villages, an initiative suggested by his subordinates. The move was part of a cleanliness policy for the villages and was carried out by the post commander at Bou Souar. Galula used Bou Souar as an example to other mayors so that they would adopt the system.[80] "Four communities are entirely whitewashed and two others are being whitewashed," wrote Lieutenant Lavail in his April 1958 report. "This idea, initiated by the post commander of Bou Souar and endorsed by Major [*sic*] Galula with the slogan 'Clean as the New Algeria' seems to be really liked by the people." It was obvious that the policy of improving hygiene and visible signs of winning the population to France were a good mix.

Action taken against the OPA and the destruction of its cells seems to have borne fruit. Admittedly, the OPA had not been destroyed completely, but its influence was reduced to a minimum (tax collecting and supply) and it seemed no longer to have the capacity to intimidate and do propaganda. The failure of the strike called by the FLN on January 28, 1957, at Djebel Aïssa Mimoun seemed to indicate a decrease in the OPA's influence on the populace. According to Galula's account: "I took a tour of the subdistrict today. Everything was normal. The peasants were in their fields, the children were at school, and the women talked at the fountains. At Igonane Ameur, to show that the populace wasn't taking part in the strike, all the men worked with picks and shovels along the road to Grand Remblai. The zone commander called me, 'Congratulations Galula. We've overflown Kabylia to report on the strike. The only zone where the pilot spotted civilian activity was your subdistrict.'"[81] Pfirrmann's report of January 28, 1957, confirmed Galula's position: "There was no strike at Djebel Aïssa Mimoun: not in the schools, not in the work sites—only the school at the village of Akaoudj (not in Galula's subdistrict) which lacked 40% of its students." At Akaoudj, the success of the strike was due to the treachery of the elected official put in place by the SAS. There is, however, another failure noted in the third company's unit history: the deserted market at Bou Souar.[82]

These two examples show that the OPA had not been eradicated completely. Moreover, the situation was in reality more ambiguous than it seemed, even for those who were conspicuous in the support for France. Pfirrmann, like Galula, does not mention the spontaneous action of the residents of Igonane Ameur to thwart the strike, but rather that of the residents of Aït Braham. "To disorganize the strike, the residents decided to work a full day without pay, cutting wood to heat the classrooms." But, for Pfirrmann, this was no sign of having won over the populace. "Make no mistake. In the old days, serious intelligence, arrests and interrogations, revealed the rebel logistic network. It doesn't seem appropriate to arrest suspects if we aren't embedded there [in the villages], as they would be replaced and we would have to begin again." This reflection of the SAS commander at Aït Braham also joins that of Galula's about Igonane Ameur. "Paradoxically, Igonane Ameur was now the only village that I hadn't systematically purged. I hated to do it, because the populace had cooperated with us openly since the departure of the OPA leader, at least in appearance." Far from being naïve, Galula recognized that a core of opposition remained that he had failed to detect. He preferred not to react. The attitude of the majority of the population was then positive and this could only reinforce the French position over the long term. Finally, the unit history of the third company reported for its part that the delegates from Mendja and Bou Souar did not attend the meeting called because of the strike. "At Captain Galula's request, to show their lack of support for the strikers," they were to cut and deliver three tons of wood to the school at Tala Ilane.

Clearly, the situation is much more complex than that seen by the optimistic Galula, who proclaimed triumphantly in the *Lettre d'informations* that "in four purged villages, five members of the OPA were killed, two imprisoned, 30 members were arrested and released on conditional liberty, and several became councilmen or *harkis*. The signs show that numerous OPA cells were destroyed: the men are smoking again, the residents go to the infirmary and chat with the soldiers. The community work is done voluntarily and without coercion." He concluded, "It is easy to evoke Sisyphus when speaking to the destruction of rebel cells. On the contrary, if this operation is properly conducted, it is irreversible."[83] The problem was that the operation to dismantle the OPA was not carried out properly in the subdistrict, as the years 1958–59 would show.

After having eliminated the OPA, local partners willing to support the army's pacification policy had to be found. The difficulty for Galula and the SAS commander was finding these partners.

FIFTH STEP: "SET UP, BY MEANS OF ELECTIONS, NEW PROVISIONAL LOCAL AUTHORITIES"

In *Counterinsurgency Warfare*, Galula writes, "Now begins the constructive part of the counterinsurgent program . . . the objective of the counterinsurgent's effort is to obtain the active support of the population, without which the insurgency cannot be liquidated."[84] Galula insists heavily on the necessity of organizing elections and selecting the right candidate. He also places equal importance on the limits of the electoral district in which the officials are to act. Indeed, if district boundaries were artificially drawn and did not correspond to how the community organized itself, there was risk of conflict among officials, even the best intentioned ones and taking local administrative action would be ineffective in the long run. Galula addressed the problem: "I do not know who was responsible for the carving of the new communes in Kabylia. I was told it was the work of a young French anthropologist well acquainted with the area and the Kabyles. All I know definitely, however, is that neither the SAS officer nor I was consulted insofar as Djebel Aïssa Mimoun was concerned. We both learned officially one day that four communes had been created in my subdistrict. . . . As it happened, large tracts of farmland owned by the people of one commune were included in another, and hamlets traditionally related to a village in commune A were now part of commune B. We also seriously doubted the possibility that four such small communes, each poor in economic and human resources, could operate efficiently. . . . Where would we find the men competent enough to administer four communes?"[85] Pfirrmann's report of January 26, 1956 confirmed Galula's position. "Investigating the repartition of the communes is proving difficult. The people don't talk. The SAS commander was warned that he would have great difficulty in getting delegates elected." Despite these problems that would weigh on community building, Pfirrmann, charged with designating new municipal authorities, found his first candidates with Galula's help in 1956. "The delegates from Igonane Ameur will be appointed soon." Here we are in Galula's subdistrict where pacification seems to be proceeding much faster than in the others, whether in terms of education or community building.

In *Pacification in Algeria*,[86] Galula tells of the difficulties encountered in finding a president of the *djemaa* at Igonane Ameur. Knowing the population well, he spotted a good possibility in Mr. Challal (a pseudonym) "in his early fifties, dignified, calm, well-mannered; I had observed on several occasions that he seemed to be respected by the other villagers; he obviously was a notable, a natural leader." He consulted the Kabyle *harkis* from the fourth company who had nothing to say against him. He tried to persuade him to stand for mayor, but he refused. Galula met with the population and proposed candidates for president of the *djemaa* and asked the people to approve his choices by raising their hands. Two names passed unremarked. He then suggested Challal and asked those who were against him to raise their hands. Nobody did, so he was designated mayor by this subterfuge and in spite of the protests of the other newly-elected officials. Galula explained that the election was for a provisional president until definitive elections could be held. Indeed, the unit history[87] and the SAS report of October 25, 1956, bear out that, on October 24, the provisional *djemaa* president was replaced by a mayor and eight delegates. Challal fled to France the same day restrictions were lifted after the November 1956 strike.

These designations cannot, however, be considered successes, as Galula did. The SAS officer, who spent two days explaining municipal delegates their roles, ended his report on a rather pessimistic note. "They do not seem thrilled to be appointed and are hoping, in elections, to go unnoted on the list of elected officials, which speaks volumes about their general mood, considering what we have to do there, in the best-controlled village." The desire to implement quickly municipal reform resulted in the designation of unwilling participants. Galula seemed to be the cause, as this happened in the village he best controlled and the one with which he had constant contact. In his book, Galula evades the problem and drops the subject of the elections at Igonane Ameur, even though the elections posed many problems. Pfirrmann, as an ex-Native Affairs officer, saw immediately that these people were not representative of the village. "No former member of the *djemaa* was among the eight delegates." In Kabylia, the *djemaa* was the village assembly including the heads of the families and elders, which manage daily village life. Its members were respected by the entire village. Igonane Ameur had to skirt both France and the FLN. In this case, forced to choose its delegates the village resolved the problem of its compromise with France by putting forward people who did not represent it. The end of Pfirrmann's report also figures in our interpretation. "The people's official explanation: the elders have all resigned or left. Mostly likely version: it seems that, according to well-known Berber behavior in such cases, the population we have chosen support us superficially to insulate the truly significant and influential people" (October 25, 1956).

Galula insisted on the election of delegates at Bou Souar. "The elections did not occasion much enthusiasm. No candidates appeared until the very last day. The villagers finally elected Bekri as mayor; among the councilmen was Gabsi, the man who had tried to give the alert when we raided Bou Souar." Although Bekri was a pro-French veteran, he was also slightly senile.[88] We can see that the delegates chosen in the two villages by Galula were very reluctant or incompetent to carry out the tasks for which they were elected.

Galula thought that all means of bringing pressure to find candidates should be employed without hesitation. Municipal funding policy must be used as a political weapon against the insurgency. Galula asked the prefect that funds be allocated in proportion to the level of cooperation shown by the population. "If this is not the case, what would be the motivation for the people to switch to our side? How could the administration consolidate its political machine if it could not protect it?" He asked that the budget be allocated to each district based on these criteria. The prefect approved of his vision and the municipalities received more money, even beyond what they could use. Was this due to the prefect who then gave similar instructions to the director of the mixed community or was it a personal initiative that backed Galula's thinking? The director of the mixed community answered the SAS commander unambiguously on the necessity of putting pressure on the populace to choose delegates. In principle nothing was given to villages with no delegates; the contrary in these villages, work sites, AMG visits, and every other form of aid, was stopped. It could be seen that at Djebel Aïssa Mimoun, the civil administration and the SAS subdistrict commander agreed on forcing the population to take sides without hesitating to use economic and administrative aid as leverage. It is therefore understandable that delegates were found at Tahanouts, Ighil Bouchene, Taguemout, Akaoudj, and Aït Braham (November 5, 1956). Pfirrmann considered this success at finding delegates as "symptoms of the developing situation," notably at Igonane Ameur and Akaoudj (November 8, 1956). The SAS officer's opinion of local leaders was favorable at first, contrary to Igonane Ameur, "At Akaoudj . . . the delegates seemed to take their roles seriously. . . . They seemed to have made a better start than at the previous villages." The efficiency of the new delegates was indicated, according to Pfirrmann, by the rise in school enrollments from 12 to 60 students (November 15, 1956). In the neighboring subdistrict, Akaoudj was also made into a municipality. But the SAS officer was pessimistic, "I hope this community building effort will be a quick success." This fear issued from the fact that the newly elected municipal officials weren't capable or motivated to undertake this kind of work. "The delegates now seem to know how the SAS operates. They are beginning to come frequently to collect mail for their constituents." The optimism wasn't as pronounced at the beginning of the report. The SAS commander thought that it was for the politicians to come to receive the money. . . . As for the competence of the new officials, the commentary is clear, "None of the delegates knows how to read or write" (December 10, 1956).

On January 7, 1957, municipal reform created four communes: Bou Souar, Igonane Ameur, Khelouyene, and Aït Braham, which forced the SAS to organize municipal elections. Galula's thinking about the community-building policy is revealed by General Garbray, the inspector of the colonial forces, in a letter addressed to Pfirrmann, January 7, 1957. "I realized today in Captain Galula's subdistrict, at Bou Souar and Igonane Ameur, that the commander views community building in the following manner: It seems premature to do community building. A. Because the population has not yet given real proof of its loyalty. B. It would be logical to draw the first lessons from Akaoudj. But if an order must be carried out, then we can build the communities of Bou Souar and Igonane Ameur soon." In early January 1957, Galula did not think that the fifth step, local elections, could begin which meant that he suspected that the OPA was still active in the villages in question or perhaps he had yet to find the pro-French minority that could destroy the OPA.

Garbray gave his opinion on Galula's position at the end of his letter. "I completely share this point of view. The question is whether this community building which affects the country's future should be done seriously, in which case it is necessary to hurry slowly. . . . Community building is an illusion; none of the conditions are set so that it may function." The slow progress of installing the candidates shows how difficult it was to find suitable ones, moreover, due to their scarcity, municipal officials would be presented on a single ballot. The administrative obligation to find someone to stand for each post made this an artificial procedure, in addition to running the risk of having an FLN supporter as the head of a new municipality. The example of Akaoudj, cited by Galula, became a negative example: the president of the *djemaa* resigned at the *sous-préfecture* a few days later, then took it up again while concealing it from the SAS officer. "We are preparing a bright future with this kind of mayor. I cannot, in fact, take the official *djemaa* president seriously, draped in an official sash, who must be paid like a fictitious *moghazni*.[89] The administration, quick to let us twist arms to illicit nominations should show the same speed in finding legal and normal means of operating," Pfirrmann commented sarcastically (January 10, 1957).

The pressure of administration, military orders in the chain of command, financial problems in paying newly elected officials (and their double standards) put the SAS officer and the subdistrict commander in a difficult situation. Pfirrmann's recriminations against the mayor of Akaoudj would multiply. "Asserting his independence and claiming money so far are only objects of this mayor's squabbles at the prefecture" (January 14, 1957). Moreover, the mayor's son participated in the school boycott. The mayor feigned surprise when we asked him if there were rebels, although there were traces proving their presence (January 21, 1957). The mayor explained that the fellaghas were in charge and that he didn't want to meddle in political issues. Pfirrmann ends his report: "I think that the mayor of Akaoudj has clearly shown which side he is on. The SAS commander's warnings went unheeded" (January 28, 1957).

If things were deteriorating at Akaoudj, at Igonane Ameur and Bou Souar the situation seemed much better. Pfirrmann praised the two communes: "The situation is much calmer at Igonane Ameur since occupation by the military and the election of their delegates under the enlightened leadership of Captain Galula, the subdistrict commander. At Igonane Ameur it was whispered that the women favored us after several months of effort from Galula's company. But I only report what I've confirmed myself, with prudence and reserve" (January 24, 1957). This was the result of Galula's policy directed at the women of Igonane Ameur and Aït Braham. He had organized childcare and even suggested the creation of units responsible for improving conditions for women. "I had stressed that Algerian women were our largest group of potential supporters provided we took the lead in their emancipation. I had learned this from the Chinese Communists."[90]

However, the process of appointing new representatives was upset by an additional factor, a reduction in military force. Pfirrmann complained of it vehemently in his report of February 4, 1957, in the middle of organizing the new municipalities (five of six to be finished), "it was the moment we chose to move a company from Djebel Aïssa Mimoun without asking my opinion, contrary to all previous instructions specifying that changes in the embedding must be agreed upon by the administrative authority. . . . It goes without saying that if the company goes, I can't guarantee anything as far as continued community building goes."

Pfirrmann reviewed the situation in each of the subdistricts of the three companies. Removing Galula's company, he wrote, "would permanently sabotage [community building] at Bou Souar and Igonane Ameur." The first company, located at Grand Remblai, deployed into mobile platoons. "Rebel bands would soon be back." The SAS commander explained that he had only four *moghaznis* and, therefore, he could not defend himself, embed elsewhere, or protect his workers or the work sites. Pfirrmann's complaints weren't enough. The first company of the 45th BIC was moved to another sector. Obviously, the SAS commander felt undermined by the civilian prefecture, as he points out: "the prefect's chief of staff declared on the way out: 'Wherever we put the military, they got up to no good.' As far as I was concerned we should have been taken back from the civilians and given back to our regiments. In any case, without the companies from the 45th BIC, there would have been no communities, no mayors, no SAS, and it would have been better just to admit it and spare us the insult." Pfirrmann's discontent is also explained by his desire to be transferred back to his original unit in the Foreign Legion;[91] but was also due to the shortage of SAS officers. He was kept in his position as SAS commander. The administrator of the mixed community's answer was clear. "You've spoken with the prefect about [the withdrawal]. There's nothing to be done about it. We weren't consulted because they knew perfectly well that we wouldn't agree, but also because the 27th DIA never did give a damn about our opinion" (February 9, 1957). Operational imperatives and the military command's contempt for the civil administration would explain why the protests of the SAS went unheard. For Galula unity of effort between civil and military activity is fundamental, though this is clearly not the case in 1957 in his subdistrict in Kabylia.

While community building seemed most well established in Galula's subdistrict, it nevertheless remained fragile. An SAS report on Djebel Aïssa Mimoun signaled that suspects arrested at Ikhlomène and Aït Braham denounced a tax collector, a municipal delegate from Igonane Ameur. Pfirrmann's bitter conclusion: "Results should never be considered definitively established" (February 28, 1957). At Akaoudj, in the neighboring sector, the situation deteriorated. Three rebels who had taken refuge there were killed while residents were in contact with the rebels. Of 40 students, only 4 attended school (March 11, 1957). If we review community building efforts, the mayor of Akaoudj worked with the rebellion and the OPA was still present. Finally, in one of the best-controlled villages, one delegate was an OPA member. The community building, judged premature by Galula and Pfirrmann, showed its limits as the villages remained under control of the OPA. The SAS commander said the same thing. "Villages have to be purged of the enemy before community building. This requires developing intelligence which takes time. Community building like that we did in certain areas was begun in spite of good sense" (March 14, 1957). This was a far cry from the optimism shown by Galula in *Pacification in Algeria*, where he stated that, in March 1957, the OPA had been destroyed in his subdistrict, except at Igonane Ameur.[92] An attempt to account for this contradiction can be found in Galula's article in *Lettre d'informations:* "It was shown that the FLN pressured people to vote for certain delegates and, in one case, to elect a president. On its own, the population eliminated these imposed delegates, except certain ones who had given evidence of sincere repentance and demonstrated a change of opinion"[93] Galula's response only demonstrates that Step Four (Destruction of the Insurgent Political Organization) was not fully accomplished, which explains why the OPA was able to disrupt the following phase. The efforts of the SAS and the army, therefore, were dispersed between fighting the OPA and a search for candidates. But arresting suspects could only disrupt the calm necessary for any community building policy.

In spite of these difficulties, Galula continued community building, extending it to another village. He took advantage of the request of the inhabitants of Ighouna, evacuated by force to Igonane Ameur in the past for not having warned the army of an ambush that had been set, to return to their village. Galula permitted their return, but required that they elect a village council. The richest villager of Ighouna was elected mayor, but two months later he tendered his resignation and was replaced by a worker returned from Saint Etienne. To avoid new problems, Galula warned them that he would hold them responsible in the event of further ambushes.[94]

SIXTH STEP: "TEST THE LOCAL LEADERS BY GIVING THEM CONCRETE TASKS. REPLACE THE WORTHLESS AND INCOMPETENT, AND IDENTIFY THE GOOD ONES. ORGANIZE PASSIVE DEFENSIVE UNITS"

In *Counterinsurgency Warfare*, Galula writes, "The ultimate results of the counterinsurgent's efforts in regard to the population depend on the effectiveness of the men who have just been elected. . . . The first thing to do, therefore, is to test these new local leaders. The principle of the test is simple: They are given concrete tasks and they are judged on their ability to fulfill them."[95] The sixth step combines military and civil activity. For Galula, testing local leaders meant testing their effectiveness in their new responsibilities, but also their loyalty. Yet the actions taken by Galula at Djebel Aïssa Mimoun seemed to be more concerned with the effectiveness of new public officials rather than their loyalty; indeed, Galula seems to have considered the OPA destroyed.

The municipalities functioned only poorly with newly elected, untrained officials. Galula asked that his subordinates who assisted the village councils not lead debates and to avoid paternalism. "True, we could run things better than they did, but it would have been self-defeating both for my immediate testing purpose and in the long run."[96] Galula is, of course, paraphrasing T. E. Lawrence, the architect of the Arab guerilla resistance against the Turks during World War I. "Better the Arabs do it tolerably than that you do it perfectly. It is their war, and you are to help them, not to win it for them."[97] Galula put a soldier, or one of the better students, at the disposition of elected officials to act as secretary to record their meetings. Galula and the SAS commander also filtered the information flowing from the prefecture and asked the prefect to provide minimal training on administrative work. They suggested the simplification of administrative procedures and asked that a collection of essential administrative laws for the mayors be compiled. The prefect promised to carry out these measures, but did not, as is shown by subsequent SAS reports. "It was then necessary to find what the people needed and, if possible, bring it to them. If the new village governments cannot implement measures to change people's lives, they will collapse and take us with them." Community building policy reflected directly on the army's and the SAS's credibility with the populace.

As he acknowledges in *Counterinsurgency Warfare*, "A certain degree of paternalism cannot be avoided initially since the elected leaders are both unknown and untrained."[98] Galula therefore refused plans suggested by the new authorities like those from Bou Souar: construction of a mosque and construction of a costly and unnecessary road. He advised instead to build a reservoir, since the village had regularly experienced droughts in summer. He refused to build a town hall, suggesting instead that a school be built. At Igonane Ameur, a school and a road for the olive harvest and to move material was built by the community. At Khelouyene, the mayor decided to build a reservoir and an irrigation system. Aït Braham built a school without taking a loan by depending solely on the volunteer labor of residents and using local materials. Pfirrmann provided funding for the purchase of tiles, windows, and a door. Hygiene improved with regular street cleaning, and latrines were built for each house.[99]

The second phase of Step 6 is military. The objective was to get the population to reinforce the military counterinsurgency effort and, eventually, to take the military's place. In November 1956, Galula acknowledged the failure of the pacification process in *Contacts*: in the event of French units' withdrawal, the rebellion would resume its previous positions. The goal of pacification, after all, was "to leave, but to leave the region in the hands of a Kabyle elite capable of holding it for us." In March 1957, in his account of pacification at Djebel Aïssa Mimoun, Galula considered that the situation had finally improved. He developed his initial thinking in the magazine at the beginning of his article in *Contacts*, "Mobilizing the Populace": "What constitutes victory in this sort of war? When does pacification end? My personal answer can be stated this way: victory is won and pacification ends when most of the counterinsurgent forces can safely be withdrawn, leaving the population to take care of itself with the help of a contingent of police and Army forces. It is therefore necessary to make the population participate actively in the counterinsurgent effort, to mobilize it in the struggle." The populace's involvement is won in four ways: "1. Organizing self-defense units in each commune. 2. Levying a *harka*. 3. Getting the population to police the area itself. 4. Preparing the local leaders to take over the propaganda work."[100]

Galula organized self-defense units at Bou Souar to protect the school and teachers. "It was a mission I could confide to them, as it was their own children who attended the school." In March 1957, he organized self-defense units at Khelouyene and Aït Braham. But in spite of the prefecture's promises to pay the volunteers, no funds were delivered and he was obliged to let them go.

The SAS archives also mention this aspect of pacification. Testing the reliability of local leaders turned into a fiasco in the nearby subdistrict. At Akaoudj, this consisted of asking officials to find volunteers for self-defense units. Pfirrmann explained, "The village refused to endanger itself and asked that we choose the men ourselves, as the delegates and the mayor did not want to be held responsible in the case of desertion" (April 4, 1957). A method which put people in danger also had financial limits. The SAS didn't seem able to afford such an ambitious policy. "The population seems to have been on our side, but to convince them, we would have had to make good on our promises (repairs, roads, wells, schools, town halls, community financing). These administrative delays made our promises ring hollow" (March 4, 1957). Security seems not to have been assured entirely for the people in danger. The minutes of the meeting with the prefect on April 5 explain that the people implicated at Aït Braham (arrested, having denounced OPA leaders, and later released) left for France without authorization. "This is becoming embarrassing for us, with respect to the healthy part of the population," explained the SAS commander.

The SAS reports provide more detail about financing the self-defense units at Igonane Ameur and Bou Souar. With compensation of 480 francs by day, the villages of Igonane Ameur, Bou Souar, Ikhalomène, and Akaoudj each agree to form a self-defense unit. Pfirrmann suggested creation of a fictitious *harka* to pay for the four self-defense units (minutes of the meeting with the prefect April 5, 1957). For Pfirrmann, the reason the populace turned toward the French was essentially due to the presence of a band of about 15 guerillas from the north, outside of the region, who had committed two assassinations. In the SAS political information bulletin of March 20 and April 25, 1957, Pfirrmann confirmed that the makeup of the militia at Akaoudj was due not to the army's persuasion, but the passage of a band which had committed atrocities targeting the population. The community deciding to protect itself outweighed any persuasion from the army. Even so, financing the militia remained a problem. On April 16, 1957, Pfirrmann asked for increased financing "or the people will go unpaid and will grow discontented." Money was the crux of everything, as the SAS officer wrote. "At Akaoudj . . . for a militiaman, it was money first, then the militia." According to the report of April 18, we learn that at Khelouyene and Aït Braham, the president of the *djemaa*, chosen by the population, had been threatened and requested immediate help from the militia. "The people requested weapons and the prefecture promised twenty rifles. The militia will not go unfunded." On April 25, 1957, the SAS report indicates that there were 9 rifles promised by the battalion and 20 rifles by the prefecture to arm four militia units. We also learn that the subdistrict commanders were against doing so. We can speculate that their opposition stemmed from the fact that, in October 1956 after a militia had been formed at Akaoudj, four guards deserted to the rebellion with their weapons.

Galula created a *harka*. According to the SAS record of April 20 1957, we know that a *harka* was operating in the neighboring subdistrict of Tahanouts during the summer of 1956 and that its official existence dated to March 1957. As raising a militia proved impossible, Galula organized a second *harka* of 25 volunteers recruited at Bou Souar, Igonane Ameur, Khelouyene, and Aït Braham. The political information bulletin for April 25 to May 25, 1957 confirms that Galula signaled the creation of a *harka* on May 1 to monitor outsiders, protect the city hall, and to keep watch over the villages. This followed calls for the formation that gave birth to plans to form a militia. Numerous volunteers were recruited by the town halls. Unreliable people were refused admission by Galula, who depended on the mayors' opinions and other locals whom he trusted. At Bou Souar, recruitment didn't take place as the population was considered too unreliable. Galula tested one of the *harkis* himself, sending a night patrol to pass by as if they were rebels. The *harki* said nothing of the incident so, the following day, Galula threw him out of the *harka*. This served as an example to the others to report such incidents.

The *harka's* mission was to protect villagers from ambushes, watching over the post offices and schools, to do propaganda work, and to collect intelligence. It guided the company on operations, searched for caches, and interpreted suspects' reactions. Galula asked the mayors and municipal councils to participate in collecting intelligence to maintain order and as well to note the names of the best informers in Khelouyene, Aït Braham, and Igonane Ameur. Only Bou Souar did the minimum necessary and Galula wondered whether he was being double-crossed and was testing them in vain.[101]

The ALN tried to react against the recruitment of *harkis*. In his *Lettre d'informations*, Galula tells us that there were attempts to intimidate the *harkis*. A spy was sent to the subdistrict to learn the *harkis'* habits. A *harki* was then murdered in April 1957 while returning home. After a half hour, the spy was unmasked, confessed, and was shot by the *harkis*. A week later the leader of the band was killed in ambush. In August 1957, another *harki* was assassinated, which led to spotting a rebel group which was then eliminated.[102]

In April 1958, efforts to create self-defense militias were tried again by the SAS. The mayors' reticence showed that the situation remained far from stable. "The idea of self-defense units as an indicator of stable pacification is not yet accepted." It seems that in the minds of the mayors, self-defense involved total commitment and confidence in the future of France that was lacking. In June 1958, two self-defense militias were operating at Khelouyene (15 men) and at Aït Braham (27 men).

SEVENTH STEP: "GROUPING AND ORGANIZING LEADERS INTO A NATIONAL POLITICAL PARTY"

In *Counterinsurgency Warfare*, Galula explains: "[local leaders] will eventually have to be grouped and organized within a national counterinsurgent political party. . . . A party is the instrument of politics, particularly in revolutionary war where politics counts for so much. The best policy may be worthless for the counterinsurgent so long as he does not possess the necessary instrument to implement it."[103] At the time of Galula's service in Kabylia, in 1956, there was no real national political party to organize the defense of French Algeria. By eliminating the *communes mixtes* and creating *communes de plein exercise* (full-status districts with elected mayors), which was the objective of Algeria's governor general, R. Lacoste, a third force[104] was created, between the FLN, fighting for its independence and the Europeans who wanted to maintain the status quo. Galula was ahead in the process of community building and supported this policy at Djebel Aïssa Mimoun. The objective of the movement in May 1958 was to unify Muslims and Europeans in public welfare committees and to create political momentum in implementing civic equality. Galula described the movement of May 1958 in *Contacts*. "Integration means the recognition of equal rights for all citizens of Algeria and their brothers in metropolitan France. It means the pooling of the material resources of Algeria and continental France."[105] The historian

R. Girardet put it this way: "integration was the key idea, the myth responding to the dreams of the crowds in Algeria to counter the mysticism of independence."[106] Faced with the insurgents' ideological power coming from the cause of independence, the loyalists also opposed the cause of integration. Galula wrote about this ideological opposition, "To deprive the insurgent of a good cause amounts to solving the country's basic problems. If this is possible, well and good."[107] It was SAS officers and subdistrict commanders who organized demonstrations of fraternization in Algiers on the initiative of Colonel Lacheroy,[108] the great theoretician of revolutionary warfare, who was stationed in the area. Galula found himself in Algiers on May 16 and spoke of "an indescribable enthusiasm. It was as if a long nightmare had suddenly ended." He met Pfirrmann, who was commanding the SAS in the Casbah of Algiers who told him, "Last week, it would have taken a whole division to move the Moslems from the Kasbah. Today they have understood, rightly or wrongly, that the Army has assumed power, and that's enough for them."[109] At Djebel Aïssa Mimoun, the SAS commander, Second Lieutenant Meneault addressed a message from his command to French citizens: "As you know, on May 13, a peaceful revolution took place in Algeria. All those living in Algeria, Muslim and Christian, are now French." Fearing a negotiation with the FLN and the abandonment of Algeria by the political authorities of the Fourth Republic, the committees of public welfare (CSP in French) were organized in every Algerian commune by the SAS, the army, and European settlers to defend French Algeria. In mainland France, Chassin tried in vain to mobilize supporters of French Algeria against the government by creating a public welfare committee in every community. Chassin threatened to march on Paris with 15,000 supporters but only managed to gather a dozen people who failed to take Saint Etienne.[110] The public welfare committees would provoke the fall of the Fourth Republic and bring General de Gaulle back to power. Committees were formed at Djebel Aïssa Mimoun as well as at Bordj Menaïel. Galula, then posted to Bordj Menaïel, was named head of the committee. Galula designated equal numbers of Muslim and European representatives to the CSP. He organized a rally at Bordj Menaïel and invited the militias, the mayors, schoolchildren, and selected women from Djebel Aïssa Mimoun to participate. Galula then moved volunteers from Bordj Menaïel to Tizi-Ouzou, where Salan and Soustelle had organized a rally.[111] In the rest of Meneault's letter he explained that on May 18 and 27, the residents of Djebel Aïssa Mimoun showed at Tizi-Ouzou "their joy at being sure of remaining French in front of General Guérin, Mr. Soustelle, Ms. Sid Cara, General Salan, and General Massu."[112]

Lacoste's third-force policy and the May 1958 movement resulted in the organization of a parliamentary group, Unité de la République, comprised of 52 of the 71 Algerian deputies. The group defended the territorial integrity between Algeria and mainland France, refused any negotiation with the FLN, and called for the economic and social development of Muslims as full citizens. The group was directed by Robert Abdesselam who was a deputy from Algiers and Lacoste's lawyer, in addition to being a tennis champion. Among the many Algerian deputies, European or Muslim, there were four from Tizi-Ouzou: A. Saadi, S. Korsi, A. Ioulalem, and H. Colonna. The Bachaga Boualam, leader of the *harka* from the Beni Boudouane tribe in the area of Orléansville also participated. He would become vice president of the national assembly. On July 20, 1959, Unité de la République counted 47 deputies as members. In September 1959, the group left the majority in protest of de Gaulle's self-determination policy.

EIGHTH STEP: "WIN OVER OR SUPPRESS THE LAST INSURGENT REMNANTS"

In *Counterinsurgency Warfare*, Galula writes, "The counterinsurgent, while concentrating on the tasks necessary for winning the support of the population, has not neglected to continue tracking the guerrillas left in the selected area after the intensive operations described in the first step . . . small scale operations could be time-consuming and not very productive. This is why it would be more profitable for the counterinsurgent to revert now to the same massive military effort that characterized the first step."[113] Galula had two ways of achieving this objective of destroying ALN bands. Either he could have participated in other companies' and battalions' operations—although he had no explicit orders to do so—or he could fight the ALN with his operations confined to his subdistrict where he had complete freedom of action.

In August 1956, an operation[114] was mounted in the area against Oudiaï and his band of 25 rebels without the benefit of an intelligence briefing on the ALN. An ALN unit was believed to be operating in the wadi Stita and was surrounded by three battalions. Two battalions conducted a sweep. Gendarmes were present with each battalion. Two platoons from Galula's company participated in order to watch the inhabitants of a village and to set up a night ambush. Neither action brought any result. Taking advantage of the night and the terrain Oudiaï's band slipped through French lines. An officer explained to Galula that successful operations began in the early hours of the night; otherwise they failed. Another cordon and search operation failed in the forest of Mizrana in October 1957, in which 160 ALN rebels were able to exfiltrate under the cover of night. Large scale operations were prone to failure, however Galula's company had no freedom of action outside of his area of operations.

As he was convinced that the army dominated by day and ALN by night, Galula modified his company's tactics to adapt to combat within the subdistrict. Four-man night ambushes were increased while night patrols were abandoned, which only advantaged an enemy lying in wait.[115] Galula was also confronted with the absence of intelligence on the local ALN commander, Oudiaï. He cordoned off a rugged ravine full of brush, where he suspected the ALN had just hidden. This, too, was a failure. Galula's company settled for shelling the ravine when lights appeared there, which was their only way to dislodge them temporarily.

Based on information from Bou Souar, Galula was able to arrest Oudiaï's cousin, a deputy commander (also called Oudiaï). The SAS reported the following: "A. Oudiaï from Bou Souar arrested October 14 [the unit history claims October 12] by the third company at the request of the battalion intelligence officer and was shot while trying to escape" (October 15, 1956). The situation in the district was far from calm, as reflected by the SAS report. "On October 19, an armed band of about fifteen individuals passed by Inkicheren and set an ambush. A patrol from the fourth company [of the neighboring subdistrict] stumbled into it. The band fled with at least one wounded. They were likely from Soltani." At the beginning of December, a band of 30 to 40 men commanded by the ALN leader Rahal clashed with a company from the 45th BIC. A single rebel was killed, while the French suffered three wounded (reports of December 3 and 6, 1956). A large ALN unit was therefore able to escape. Galula's outposts at Ighouna and Igonane Ameur were also harassed a few days later (December 1, 1956). Even in spite of the death of the deputy chief of the ALN, the situation remained fragile in the area around Djebel Aïssa Mimoun.

Knowing that his units were dispersed and therefore less effective, he raised a commando composed of men taken from companies of the 45th BIC responsible for tracking down fellaghas north of the subdistrict.[116] South of Galula's subdistrict, the 1/93rd RAMA crossed paths with Oudiaï's band. The commando from the 45th BIC was called in as reinforcement, but arrived after the fighting, just in time to recover weapons. Oudiaï's body was located, as Pfirrmann found out belatedly: "Commander Oudiaï's death during an operation still unconfirmed" (January 31, 1957). In the *Lettre d'informations*,[117] Galula explains, "In December 1956, the rebel leader was killed along with ten of his men during a night ambush." However, contrary to what he writes in his book, Galula doesn't exactly credit in *Lettre d'informations* his units and tactics, but rather a neighboring unit. He wanted, rather, to take psychological advantage of the death of Oudiaï to show the bodies of the fellaghas to delegation from each village (under the pretext of identifying them) to quell rumors that Oudiaï had escaped. Argoud used public display of bodies to make an impression on the populace.[118]

If the situation had improved at Igonane Ameur and at Bou Souar, owing to the luck of a successful operation, the situation was different across the rest of the district. The SAS commander explained that the ALN seemed to be adapting and had taken the offensive. "The atmosphere at Aïssa Mimoun village, which had improved in November and early December, seems to have once again deteriorated over the last few days" (January 24, 1957, covering the period from December 20, 1956 to January 24, 1957). "The ALN command was overhauled with the introduction of new leaders who increased activities. As I had feared, the 45th BIC did not keep up with their [the ALN's] tempo after the end of November. One month afterward, the rebels returned. Akaoudj, until then, epitomized village community-building. Understandably, the rebels made a concentrated effort to sabotage it." At Akaoudj, an official quit and the school suffered a boycott. "The bands aren't completely destroyed. With three day's effort they undid months of work." Pfirrmann didn't think that patrolling was enough, but that reinforcements and rapid response units were needed.

According to Galula's account, the OPA cells had been destroyed and the ALN was isolated from the populace. The ALN was itself obliged to devote its time to collecting taxes and supplies from remote farms and in nearly abandoned hamlets. After two months, the nine ALN members reached the Mizrana Forest, a traditional safe haven, far from the army's reach. Two deserters told Galula, "his *djebel* was considered a lost area by the rebel chiefs in the Mizrana. The fellaghas were forbidden to cross it without express orders."[119] In fact, SAS reports confirm two public rallies on May 2 and 21, 1957, "a psyops operation with loudspeakers and speeches from the two." The SAS reports of March 20 to April 25, 1957 are much less optimistic about the general situation. "The region is permeable to infiltration by small rebel groups and [our] military presence is too dispersed." An operation was conducted near Aït Braham: four rebels from Djebel Aïssa Mimoun were killed, among them the political officer, the source of threats against municipal delegation heads (SAS report dated April 25 to May 25, 1957).

From September 1957, as Galula explains in *Lettre d'informations*,[120] there was a "weak recovery of rebel activity conducted by a band of seven outlaws," who enjoyed no support from the OPA. They traveled the sub-district by night and confined their activities to harassing an army outpost. The inhabitants refused to pay taxes to the ALN, explaining that there were too many traitors and the army's control was too tight. This was indeed confirmed by Lieutenant Lavail, an SAS commander. "The fellaghas' families no longer receive benefits from the FLN, as the villages no longer pay the taxes." The situation was still far from calm: A delegate from Aït Braham was assassinated and another was attacked in his home (August 25, 1957).

As far as unit organization went, Galula handed over his command in February 1958 to Captain Simon. Galula wanted to mount a final operation to remove the remaining rebels, the Ben Smail band. The SAS report of March 1958 states that on February 22 the company commander and a *harki* were killed in an ambush, but, "the general population continues to place its trust in the army and the SAS." According to Galula, Simon was killed near Tala Atmane. His death was due to two errors: moving at night with too large a unit must have raised attention; moreover, as he was leading from the front, Simon was the first one hit in the ambush. Guérin decided to put Galula back in command to raise the soldiers' and inhabitants' morale. Based on the fact this band must have had local support, Galula decided to target the OPA cell at Tala Atmane and arrested four villagers. Based on indications, he organized a sweep in the area of Akaoudj and succeeded in flushing out five members of the ALN, three of whom were killed, along with the local chief Ben Smail.[121]

In April 1958, Galula left Djebel Aïssa Mimoun for good and conferred the subdistrict to Captain Herrmann. Galula's fight at Djebel Aïssa Mimoun was not simply a matter of military operations and civil-military activity, but also an intensive communication effort with political authorities and the media.

CHAPTER 3

David Galula and Media Counterinsurgency

> If we do not inform the people, others will do it for us, and not in the way we would want.[1]

With this thought, Galula criticized not only media outlets that belonged to or supported the rebellion but those of mainland France like *Le Monde, L'Express, France-Observateur, Témoignage Chrétien, France Soir,*[2] and of course the communist *L'Humanité*. A reading of *Counterinsurgency Warfare* could make one think that Galula was only interested in three audiences for communications operations: the populace living in contact with the rebels, the insurgents, and loyalist forces. It would nevertheless be an error to suppose, as does *Cahier de la recherche doctrinale* from the French doctrine command, "Galula was more interested in the in-theatre population than what was being said in the rear."[3] In several passages in *Pacification in Algeria* Galula shows his preoccupation with the influence of newspapers on public opinion in France as well as in Algeria.

Djebel Aïssa Mimoun did not go unmentioned in the press of the time, nor by the civilian or military authorities who brought journalists there. The SAS and the Djebel Aïssa Mimoun subdistrict were models shown to the mainland press and parliamentary delegations. On December 4, the Parliamentary Committee on National Defense and Gouraud visited the community leaders and the schools. On December 13 it was the turn of the Group of Independent Deputies and Farmers to visit the SAS and the villages. Pfirrmann was critical of these junkets. "Perfectly useless visits, if the newspapers depended on only that to inform their readers" (October 25, 1956).[4] A month later, it was a journalist from the *Saturday Evening*

Post who visited the SAS for about 20 minutes (November 26, 1956) who asked questions about the area around the village, its people, and rebel activity. At the beginning of 1957, Galula sent invitations to journalists to come view the progress made in pacification. None came, with the exception of an American reporter from *US News and World Report,* who stayed for four days and "got a better view than he might have had elsewhere."[5] Galula tried to use all the media: he obtained a recorder and interviewed a young FLN member in the hospital who had been wounded during an operation. The interview was judged interesting enough to broadcast on Algiers radio over several days.[6]

The newly created municipality of Igonane Ameur put in place by Galula, was also visited by the *préfet* who, happily surprised by the good relations between the villagers and the military, invited Lacoste to visit Bou Souar at the end of February 1957. Lacoste accepted the invitation but cancelled at the last moment due to a cabinet meeting. In his place he sent his political affairs director Lucien Paye, future minister of education for the Debré government of 1960, who came with the *préfet* and Gouraud. Paye, returning to Algiers, claimed it was a put-up job: "the populace wants independence and nothing else. So don't tell me that they're sincere [about French authority]." Galula explained that he had been shocked to learn that Paye, chief of staff to the governor general of Algeria, did not believe there was any solution other than independence for Algeria.[7] This should not have been surprising as Paye had been charged by Guy Mollet's government with contacting the ALN leaders in the Aurès mountains during the summer of 1956. These talks failed as the FLN required recognition of Algerian independence as a precondition to negotiation. Paye was then ordered, along with A. Chandernagor, to draw up the future status for Algeria. The plan, which provided for free-and-secret elections, the creation of a single assembly in Algeria, and territorial autonomy was revealed by *France Soir,* September 16, 1956. Mollet canceled the plan and Paye tendered his resignation, which was refused.[8] Galula did not seem to have been aware of Paye's past when he visited the subdistrict six months after the affair came out in the press. Other politicians more amenable to Galula's ideas visited the subdistrict including the minister of defense, M. Morice, who visited in September 1957 with Salan and Guérin.

Galula also criticized the negative influence of the media on the populace, so much so that he sent a sergeant to inquire at the bookshop at Tizi-Ouzou for the number of copies sold of *Le Monde* and the names of the people who bought them. This investigation revealed that 14 were sold in one hour, 12 going to Kabyles. Galula claimed that he wasn't alone in his opinion about the press. He reported that during a meeting of SAS officers of the *sous-préfecture* at Grand Remblai that he attended, SAS officers complained of the bad influence *Le Monde* was having on the citizens in their districts. He noted their reactions: "'Very bad in my area . . . four copies are bought every day.' 'Worse in mine, six copies,' said another. 'It's fine in mine, only one copy.' 'The circulation of this newspaper was literally an accurate barometer of the success of pacification. Not one copy was read in Aïssa Mimoun, fortunately.'"[9]

Galula himself would be criticized in *Le Monde*. "An early report of mine on conditions in Kabylia had been expurgated[10] and printed in a restricted Army bulletin in Algeria [*Contacts*].[11] *Le Monde* got hold of it and devoted two pages of its valuable space for three days showing how 'fascism was guiding the French Army in Algeria.' *L'Humanité* . . . promised to disclose the name of this Captain from Kabylia. I was prouder than if I had been awarded the Legion of Honor."[12] Galula saw his actions called into question, but the criticism did not issue from a single journalist. A student from the *Insitut d'Etudes Politiques* in Paris, author of a 1953 study on agricultural problems in Morocco, adopted the pseudonym Serge Adour. His real name was G. Bélorgey, a social activist working on the France-Maghreb committee. He was admitted to the *Ecole National d'Administration* after his time in Algeria, later pursuing a career in the prefectural government within the ministries, finally serving at the helm of large public enterprises. He finished his career overseas, where he was the director of overseas French broadcasting.[13] The article Bélorgey published was drawn from his 14-month experience as a second lieutenant of reserves on the Moroccan-Algerian frontier, from May 1956 to June 1957. Bélorgey served as intelligence officer of the Second Algerian Spahis from April to June 1957 in the Mostaganem sector, where he witnessed torture and summary executions.[14] On returning from Algeria, he wrote up his experiences in a 250-page typescript,[15] which he sent to the director of *Le Monde*, H. Beuve-Méry. For the third anniversary of the war in Algeria, *Le Monde* serialized the extracts of the typescript in six articles called "Algeria: from Utopia to Totalitarianism." The articles were published in *Le Monde* from October 31, 1957, to November 6, 1957. Bélorgey's title alludes to the 1951 publication of Hannah Arendt's *The Origins of Totalitarianism*. Arendt's concept of totalitarianism is not confined to fascism or Nazism, but includes communist Stalinism, which she places at the same level as the other two. She notes two causes in *Origins*: anti-Semitism and colonialism (or imperialism). S. Adour conflates totalitarianism and fascism just as, paradoxically, *L'Humanité* is blind to the fascism in Stalin's totalitarianism. The November 5, 1957, issue of *L'Humanité* included excerpts of the articles by Adour under the title "A Second Lieutenant Testifies." Adour responded in *Le Monde*, November 6, 1957, criticizing the use of his articles by *L'Humanité*, which had excerpted his sentences out of context. He explained that the gulags and repression of the Budapest uprising in 1956 were worse than atrocities committed in Algeria and went on to denounce *L'Humanitié*'s silence on the crimes of communist countries.

If Adour's typescript is a prolonged reflection on the Algerian War, supported with numerous specific examples, *Le Monde* only retained the conceptual framework more often than not. Bélorgey kept his letter, dated

December 8, 1957,[16] to the director of *Le Monde*, Beuve-Méry, in his archives and later admitted that the article in *Contacts* essentially allowed him to write "certain passages of the fifth article on Algeria" (fifth in a series, published November 5, 1957, under the title "The Limits of Pacification"). Indeed, as published in *Le Monde*, it begins with a reference to *Contacts*. "This article was received very favorably by the officer corps of the French army in Algeria." Adour cited the four preceding articles, which would have meant that certain points from Galula's article would have been used in previous articles. In his letter to Beuve-Méry in December 1957, Bélorgey justifies the reference to the article in *Contacts*. "This item was unanimously approved by the unit leaders I knew. That was when I left Algeria, the last noise about pacification. It was universally admitted that the difficulties and limitations presented by the Captain in Kabylia [Galula] were borne out in our sector."[17] By the *Le Monde* article, but especially by this letter, we learn that Galula's *Contacts* article had a major impact among officers in Algeria, even in sectors where the population and geography was very different, like at the Moroccan border where Bélorgey served as a second lieutenant. One might wonder what could explain the success of Galula's article, as *Contacts* published dozens of articles every month that did not meet with similar attention.

Galula's impact on officers in the sector came from his tactical simplicity, the phasing of operations, assessment of constraints, proposed solutions, and, especially, the ability to profit from tactical implementation elsewhere. Bélorgey, in his letter of December 8 to the director of *Le Monde*, explained that the same difficulties were encountered on the Moroccan border as those mentioned by the Captain in Kabylia: "the [lack of] opportunity to destroy the large bands, apathy of the populace, the responsiveness of networks, need for standard procedures, firmness, and propaganda." It was perhaps the pedagogical approach Galula adopted to talk about counterinsurgency on the subdistrict level that seems to have convinced French officers—the originality of his thinking that other counterinsurgency theorists had pushed much farther, but they were unable to popularize them among the officer corps. A few tactical successes in Kabylia also seem to have played a role. "We even considered the Captain in Kabylia as privileged to have successfully got to point three [control of the populace]," continued Bélorgey in his letter to Beuve-Méry.

In the *Le Monde* November 5, 1957, Adour presented Galula's four points of pacification, citing long extracts from his article in *Contacts*. He criticizes Galula on several grounds. If the policy of rallying to the population fails, it will be necessary to occupy the country over the long term, which he sums up with the following: "If we don't rally them, we can't leave." The military occupation necessary for any support is estimated by the leadership Bélorgey was familiar with during his military service in Algeria. Bélorgey saw this vision as utopian, a term that he would integrate into the title of his series of articles. Adour then criticizes the propaganda methods adopted by Galula. In his *Contacts* article, Galula suggests showing off the bodies of ANL members to the population, as well as to supporters and prisoners. Adour's retort was final: "We exploit the corpses to demoralize [the enemy]. But we are also creating heroes and martyrs." Adour, along with Galula, also criticizes the naiveté of propaganda slogans. He especially criticizes propaganda that proposes no political reform. "This propaganda is therefore moralistic and not about political renewal." Adour contradicted Galula about the fact that, in the case of the withdrawal of auxiliary troops having pacified a sector, "without doubt, the underground will easily find their strength again and armed groups will again emerge." For Adour, pacification's success could only be temporary with the populace playing to both sides. It will pretend to be pacified and the OPA will remain quiet. Adour also criticized the system of punishments instituted, which transformed Algeria into a vast reformatory for delinquents. About the *Contacts* article, Bélorgey wrote in the margins that the system resembled Soviet criminal codes. In sum, the refusal to accept differing views lead strait to totalitarianism. "Any opinion that does not correspond to our policy is considered a public danger and treated as such." Adour asserted that the army had assumed the role of a one-party totalitarian regime:[18] "the general image given by its behavior and actions, authoritarian structure, exclusive responsibility respecting hierarchy above all else." To paraphrase Adour, the army's totalitarian attitude amounted to local paternalism, which consisted of punishing the bad, attracting the good, and winning the indifferent.

Adour criticizes two further points about counterinsurgency at the end of his *Le Monde* article. Rebel bands can never be destroyed completely: "After a certain point the rebellion becomes too diffuse, too fluid, and weak, but practically indomitable." He criticizes the importance given to political factors in counterinsurgency, which consists of eliminating political oppositions and developing friendly forces. Adour also refers to this as sociological warfare in his first article in *Le Monde* (October 31[19]), referring to the expression Galula used in *Contacts.* The political factor of revolutionary warfare prevents, according to Adour, the emergence of "public order and peace of mind," essential to establishing a democratic solution "of reconciliation, elections, and negotiations with elected officials." The failure of pacification prolongs the war. It also prevents the organization of elected officials representing Muslims and the beginning of negotiations to end the Algerian War.

Adour's article raised many reactions. Among them, was a very reasoned reply in *Lettre d'informations politiques et économiques* edited by A. Noël.[20] This was a four-page newsletter published in yearly editions of 100. Three issues of *Lettre d'informations* (numbers 573, 574, 575) of December 1957 dealt with the response to Adour's articles, in which he was criticized for "truncated quotes, taken out of context so as to completely change their meaning and deliberately changing the dates to make events that had taken place a year before seem current."

Letter d'Informations explained to its readership that it would reveal a few excerpts of the texts and that it would describe the actual situation in the subdistrict from November 1956 to November 1957. Among these examples, the journal discussed the mistaken date assigned to the *Contacts* article that, though published in 1956, *Le Monde* made to seem to be about events in April 1957 (the publication date). According to Noël, *Le Monde* deliberately confused the reader, "although they [the citations] were out-of-date by April 1957." According to *Lettre d'informations* Adour was mistaken in taking stock of the pacification effort based on this article, when in reality the effort was just beginning in November and therefore had not yet produced its effect. The notion, therefore, that pacification was precarious or amounted to military totalitarianism was false. Bélorgey responded to Beuve-Méry on December 8, 1957, with his objections to the *Lettre d'informations,* pointing out that, given the publication date of the article in June 1957, the validity of the analysis had been widely recognized. Moreover, he explained that *Contacts* had not seen fit to print additional information three months after publication beyond a footnote dated February 1957. The dispute over the mistaken date would not be relevant. A reading of the article, typescript, and correspondence between Bélorgey and the director of *Le Monde* show no intention on Bélorgey's part to falsify dates.

Bélorgey challenged the progress of pacification: he did not believe that the population gave intelligence freely, relying on his own three-month experience as an intelligence officer. "There was an unbroken wall of silence," he wrote. He thought that the election of delegates could only take place under threat of resettlement. It therefore became "a superficial pledge of obligatory support," moreover "the election of delegates, more precisely, the appointment of officials leads directly to a deep decay." Bélorgey's argument, the election of officials under the threat of expulsion of the population, is unconfirmed by the archives. It is nevertheless true that financial and social pressures were used to force elections. As for Bélorgey's last thought, explaining that elections are not inconsistent with the deterioration of the situation, is confirmed by events at Djebel Aïssa Mimoun.

According to *Lettre d'informations,* the passage on punishment and the absence of a coherent penal code across sectors was distorted. *Le Monde* presented as established practice what was really a range of possible sanctions. In Bélorgey's letter to Beuve-Méry, he admitted to "forcing the Captain in Kabylia's statements," by condensing them, but that he also relied on the realities he observed in his sector. The establishment of a common code showed Bélorgey the will to regularize military practice "confusing military and judicial powers." Additionally, Bélorgey explained that what jarred the officer in Kabylia was not the penalties in themselves, but the incoherence in their application. For Bélorgey, the penalties, like beatings, interrogations, and forced labor, suggesting colonial methods more than pacification, in which the populace's humiliation became "the bedrock of nationalism and the wellspring of rebellion."

In number 574, *Lettre d'informations* responded to Adour with a monograph on the territory commanded by the Captain in Kabylia. The articles were unsigned. The director, Noël, neglected to put his name at the end of each of them. A few clues suggest that the response came from Galula. The categorical statement might make us think so: "The Captain in Kabylia has in fact never inflicted a beating; he is the enemy of ineffective interrogation He pays for all labor. Not only is it not his habit to impose such sanctions, but he doesn't impose them anywhere. He imagines that, hypothetically, they might be practiced in other sectors." Finally, if the *Lettre d'informations* provides a monograph on the subdistrict, it was whoever commanded it at the moment who obligingly forwarded the information. The dates and the facts are indeed very precise. One fact, leaving no doubt as to the author, appears in the article: "Villagers who were approached [to collect the FLN tax] also sought us out to explain the pressures they were under." Further on, "in fact, over the last six months, the Captain in Kabylia was more embarrassed by the abundance of intelligence than by its scarcity." In number 557, Noël wrote: "The Captain . . . reported there were two tasks he had to do." After explaining how he managed to destroy the ALN and OPA bands, he turned to municipal reform. Once the communal delegates were nominated, elected, and trained, the army and the SAS were removed from municipal administration. Galula made an ironic retort to Adour about totalitarianism: "There may be here the only historical example of a totalitarian regime (to adopt the language of *Le Monde*) which vanishes as soon as its objectives are achieved." On this point, Galula is excessive, as it is not borne out by the facts, especially when elected officials were illiterate. In number 578, the training of *harkas* and protection of the population are brought up. Under the title "Bonbons," referring to Adour's article, Galula explains building schools and the free clinics.

The manner in which Noël calls *Le Monde* "an outlet for defeatism," "conspirators for giving up," and an "evening newspaper of French defeatism," approximates Galula's view of the journal. As Galula put it, the more the journal was read, the harder pacification became. This thought would be found later in one of his books.[21] Moreover, Galula did not believe the articles by Adour was the work of an officer, owing to his lack of "accurate, personal memories of his experiences," believing it to be a composite written by a journalist. Galula's analytical error owed to the fact that the director of *Le Monde*, Beuve-Méry, who preferred publishing only general thoughts on the conflict in Algeria rather than the numerous factual claims found in the 250-page typescript. Not all officers shared Galula's opinion about Adour's article. J. Lanoire, a reserve officer and teacher in civilian life, served as SAS commander at Zelemta (in the Mostaganem region), wrote to Adour to congratulate him and to share the same feeling on the Algeria situation.

Adour's series of articles in *Le Monde* caused a reaction in political circles, particularly during parliamentary debate in November 1957 granting special powers to the army and the use of torture during interrogations in Algeria. The debate between communist deputy Pierre Cot and Gaullist Jacques Soustelle showed that both had read Adour's articles.[22] Thus, unintentionally, Bélorgey, through Adour, popularized Galula's operations in the parliamentary sphere. The paradox concerning the revelation of Galula's counterinsurgency methods is that, even if it was recognized and dissimulated among officers of the time, by means of *Contacts* and *Le Monde*, their author remained anonymous save for the pseudonym Captain of Kabylia.

The main media criticism of the French army in Algeria consisted of denouncing torture and summary execution explained away with the phrase "shot under pretext of an escape attempt." Adour, himself a lieutenant and reluctant intelligence officer, was explicit. "Why deny it? Torture is being used and everybody knows it." The same phrasing later appeared in *Humanité. Le Monde, France Observateur, L'Express,* and *Témoignage Chrétien,* all led a very active anti-torture campaign along with members of the military, officers like General de la Bollardière who protested against its use in interrogations.[23] Galula was very clear on the question: "As the insurgents don't hesitate to employ terrorism, the counterinsurgent must do police work. . . . if anyone seriously believes that his purity will allow him to get information, all I can say is that he will learn a lot once he is faced with the problem. I don't like doing police work, but it is vital, so I did it. My only interest was to remain within decent limits and do no damage to my more constructive pacification work." Galula refused to use torture, preferring other methods to obtain information. In *Lettre d'Informations,* Galula wrote of the effectiveness of collective interrogation. In effect, a single person arrested and interrogated will say nothing, because he will later be identified as the source and then condemned to death by the FLN. If it is the entire group which speaks, it is impossible to target an individual. "Destruction of terrorist cells was carried out without having to resort to torture."[24] A second method of interrogation is described in his account of Algeria. Galula used psychological pressure on detainees, locking them in an oven and threatening to light it to make them speak.[25] In general, Galula said, interrogation of prisoners was poorly conducted by untrained officers and this led to the use of torture. He saw the creation of the DOP (*détachement opérationnels de protection*) as the answer. "If I were to state now which was our single most important improvement in our counterinsurgency operations in Algeria, I would flatly put the DOP first."[26] Indeed, the DOP detachments staffed by trained intelligence specialists produced results. Delivering prisoners to the DOP, however, absolved Galula of the question, as the DOP was known for using torture to make prisoners talk.[27]

A contrast could be drawn between the respectful methods of Galula's and those of Trinquier, who advocated emergency measures to fight the guerillas.[28] A hasty reading of *Pacification in Algeria* shows few instances of extrajudicial executions.[29] No planning had been done by the army or law enforcement to accommodate prisoners, who were detained at the posts. It wasn't until 1957 that two prison camps were built in Kabylia. Without proper detention facilities, there were attempts to escape from Djebel Aïssa Mimoun that ended in the death of the fugitive.[30] The unit history of the 3/45th BIC cites four cases: October 12, 1956, Oudiaï (cousin and deputy of the ALN leader) was arrested by a patrol and shot while attempting to escape. An investigation was conducted on October 15. On the same day, another rebel was killed during an escape attempt. On November 7, a suspect was arrested at Aït Braham and killed while escaping. On March 14, 1957, a patrol trying to locate an arms cache based on information from detainees and was confronted by a developing group escape. The suspects were killed[31] (among them four rebel leaders, according to the SAS report of March 14, 1957). Was this due to bad luck or poor oversight of the prisoners, as suggested by the SAS commander at Aïssa Mimoun? Pfirrmann, when questioned about the dead fugitives explained that the prisoners had been tied to the barbed wire and guarded by a sentry, but the escape was easy.[32] That it was an execution is a hypothesis that cannot be ruled out as it might be understood by the administrator of the *commune mixte* of Mizrana (equivalent of a *sous-préfet*), who said, "What happens to the arrested workers? You know they can be held if necessary even if they don't try to escape" (October 14, 1956).[33]

CHAPTER 4

Counterinsurgency at Djebel Aïssa Mimoun after Galula: "A Slow Deterioration"

In March 1958, the SAS report remarked the dissolution of the 45th BIC and the Second Company's withdrawal from Akaoudj and Tahanouts. The village mayors requested in vain that the company remain. Evidently, the neighboring company to Galula's was well thought of, too. An OPA cell became active at Akaoudj and was dismantled quickly. But the report mentioned that children fled an approaching patrol, something which had never been seen before. The population was being taken over by the FLN. A month later, in April 1958, Menault,[1] SAS commander, noted that the situation had improved in the villages left behind by the Second Company and that Khelouyene, Aït Braham, and Igonane Ameur, all communes in Galula's subdistrict, were considered as the three best.

If the June 1958 report acknowledged a surge of enthusiasm with public meetings at Tizi-Ouzou with the population of Djebel Aïssa Mimoun, it was quickly followed by "a rebel propaganda offensive which put the population in awe of the FLN." The FLN issued instructions to avoid military posts and the SAS. Galula's three communes seemed to have been spared, possibly thanks to the two militias who were able to stand up to FLN pressure. The inhabitants of Bou Souar, who had received so much attention from Galula, along with those of Tahanouts and Akaoudj, no longer visited the SAS and soon fell under the influence of the FLN. In July 1958, Meneault's report was more optimistic: A serious cleansing took place at Akaoudj and Tahanouts, "the mayor of Akaoudj was changed and the ALN zone commander was captured. A psychological warfare campaign was conducted at Tahanouts." As far Bou Souar was concerned, the deterioration seems to have been due to the post commander, who was replaced. A few months after Galula's departure, the rebellion tried to regain the initiative and managed temporarily to take advantage of troop rotation and the lack of awareness in the new officers. But the SAS and army seemed to regain control of the situation. Menault also explained, "rebel terrorism . . . has practically disappeared." After nine months of working in the SAS, Meneault seemed to have a clearer vision of elected officials: the new mayor of Akaoudj seemed to resist rebel pressure. The officials at Tahanouts and Igonane Ameur remained "very average, their authority seems to be supporting both sides." At Bou Souar, the situation remained poor (August 1958). Igonane Ameur, the village where pacification was considered a solid success by Galula, was double-dealing, even though it was a just a few months after the public meetings of 1958 and the village had an embedded army unit and a militia. The SAS report for November 1958 was pessimistic one month after the successful referendum for the constitution of the Fifth Republic. Meneault writes of a slow deterioration: "The rebels are obtaining broader support from the population. People reluctant to pay their fines [to the FLN] two months ago, now do so without question." A band of seven or eight rebels collected the fines and conducted psychological operations.

Galula claimed to have returned to Djebel Aïssa Mimoun several times to see how the situation was evolving. He explained that his successor, Captain Herrmann, who was subdistrict commander in April 1958, stepped on a mine placed near the village of Ighouna, a village he had allowed the resettlement of on the condition that the army would be warned of any ambush attempts. The owners of the two houses closest to the ambush had been bound and gagged, as the ALN was afraid of being reported.[2] Galula, however, did not see this casualty as a part of the slow deterioration of pacification. The report of November 1958 mentions the ambush of November 25 during which the first company's commander was killed in an ALN ambush between Igonane Ameur, Khelouyene, and the SAS post, along with four others. This ambush mounted in the midst of the SAS and the army, in the best-monitored and longest-controlled zone, shows that after Galula's departure, counterinsurgency had become less effective. Lieutenant Perrot, SAS commander, provided further information that the ambush was carried out by a commando of 30 well-armed men who had taken over the population by virtue of their spectacular ambushes (December 21, 1958). A further ambush, targeting a colonel and a captain, is mentioned on December 13. "The SAS was outnumbered, overmatched, and outgunned by the HLL [fellaghas]." The initiative had passed to the ALN, who began the offensive, taking advantage of the reduction in military force. Perrot noted as well "a wavering among the *harkis*."

The morale report for 1958 made by Perrot gives an overview of the situation: At Akaoudj and Bou Souar, the mayors' actions were harmful and they were arrested by the company. The mayor of Tahanouts was hesitant.

The mayors of Khelouyene, Aït Braham, and Igonane Ameur were good. Akaoudj fell outside of Galula's responsibility, as it was situated in the neighboring subdistrict. With respect to the mayor of Bou Souar, Galula considered his nomination a bad idea. "In the lottery—for it was a lottery—I had drawn the bad ticket." He was unable to convince the *sous-préfet* to fire him and was instead asked to put up with him as long as the situation didn't deteriorate.[3] At Akaoudj, where Pfirrmann had asked in vain for the firing of the mayor for his support of the FLN. Later, Pfirrmann received the same response from the director of the mixed community (February 9, 1957). In terms of insecurity, the report for 1958 indicated a resurgence of terrorism as manifested by three large ambushes in February, November, and December targeting the officers in charge of the sector.

The *harkis* recruited during Galula's deployment were not entirely reliable. "Increased scrutiny of their individual actions uncovered some who sold ammunition and collected intelligence for the rebels." This meant that the rebels knew the defenses and movements of the SAS and the army, which would explain the successful ambushes. Successful intelligence gathering was no longer limited to the French.

Finally, the referendum of September 1958 was marked by massive turnout including the women's vote. The FLN responded with "surveillance, supply, and intelligence provided by the women." The FLN tried to thwart the army's employment of women by involving them in the fight for independence by effective counterpropaganda. There are previous reports that give evidence of FLN action toward women. An SAS report notes a return of women to the home and asks: "Is this a sign of pacification or evidence of the rebels' repression of women?" (April 20, 1958). The SAS commander never answered, but it can be supposed that this was indeed an FLN effort to counter the army's influence on women. A report of February 1958 shows how women were used in the FLN's fight against the French army. "There is a deficiency in the repression of pro-rebel women's action which is so serious that pro-French women are extremely worried." The sector's military authorities had not seemed to have found a response to the FLN's use of women.

So after this slow deterioration of the situation with the Djebel Aïssa Mimoun SAS, the deterioration accelerated. Galula's operations did not have a long-term effect. Nobody could have taken over the counterinsurgency successfully at Djebel Aïssa Mimoun. The fight against the ALN and OPA, the recruitment of reliable officials, the enlistment of *harkis*, supporting the role of women, were failures over the long term. Galula had employed his tactics too quickly. He obtained short-term results at the cost of creating new long-term problems. Unreliable elements were integrated into civil and military organizations that were not sufficiently vetted or purged. He had left alone members of the OPA or FLN sympathizers who would turn against France at the first sign of weakness in the military.

Galula, obviously, does not bear all of the responsibility. His dependency on district defenses, the absence of reinforcements for his subdistrict, the increase of his subdistrict's size, the administrative pressures of rapid community building, too much latitude given his subordinates who failed to detect the duplicity on the part of the *harkis*, the mayors, and population, also bear some responsibility. It can be assumed that Galula's communications efforts with journalists and political and military authorities came at the expense of rigorous daily operations.

On his return to Djebel Aïssa Mimoun in May 1959, Galula had this to say: "My area had visibly retrogressed to the average level of most of Kabylia in 1959, clearly above the situation as I had found it when I arrived in 1956, but below the one I had left [in 1958]."[4] This may be regarded as very optimistic vision as, by 1959, Galula's remaining counterinsurgency concepts had failed. For 1959, Perrot saw "rebel propaganda circulated through the population freely" (second quarter report, 1959). In December 1957, Galula made the following remarks about the municipalities in *Lettre d'informations*: "Communal affairs are handled directly by special delegations on one hand and the commanding officer, SAS commander, and the *sous-préfecture*, on the other. The military was completely withdrawn from the administration."[5] If the military was withdrawn in favor of the SAS officer, this does not mean that the delegations were effective. After working this way for two years, Perrot's opinion about the officials was final: "mayors and councilmen are interested in municipal problems, but the communes are more figurative than real in our area" (third quarter report, 1959). The reason for this was simple: "the current administrative organization seems to have been installed too hastily, even prematurely" (fourth quarter report, 1959). The result of this too-hasty community building was that the officials were not true representatives and were unable to execute their responsibilities, according to Perrot. Additionally, there were five communes and a special delegation for 7,121 inhabitants depicted as "an incoherent plurality of local civilian authority" (fourth quarter report, 1959). The municipal structure of Djebel Aïssa Mimoun was therefore artificial, anarchic, and seemed to be going nowhere fast. Galula's goal had been to build on local pro-French support to counterbalance the FLN. No longer trusting the elected officials or believing in their effectiveness, "certain military authorities preferred to manage the population directly, for the sake of efficiency and establishment of military discipline" (third quarter report, 1959). This paternalism undermined Galula's and the SAS's idea of integration, whose goal was to put Muslims and Europeans on equal footing. It was a regression that only could have raised the population's frustrations as the policy returned Muslims to a subordinate position—as Adour had written in *Le Monde*—and risked losing them to the rebellion. The absence of training for elected officials and their lack of understanding of administrative procedures largely explain the impossibility that the new municipalities function normally, as in mainland France. By ignoring the culture of the governed, unmanageable local structures were created that had to be entirely managed by the SAS. The result was that six municipalities were too small to be properly managed. Perrot suggested combining them into two (first quarter report, 1960). The measure was adopted partially at the end of 1960 with the amalgamation of three communes into one (fourth quarter report, 1960).

Galula had insisted on the need for units to address the population and work with the SAS. In 1959, Djebel Aïssa Mimoun regressed and Galula's basic principles largely were forgotten. Perrot wrote, "there was no real cooperation between military units concerned with the day-to-day and the SAS whose objective was the future" (third quarter report, 1960). This was due to the failure by the army to understand the SAS's mission and administrative methods, according to Perrot. This suggests that, in 1959, the 15/9th RIMa only dealt with operations and in the best of cases, developed municipal infrastructure, without consulting the population or coordinating with the *sous-prefecture* or the SAS. Galula was aware of the problem when he returned to Djebel Aïssa Mimoun in May 1959. "His successor [the company's second commander after Galula] . . . contented himself with military activity, he let the SAS officer . . . handle all the work with the population."[6] At Djebel Aïssa Mimoun, the Ninth RIMa was relieved by the 2/93rd RAM (*regiment d'artillerie de montagne*) in the third quarter of 1960. The SAS commander considered, "the unit was too operational, which meant it became disinterested in pacification, and was threatened by becoming cut off from the population" (first quarter report, 1961). Galula's opinion of another company from the same battalion, the 1/93rd RAM, was prescient in 1957 (before operation JUMELLES, July 1959–March 1960 which disrupted the ALN): "The troops are in insufficient contact with the population. Operations are conducted practically every day. No unit smaller than a company was deployed and no unit smaller than a platoon could move safely." It is surprising that there was no reaction at the sector level or by command in Kabylia about the accelerating decline at Djebel Aïssa Mimoun, even if only just to analyze mistakes. Considered for years a model *sous-quartier*, Djebel Aïssa Mimoun lost every aspect of a pacified area. By the third quarter of 1959, according to Perrot, only Khelouyene and Aït Braham remained out of rebel hands. Igonane Ameur, Tahanouts, and Akaoudj supported the rebels, and Bou Souar collaborated with them.

By the third quarter of 1960, Perrot nevertheless noted a slight improvement in the situation. "The rebels failed to retake [the area]. The defense militia interferes with them significantly." The ALN was estimated at 20 to 25 men in the Aïssa Mimoun area. It was strong enough to pressure elected officials (third quarter report, 1959), influence the population (second quarter report, 1960), and collect tactics (second quarter report, 1960). The public perception of those who openly chose to support the French was an ominous sign: "relations between the *harkis* and the population are mediocre" (third quarter report, 1960). Additionally, for those who switched sides, the situation was not nearly as clear: of the four militias, one wasn't working: "the Khelouyene militia was a sham since no guard was organized" (first quarter report, 1960). The *harkis* also had suffered defections in the same village, while the *harkis* at Khelouyene quit without reason (second quarter report, 1960). The militia at Tahanouts was judged unreliable; it was disarmed and its commander, an FLN tax collector, was arrested (first quarter report, 1961). Of the four defense militias, two had been infiltrated or were dysfunctional. Operationally, the situation was improving: 14 ALN members were killed during an operation at Aït Braham (second quarter report, 1961). However, after the third quarter of 1961 with the shift in de Gaulle's policy and the independence process, half of all military posts at Djebel Aïssa Mimoun were closed: schools, clinics, militias, and town halls gradually disappeared; however, for a long time pacification policy had only been a shadow of what it had been before Galula's departure.

Blaming Galula for the failure of counterinsurgency at Djebel Aïssa Mimoun would be absurd. The responsibility lies clearly with the two units that succeeded Galula's who neglected the population in favor of military operations. Galula cannot, however, be excused from all responsibility: indeed, he helped sow the seeds of counterinsurgency's failure by recruiting unreliable officials, militia members, and *harkis*. His successor's lack of overall vision and poor tactics only aggravated a fragile situation. Failure came at the sixth step of Galula's theory. It is likely that this phase required more time than Galula had. His unit was called upon to maintain order at Tizi-Ouzou[7] (February 1957, April 1957) and participated in a sweep in the Mizrana Forest (August 1957). He saw the limits of his *sous-quartier* expanded to include two new villages (September 1957). The events did not leave him sufficient time to test the elected officials (March 1957) or the *harkis* (April and May 1957). But Galula was also busy communicating his operations (the report on the pacification in Kabylia was written in March 1957) and conducting numerous civil and military visits to his *sous-quartier*.

CHAPTER 5

David Galula and the Battle of the Airwaves (1958–1962)

Galula wrote *Pacification in Algeria* based on his experience as subdistrict commander at Aïssa Mimoun, and then as deputy battalion commander in the Bordj Menaïel sector. He makes no mention, however, of his activities between 1958 and 1962. It is stated in the preface to the book published by RAND, that he served on the national defense staff in Paris, dealing with unconventional warfare, particularly in the Algerian War.[1] In his preface to *Counterinsurgency Warfare* [French edition], de Montenon makes reference to this part of Galula's life citing, more precisely that Galula served "the council chairman (of the national defense staff, information division)," but he says this period was relatively brief.[2] Galula's American biographer, Marlowe, whose work is based on memories of Galula's widow, who explained that he had been requisitioned by the psychological warfare branch of the Ministry of Defense. He would have worked for "the intelligence services of the French army, the G2"[3] in Paris, before and after his staff training at Norfolk in 1960. However, Galula's widow does not remember exactly the exact nature of his work.[4]

Originally, Galula was to have been transferred in June 1958 to the psychological warfare group (G5) in the Ministry of Defense, called the *Service d'Action Psychologique et d'Information Générale de la Défense Nationale et des Forces Armées* (SAPIDNFA). The service to which Galula was assigned was established by the minister of the armed forces, Bourgès-Maunoury, in January 1956 and placed under the direct command of the commanding general of the general staff. Galula reported to Colonel Lacheroy, the revolutionary warfare theoretician. This group directed the psychological warfare of the armed forces, disseminating information to print media, radio, and film.[5] The name changed to the Division of Information in August 1958 and was governed both by the prime minister's staff and by national defense staff. This Division of Information reported to the Executive Committee of Broadcast Warfare,[6] also called the Broadcast Radio Steering Committee. According to the meeting minutes of August 4, 1958, the committee was created in July 1958 after a decision by the Council Presidency (prime minister) of the Psychological Warfare Committee and put into practice during a meeting, which took place August 4, 1958, by minister of information Soustelle, the former governor general of Algeria, formerly of the Free French secret service, anthropologist, and founder of the SAS in Algeria. The committee functioned as an inter-ministerial department grouping the ministries and state bureaucracies concerned with information warfare (RTF French Radio and Television Broadcasting, the Ministry of Information, Ministry of Overseas Territories, and intelligence services) coordinating their activities at a weekly meeting. Galula would work for this committee between 1958 and 1962.

Several reasons could explain the transfer. Galula's intense lobbying of his superiors eventually succeeded. He wrote a report on pacification in November 1956, making a tape recording of it for General Ely who was then the chief of the general staff of the armed forces from February 1956 to February 1959.[7] This report was also heard by minister of the armed forces Bourgès-Maunoury. These two political and military authorities led the SAPIDNFA, where Galula was to end up. In March 1957, he wrote a second report that was approved by Generals Lacomme and Guérin, who passed on his theories to the chief of staff for Salan, General Dulac.[8] Other reasons for his transfer owed to his specialization in psychological warfare, the theory he had developed through his articles and that he had applied in the field at Aïssa Mimoun. Galula was interested in the latest audiovisual technology, as can be seen by his choice of making his report to his superiors in the form of a recording. In *Pacification in Algeria*, he explained that he had made a recording of an ALN prisoner later broadcast on Radio Algiers.[9] His article published in *Contacts* discussed the importance of slides depicting general information and the fact that he lacked a "projector and unexposed film."[10] In his report on techniques of pacification in Kabylia of March 1957, circulated to his superiors, Galula asked that a team of journalists, photographers, and cameramen be attached at division level. If, in *Counterinsurgency*, he ignored the various methods of propaganda, with the exception of the mimeograph (the photocopier's antecedent),[11] he did categorize propaganda objectives: loyalist forces, the population, and the insurgents.[12] Over 50 years later, Petraeus and Nagl appreciated Galula's prescience: "It is about maintaining control of information and public opinion; Galula had foreseen this well before the advent of the Internet."[13]

COMMUNITY PROPAGANDA AND COUNTER-PROPAGANDA ON THE AIR IN ALGERIA

The importance of radio in the political life of de Gaulle should not be underestimated, as explained by the historian Martin. The call to resistance of June 18, 1940 was broadcast over the BBC. Radio Brazzaville, then Radio Algiers in November 1942, were the voice of France and of resistance within the French Empire. During the Algerian War, had Radio Algiers not been taken over by the military in May 1958, and "the near-instantaneous broadcast of its propaganda throughout Algeria," the country would have never fallen into the hands of the military insurgency. Moreover, "the intervention of Radio Algiers was more important in the eyes of the mainland population as essential for transmitting the messages of the Algerian government" in calling for de Gaulle's return to power. "Radio Algiers contributed to shaping opinion in two ways (on the theme of fraternization . . . and causing worry with its martial tone)." In April 1961, during the attempted generals' coup against de Gaulle and his self-determination policy for Algeria, de Gaulle's radio address of April 23, 1961, calling for the disobedience of draftees, put an end to the revolt.[14]

Radio's sharp rise in importance coincided with the transistor's arrival in France, imported from the United States in 1955–56. In 1960, a million and a half transistor radios were sold in France. Additionally, Martin writes of the importance of this media over others, citing the study done by E. Veron concerning the Three-Mile Island accident in 1979 wherein, "the impact of live reporting contributed to the dramatization of the information," as well as the "the frequency of bulletins allowed an acceleration of the news cycle." Finally, the distance and time between the event and the report was constantly being reduced through live radio.[15]

At the end of the 1950s and beginning of the 1960s, radio was taking on more and more importance on the African continent. On June 21, 1957, *Le Monde* explained that "The Voice of the Arabs" broadcast from Cairo was listened to in cafés throughout the Arab world and that taxis from Baghdad to Damascus were tuned in to Cairo.[16] Radio L from Cairo also broadcast "The Voice of Free Algeria," which evidenced "calculated violence perverting the opinions of Muslim Algerians, despite, or because of, its systematic disinformation. Its influence is most felt in the rural villages where we find that it encourages open insult of Europeans." Soustelle, governor general of Algeria, fearing a negative influence over Muslims ordered on May 18, 1955, "blocking battery operated transistor radios at customs and at vendors, whose sale is now subject to official authorization of the *préfecture*." This measure failed, with antennas going up in Tunis, Rabat, Damascus, Tripoli, and Baghdad: "Arab solidarity is in play against France."[17] In French Cameroon, restive with UPC guerillas, "the period was marked by a passion for transistor radios." The SDECE (French secret services) reported in March 1958 that "The Voice of Free

Cameron" was broadcasting in French and Arabic from a "new radio station with Czech equipment set up near Cairo."[18] Galula, during a mission
in sub-Saharan Africa, explained, "The radio market is developing, buy-
ing a receiver came right after the motorbike for blacks with means . . .
the use of transistor devices is spreading, especially in Mauritania, where
they are smuggled in (report of December 23).[19] Ely explained in a note
addressed to the prime minister on November 18, 1959, "radio, in the territories with a 20% literacy rate, can be regarded as the newspaper of the
illiterate. In Algeria, as in sub-Saharan Africa, while reading newspapers
is reserved for a small intelligentsia, every rural village has at least one
receiver."[20]

Ely, Galula's direct superior, had always had keen interest in psychological warfare, as he writes in a note, May 31, 1957, "I emphasized the
need to express policy in terms of psychological warfare and to draw up a
plan of action using every resource of this new technique."[21] The archives
of the division of information belonging to both the prime minister and
the defense minister were partially opened,[22] allowing us to see the nature
of broadcast warfare more closely. A division of information record dated
April 20, 1959, outlines the needs of national defense and broadcasting; the
author explains: "Of the current forms of warfare, broadcast warfare is not
the least dangerous as it is permanent and knows no boundaries or lin-
guistic barriers. It is particularly prevalent in countries with low literacy.
Its only obstacles are spectrum congestion and potential jamming." Noting
that the propaganda of hostile states (Soviet satellite countries, Egypt) is
spread primarily through radio, it is not possible for the military to remain
in a passive attitude (jamming), but that they should take the offensive, responding with counterpropaganda. The note's author believed that French
national radio wasn't suitable for counterpropaganda and requested the
creation of "a kind of unofficial Radio Free Europe" but this proposal
never saw the light of day. Two years later, the situation had not changed.
Ely explained in a note to the prime minister on January 20, 1961, that radio
"must be used for other purposes: External contingencies impose 'broadcast warfare' on us. Jamming is only a passive response." The committee
of defense information had as its mission to jam enemy transmissions
and to propose government approval of themes of ideological struggle in
France's interest." Ely gave an example of radio propaganda used against
a country. "If the government wants to worry Morocco," the suggested
themes of the campaign are: "Moroccan racism and the situation of Jews
in Morocco, financial mismanagement and embezzlement in Agadir, and
the funds collected for the FLN."

If the idea of counterpropaganda seemed promising, it had an important material drawback: the low number and antiquity of African and
Algerian radio stations, both for jamming and broadcast. According to a
report from the General Information Service and War Planning Office of
July 29, 1957 that took stock of short wave transmitters: Radio Moscow

has 60 transmitters, Radio Free Europe (UK) 22, Voice of America (from Tangiers and Salonkia) 29, France has 17 (13 on the mainland and 4 at Brazzaville), and Egypt has 1.[23] On January 20, 1961, Ely wrote a note addressed to the prime minister explaining that France was only 14th in terms of broadcast hours behind the Vatican and at the same level as Portugal. Ely described the effort in radio frequency hours/day (HFJ): while France offered 202 HFJ in 16 languages and 18 in French; the British broadcast 622 HFJ in 38 languages, 178 in English; the Americans 539 HFJ in 37 languages; and the USSR, 447 HFJ in 56 languages. The French broadcasting effort was largely outclassed by other powers. In Algeria, on the other hand, there seemed to be enough equipment with the Algerian television network, the channel Radio France 5, the high-power transmitters at Oran and Constantine, and the prefecture networks, all set aside for the Battle of the Referendum. To this was added powerful jamming of foreign transmissions with 18 jamming stations, making for a total of 80 shortwave jammers. But Ely recognized a gap in the jamming on the Moroccan border against Radio Tangier (an old Voice of America transmitter).[24]

Any effective radio counterpropaganda must address infrastructure problems. Here is where Galula came into play. Although one might expect to find Galula in Algeria, paradoxically documentation of his actions comes from sub-Saharan Africa. Indeed, broadcast information was a problem concerning the entire French African Community. Many documents were copied to now-Major Galula, like the one dated October 13, 1958, by Vice Admiral Fourquet, chief of staff of National Defense to the Minister of Overseas Territories, raising the problem of radio equipment in overseas theatres. The note describes equipment in the AOF (French East Africa: eight territories of the French Community that stretched from Senegal to Niger and the AEF, including French Equatorial Africa: four territories in the French Community stretching from Chad to Congo-Brazzaville) concerning the financial needs of French overseas broadcasting to equip themselves with eight short-wave transmitters of 100 kW. Fourquet, now director of the telecommunications coordinating committee of National Defense, received a letter from Major General G. Andrier of the air force, dated February 17, 1959, ordering the construction of eight short-wave transmitters to "intensify broadcasts to the French Community and abroad," and he asked that medium-wave broadcasting not be forgotten. The territorial priorities were: "1. Tunisia, 2. Morocco, 3. the rest of Africa, in particular Guinea, 4. the Middle East." No explanation was given for the order of priorities, but it isn't difficult to guess. Tunisia and Morocco border Algeria and served as rear-area bases for the ALN. Furthermore, these new states were using radio to criticize the French presence in Algeria. In 1958, FLN Radio, the voice of fighters in Algeria, transmitted from Tunis and Rabat.[25] On November 18, 1959, in a note to the prime minister, Ely recognized the North African theatre as a "considerable discrepancy [with regards to radio] in favor of the FLN, in particular in terms of short-wave (where their volume is double that of ours). Currently, this imbalance is neither compensated by jamming or by medium-wave superiority."[26]

The French presence in Africa was also challenged by the United States who feared that if France clung too tightly to its territories, African elites would go over to the communists. Similarly, the USSR supported decolonization movements throughout the world to weaken states allied to the United States, France, and Great Britain. Finally, Egypt's Nassar, who had taken on a leadership role of nonaligned states had his own interest in countering French influence in North Africa. Egyptian minister of foreign affairs in charge of propaganda, M. Hatam, declared August 10, 1959: "Radio is an effective weapon against imperialism." Indeed, "more than 30 movements of national liberation used Cairo as a broadcasting base during the independence movements of the 1960s."[27]

In French-speaking Africa, Guinea posed the greatest problem for France. In the AOF and AEF, Guinea was the only African state to reject the French Community proposed by de Gaulle in 1958. The objective of the Community was to give more political autonomy to African states colonized by France and to effect a political transition from colonial administration to independence. Fourquet's report of October 13, 1958, to the Minister of Overseas Territories foresaw trouble in Guinea in terms of radio propaganda: "Guinea risks becoming a new site of infection."[28] Indeed, when Sékou Touré's Guinea was the first to become independent, it chose the Soviet camp. Touré's regional ambition was to spread Guinea's model of communist independence to other African and Community states. As general secretary of the Communist General Union of African Workers, Touré had influence with West African unions and could use them to destabilize the new states of the French Community. Guinea also supported guerillas in Cameroon, the UPC (Union des populations du Cameroun). Founded in 1948, the Marxist separatist party in Cameroon chose to fight a guerilla war for independence in December 1956. Composed of 3,000 to 4,000 guerillas, they were defeated in September 1958. The rebel leaders then broadcast propaganda from first English-speaking Cameroon, then Sudan, Egypt (1958–59), then Guinea.[29] After studying the archives of the Ministry of Foreign Affairs and the records concerning the UPC, the historian M. Michel explains that the UPC's reorientation characterized by "the systematic use of the radio . . . in order to get their opinions across to the international community, but also to their listeners in Cameroon." A report by French security signaled, "Arab and Soviet broadcasts were sufficiently powerful to be heard in Cameroon where they had an audience."[30]

Card file no. 182 (January 14, 1959) issued by the Division of Information shows Galula's mapping of the adverse influence of radio in North Africa, according to their broadcast power and hours on the air. Cairene and Moroccan radio, with transmitters at Sebra Atoun, Tangier (the transmitters at Casablanca and Rabat seemed to have been less powerful), and

Tripoli. Broadcasts from within the communist bloc from Moscow and Prague were also influential. Transmitters in Ghana and Guinea figure in the report but played lesser roles.[31] Had the army exaggerated the danger? F. Benhalla, a former RTF journalist and also its former director, spoke of the radio war and radio bombardment. He argues that the radio employed during World War II and the wars of decolonization was "an instrument of war," later during the Cold War as "a means of psychological warfare."[32]

The transmitter in Ghana was explained by the policy pursued by Nkrumah, president of English-speaking Ghana (a former British colony). Since 1957, Nkrumah's Ghana was the diplomatic and economic enemy of Houphouët-Boigny's Côte d'Ivoire, who was a great supporter of France's policy in Africa. Fourquet's report of October 13, 1958 to the Minister of Overseas Territories also foresaw trouble in Ghana in terms of radio propaganda. "The danger of subversive broadcasting . . . can only grow as Ghana has built a powerful station."[33] The Ghana transmitter broadcasted in English, French, Arabic, Swahili, Houssa, and Portuguese: "all languages commonly spoken and understood in Africa."[34] In December 1958, Nkrumah organized a conference in Ghana gathering together all the independent African states and movements. Representatives of the UPC and the FLN were in attendance.[35] Nkrumah even financed a separatist party in 1959 in the Côte d'Ivoire to cause trouble and gave the party refuge in Ghana. While away in Beijing in 1966, Nkrumah was ousted in a coup. The elections brought Dr. Busia to power, with the support of Houphouët-Boigny. Nkrumah sought refuge in Guinea where Touré put Radio Conakry at his disposal to spread inflammatory rhetoric.[36]

These examples demonstrate perfectly the influence of radio on the struggles for independence in French-speaking Africa and Algeria and its use by its adversaries.

GALULA'S CONTRIBUTION
TO BROADCAST WARFARE

Galula's missions within the Division of Information were very diverse and extremely precise. The record is not complete, but unsigned and fragmentary slips of information are sometimes marked by Galula's pen. The minutes of the meetings of the Radio Steering Committee Galula attended also exist. The Radio Steering Committee's inter-ministerial meetings brought together the heads of technical departments of the RTF, editors of Arabic and Kabyle language programming, and personnel from the Ministries of Foreign Affairs, Algerian Affairs, and Information. "It is difficult to establish a list of all the organizations with at least some interest in a psychological warfare that, without effective direction or even simple coordination, could make itself felt." He suggested the creation of "a departmental agency with the delegations to the head of government, but with a permanent working body for the conduct of psychological warfare." In a memo dated February 21, 1958, he reiterated his suggestion: "It is necessary, as I have repeated for a year, to establish a body which, by the authority of the head of government, will be responsible for psychological operations in accordance with the most important French policies and interests."[37] The historian A. Sabbagh sums it up pithily: "Five ministerial angels watch over the radio from near and far: Foreign Affairs, Interior, Information, National Defense, and Algerian Affairs."[38]

Of these weekly meetings we are left with only a dozen reports for the years 1958 and 1959, which is enough to give us an idea of how the department worked and what Galula was doing. His thinking guided a working group, seeking inter-ministerial solutions to broadcasting problems, as his superiors on the national defense staff wrote of him in 1958. Galula "applies himself with great tenacity to problems and always looks for concrete solutions."[39]

For the Algerian theater, the Radio Steering Committee had an offensive and defensive role when it came to foreign broadcasting. Offensively, psychological warfare took the form of Kabyle language programming. Galula attended a meeting on August 12, 1958, to examine the implementation of four shortwave transmitters to increase the broadcast power of Arabic language programs and extend it to 14 hours a day, adding 5 hours of Kabyle language programming. This broadcast project was codenamed KY, as mentioned in the minutes of August 19, 1958. Mr. Colonne, director of Arabic programming at RTF, was to start the broadcasts in September 1958. In terms of defense and in an area totally ignored by historians of the Algerian War, there was the jamming of Arabic programming in mainland France (meeting of September 22, 1958). Muslims in mainland France listened to the following stations: The Arab Voice (Cairo), Damascus (Syria), Budapest (Hungary) over shortwave between seven o'clock in the evening and midnight. Noting "the propaganda was very violent, very virulent (calls for murder) and amplified the actual facts of terrorism," it was necessary to jam these stations. Jamming tests were carried out successfully over three days in Moselle. The objective was to extend jamming over the places where the Muslim population was concentrated in the departments of the Seine, Seine-et-Oise, the Bouches du Rhône, Rhône, and Moselle. The committee considered five jamming sites with five transmitters, but had to wait 18 months before receiving them. Over the short term, reserve transmitters were pressed into service. Noise generators would be delivered within the month. The committee fixed the area to be covered and set the hours for jamming.

The problems with radio weren't confined to the Algerian theatre. They also included supporting French interests worldwide, including Asia and Africa, wherever they were challenged by communist states or others hostile to the French colonial presence. It is no surprise that Galula's operations extended to these places as well. At the October 17, 1958, meeting of

the Radio Steering Committee, concerning Southeast Asia, Galula was ordered to investigate whether Radio Bangkok might serve as a musical and
cultural outlet for RTF. At the same meeting Galula suggested jamming
broadcasts from Cairo to Tunisia to support Tunisian president Bourguiba
against Egyptian president Nasser. This note was subsequently crossed
out, with a handwritten request that RTF study the material requirements
of jamming Radio Cairo. This last point demonstrates Galula's power to
influence policy by choosing to neutralize a broadcaster to support a diplomatic objective (creating dissention between two of France's adversaries
in the Maghreb). At the next meeting on November 5, 1958, it appears that
the jamming turned out to be impossible. Galula then suggested creating
"a parallel station for the Maghreb and Guinea."

For 1959, the traces left by Galula are thin, but we can nevertheless get an
idea of his activities. In January 1959, a meeting was organized to review
the penetration made by enemy broadcasting. The task was to broadcast
counterpropaganda on the same frequencies. While this was technically
possible in material terms (available transmitters) the meeting concluded
in failure. The committee recommended further testing and continuing
jamming with existing available transmitters. According to the report of
October 13, 1959, Operation SOPHIE was to consist of eight 100-kW transmitters to broadcast propaganda and conduct jamming and intrusive operations. They were to be put into action within 18 months, that is to say
at the beginning of 1961. Galula suggested that only two of the transmitters be used for intrusion and commented that the first jamming attempts
seemed very effective.

Only the agenda for the meeting of April 8, 1959, remains. On it were
three items: jamming, special broadcasts [for Algeria?], and special programming for Morocco and Tunisia. Galula was responsible for present-
ing the jamming effort. One might think this was his area of expertise,
especially as he was to deal with the problem of a radio station at Nador
in Morocco a few months later. The FLN claimed to have installed it
in Algeria (report of July 22, 1959). "Four solutions were discussed:
1) Take aerial photographs, pass them to the press, let the FLN continue
to operate until tangled up in their lies, and then expose them; 2) Mount
an operation to destroy the station and pin it on FLN dissidents in Morocco; 3) Employ diplomatic means [threatening to destroy the FLN sta-
tion]; 4) Put this item on the agenda of Franco-Moroccan talks and use
it as a loyalty test for Morocco." The four solutions were annotated by
hand. The first inferred the participation of the air force and the media,
which was marked "done." The second solution was marked "not excluded," and that the secret services, the SDECE, needed to be notified:
"SDECE, of course." The third and fourth solutions were approved. This
report concerned several ministries and was forwarded to the national
defense staff, to the Ministry of Foreign Affairs, to the Ministry of Armed
Forces, and to the SDECE.

Andrier, in reaction to broadcast propaganda from Arab and African countries against the French presence in Algeria and the French Community, requested permission from Fourquet to lead a counterpropaganda effort against these countries in his letter number 0085 DN/PSY of February 17, 1959. He asked consideration of three options: "building a powerful transmitter in mainland France covering North Africa, constructing several medium-power transmitters (50 kW) two in Oran oriented toward Morocco and one in Constantine oriented toward Tunisia, or the installation of a medium-power transmitter on a ship. The operational, technical, and financial angles of these three solutions are under study." The national defense staff assigned an engineer and Galula to assist the Telecommunication Steering Committee. Galula seems to have worked with this group on the operational aspects described in an attachment to the letter. The team was to determine "objectives taking into account French and foreign broadcasting's coverage of the territories concerned, geographical areas to be served, and the origin of programming."

In his June 19, 1959, letter, Ely wrote to the Minister of Information suggesting the creation of a channel devoted to Muslims in the greater Paris area. Galula worked on this parallel channel (June 19, 1959, note addressed to Ely, two memos addressed to General Nicot, Head of Radio-electronic Enforcement September 15 and 28, 1959), on the American model of the Radio Free Europe and Radio Liberation networks. Half of the 340,000 Muslims living in mainland France were in two departments (Seine and Seine-et-Oise). Based on the idea that RTF's Arabic and Kabyle were insufficient and that jamming foreign broadcasts in Arabic was very effective (June 19, 1959), it was important to take advantage of the improved state of mind of Muslims to build a transmitter where they lived, keeping to the Paris region with a weak transmitter borrowed from the RTF but autonomous in terms of its operation. Galula remembered that this plan had been proposed in December 1959 to Soustelle and, in April 1959, R. Frey, the new minister presented it to the ministerial council.[40]

In a November 18, 1959 note addressed to the prime minister, Ely suggested the establishment of "radio equipment on a North-South axis between Paris and Brazzaville via Tamanrasset" and "worldwide installation in the Tropics where the propagation of short wave is easier to do with a belt of short-wave stations: Comoros (to Djibouti), Reunion Island (to Djibouti), Noumea (to Saigon and the French islands farthest east in the Pacific), Martinique."[41] To implement this project, Ely expressed his opinion in his October 19, 1959, letter to Nicot, head of the group charged with radio-electronic enforcement,[42] and sent a mission to study the radio situation in Africa including Majors Galula (from the Division of Information) and Le Gall (Telecommunications and Electronic Warfare) to sub-Saharan Africa, while other experts from the same two services were sent to Algeria in 1960.[43]

A 22-page report on the fact-finding mission in the French Community in Africa, Madagascar, and the coast of French Somaliland (Djibouti) from November 8 to December 2, 1959, was prepared by Galula and Le Gall. Studies were conducted in Senegal (Dakar, Saint Louis), in Côte d'Ivoire (Abidjan), Yaoundé (Cameroon), Fort Lamy (Chad), Brazzaville (Congo), Antananarivo (Madagascar), and Djibouti. The mission's objective was to improve radio propaganda in the territories of the Community and to study countermeasures to be applied against subversive broadcasts.

According to the report's authors, African states in the Community had 300,000 radio receivers, or more than 3 million listeners. Radio Moscow, Beijing, and Cairo were all received over the shortwave. The Voice of France was broadcast to those Community states who enjoyed good relations, which wasn't the case for Radio Mali (the most subversive), Sudan, and Senegal. The programming of these stations was cultural with no news broadcasts. The infrastructure was composed of 11 RTF shortwave transmitters at Issoudun in mainland France, but which were obsolete and only broadcast two to three hours of programming for sub-Saharan Africa, and RTF Brazzaville with two transmitters, dedicated to jamming transmissions from Algeria. Mainland RTF was inaudible, the authors recommended technical diagnosis. In addition, programming wasn't tailored to the audience, the authors recommended revisions to content and rescheduling. They required the recruitment of personnel with knowledge of sub-Saharan Africa, due to competition with African stations and to use local correspondents to raise interest in the programming. Finally, they suggested increasing Swahili and Hausa broadcasting to draw an audience of tradesmen who were "the natural informants and propagandists of rural populations." Galula made occasional notes on the state of radio in the seven African countries they visited. He referred to areas for jamming and coverage, RTF audibility levels in mainland France and Brazzaville. He also mentioned the situation of adverse stations, that in Mauritania there was subversive broadcasting: Radio Mali was first, broadcasting to an audience of 200,000. The Voice of the Sahara [Morocco] came in second with an audience of 450,000. Conakry was third, Moscow fourth, Beijing fifth. These last two stations were listened to by 5% of the population along with intellectuals." For Radio Beijing and Moscow, the programming was the easiest to tune in to. Galula put their influence into perspective: "Right now they aren't particularly dangerous as they aren't adapted to African audiences," but both states were making efforts to establish themselves in Africa by setting up specialized institutes or scholarships for African students. "This effort will inevitably bear fruit," Galula warned. France maintained its territorial interests in Africa, but Russian and Chinese competitors threatened its preeminence in particular with the literate elite. The Americans were still in the picture, as a report for 1960–61 showed. Voice of America was to install six shortwave 500 kW transmitters on the east coast of the United States, each directed at Africa.

To Galula, the most harmful African radio stations were "Radio Mali, which exceeds the virulence of Conakry [Radio Conakry, Guinea]. Its propaganda primarily targets the Côte d'Ivoire, but may turn to the Upper Volta [Burkina Faso] and Niger in the near future. The Côte d'Ivoire felt threatened enough to request that this broadcasting be jammed even before Radio Conakry." But Mali, a member of the French Community, then posed a diplomatic problem for France. Galula suggested, "If countermeasures are adopted they should issue from the authorities in Abidjan [Côte d'Ivoire], without France being openly implicated." As for jamming, Galula explained that it could not be entrusted to the Mauritanians, but "the Mauritanian government would be happy to have them jammed without them being implicated" (Memo from Galula at Saint-Louis, November 11, 1959). Galula's report shows the French radio communications strategy with Community states. France could decide to jam a station but the neighboring countries would refuse direct involvement, preferring that France do the jamming itself. Or an African country could decide to jam a station and France refused to get involved, preferring that the country do it itself. Galula suggested the following procedure when the jamming could be undertaken jointly: "The most reasonable solution is to inform the threatened states that France can lend them the necessary jamming equipment [low-power network jammers] and train personnel to use it. . . . France retains overall control." According to Galula, the high commissioner of Dakar surveyed the states of the AOF about this proposal and only Senegal and Sudan [Mali] refused. The former AEF states were favorable. Galula's proposal was in effect to relocate jamming from mainland France to the African states while maintaining control over how the material was used. The jamming would be locally limited and would only affect urban centers.

In the case of Radio Conakry, of most concern to France, the report explains that the states most at risk were Côte d'Ivoire, Upper Volta [Burkina Faso], Niger, Dahomey [Benin], and, to a lesser extent, Gabon and the Congo. The most important states to protect with jamming were the first four of these (Galula's Dakar memo, November 9–10, 1959). Galula reported the construction of a Czech transmitter at 150 km from Conakry. "The fear is that no territory of the Community will be free from its influence." He also noted, "Their reliance on this instrument is surely due to the fact that the Cameroonian leaders of the UPC transferred their headquarters from Cairo to Conakry." Radio Maroc (Voice of the Sahara) was considered dangerous to Mauritania, while Radio Cairo held influence over Muslims who spoke Somali, Swahili, and Fula. This station threatened the territories of Chad, the north of Cameroon, the French coast of Somalia, the Comoros, and Madagascar.

Galula detailed the jammer infrastructure to develop in the former AOF: seven jammers in Mauritania on the two frequencies used by the Moroccan station Voice of the Sahara; eight jammers in Côte d'Ivoire on

Radio Conakry's two frequencies; a jammer for the four frequencies of
The Arab Voice of Cairo; with five jammers in Chad dedicated to two frequencies of The Arab Voice. For Upper Volta (Burkina Faso), Niger, and
Dahomey (Benin) he suggested four jammers in each country dedicated
to the two frequencies of Radio Conakry. He had no suggestions for East-
ern Equatorial Africa and Madagascar. He recommended five jammers for
Cameroon. He evaluated a need for 68 total jammers at a cost of 2 million
new francs. Galula concluded that it would be useless and difficult to jam
everything and that no further development of the initial system should
be sought. He explained that jamming a program didn't prevent it from
being listened to and he proposed a radical solution, that of Houphouët-
Boigny who said, "low-cost receivers receiving only one or two friendly
frequencies should be manufactured."

As for French influence from the mainland RTF or Brazzaville, Galula
noted that the two and a half hours of programming were inaudible in
sub-Saharan Africa and unsuited to African audiences. In any case RTF
Brazzaville lacked the means for broadcast as its transmitter served as a
jammer for Algeria. Galula's thoughts were final: "We won't capture an
African audience with two and a half hours of programming or even with
five hours. We must be a continuous presence on the airwaves, with such
power that the listener will get hooked on our programs." Galula suggested the establishment of a kind of Radio France Internationale, which
was actually created in 1975. The proposed solution of increasing the trans-
mission capacity would be developed at the Saharan site at Tamanrasset
with two medium-wave transmitters, two short wave ones, and a 20 kW
tropical band transmitter. Medium-wave transmitters would be heard in
Tripoli, Libya, in Dakar, Senegal, and from Algiers to Cotonou, Benin. The
only drawback was that the time necessary for their construction was estimated at two years, which meant their implementation would not take
place before 1962.[44]

MEETINGS AT THE DIVISION OF INFORMATION:
GALULA MEETS MR. AFRICA AND THE FOUNDER
OF PSYCHOLOGICAL WARFARE

In the interministerial meetings of the Radio Steering Committee,
Galula crossed paths with very influential people and it is necessary to
know how their activity impinged on Galula's.

It was there that Galula met Lacheroy, the great theorist of revolutionary
warfare and the director of the of the psychological warfare and information services in the National Defense. Very close to Minister Bourgès-
Maunoury, he developed the public affairs sections at every echelon of
the French army.[45]

It is interesting to draw parallels between these two officers who had
so much in common before the Algerian War, a war which would drive

them completely apart.[46] Comparing the beginning of their careers, we see Lacheroy[47] was much older than Galula. He was from the Morocco and Syria class of 1925–27, while Galula was from the Franco-British Partnership class of 1939–40. The two officers chose commissions in the colonial infantry. Lacheroy served in French West Africa for two years (1928–30) and in Upper Volta (Burkina Faso) in a Senegalese light infantry regiment. From 1932 to 1935 he served in a camel unit in Syria. While working with a tribal chief, he discovered the accounts of Lawrence of Arabia and his guerilla actions against the Turks during World War I. It was during his time in Syria that Lacheroy read this theorist and practitioner of Arab guerilla warfare against the Turks. Similarly, it was only once Galula was in China that he learned the theories and practices of Mao Tse Tung. If Lacheroy discovered T. E. Lawrence through the stories of a tribal chief, Galula still had an advantage over Lacheroy: as a privileged spectator, he analyzed the daily guerrilla tactics of Mao and his rise to power in 1949.

Subsequently, Lacheroy found himself in Morocco, assisting Groussard in the intelligence section responsible for watching over the Moroccan nationalist movement of 1937. It was there that Lacheroy learned collection and exploitation of information. Galula as well would learn from his time serving in an intelligence section later on in China after being recruited by Guillermaz in 1945.

These two officers crossed paths during World War II. Both ran afoul of the ideology of the Vichy regime. In 1940, Lacheroy was imprisoned as a suspected Gaullist agent. In December 1940, he was freed through the discrete intervention of Groussard, founder of the GILBERT network working in liaison with army intelligence services. In 1941, the same Groussard very probably recruited Galula to his network after Galula was dismissed from the army after the adoption of anti-Semitic laws. Even if this were not the case, Galula could have been working for army intelligence, under Rivet. The two officers were involved in the fighting in Italy and both found themselves in de Lattre's First Army during the liberation of France and later on the Rhine and into Germany.

After 1945, Galula's career followed an unusual, seemingly less prestigious route, in the intelligence section in China. Perhaps the years spent undercover as an intelligence officer accentuated Galula's individualistic character, making it difficult for him to return to more traditional and rigid regimental work. Lacheroy's career was more conventional: he returned to Côte d'Ivoire, and from 1946 to 1949, he carried out pacification operations building schools and roads to improve the lives of the population. He also helped to suppress the 1949 insurgency in Côte d'Ivoire.

Meetings with de Lattre in Tunisia and Salan in Senegal during World War II would have a huge impact on the rest of his career. He was called upon by de Lattre to serve in Indochina in 1951 and commanded there for three years in the Bien Hoa sector in Cochin. He conducted many operations against the guerillas and paid close attention to the reports from the intelligence section to understand the basis of this new type of conflict. Based on his experience in the field, Lacheroy drew up his theories under the heading parallel hierarchies to explain the governance methods used by the Vietminh. From this, he explained the workings of revolutionary warfare. An excellent speaker, he began to frequent conferences in 1952 to publicize his theories that had had great success among officers serving in Indochina. Only participation in the French-Indochina War separated these two officers.

Unlike Lacheroy, Galula would never fight in Indochina. The latter was only able to meet officers who had fought there or those of other nationalities who had fought guerillas in Malaysia, the Philippines, Greece, and even Korea. He got his information from the press or by reports about other theatres of operation. He studied the tactics of Maoist guerillas used by the Vietminh in Indochina. His distance from the theatre of operations in Indochina meant he would remain obscure among his peers in his analysis of revolutionary warfare. Perhaps this is why Galula invariably summed up his experiences as an observer of guerillas before giving a speech or writing an essay.

Named director of the Center for Asian and African Studies in 1953, Lacheroy trained officers who were to serve overseas. He taught his theories which were well received by the military hierarchy and by General Guillaume, chief of the general staff of the armed forces. On August 3 and 4, 1954, *Le Monde* made Lacheroy's work known to the general public. By 1955, he convinced the general staff of the correctness of his theories on revolutionary warfare. P. and M.C. Villatoux explain, "the role of Colonel Lacheroy in the discourse surrounding revolutionary warfare remains decisive." As Lacheroy's media star was rising, Galula remained in the shadows. In the cosmopolitan surroundings of Hong Kong, he met Chinese fleeing the communists, British officers returning from Malaysia, American officers on their way to the Korean War, senior American officers just passing through, American and British diplomats, and journalists. His billet was simply that of an attaché observer, far from any action, except when he was asked to leave for Greece as a UN observer. Once in the field, Galula still found himself a passive spectator to the fight between the Greek army and Greek communist guerillas.

The Algerian War was an opportunity for Lacheroy to apply his theories. In 1957, he was director of the Department of Psychological Warfare and Information of National Defense that was a vehicle for his theories. The creation of a psychological warfare intelligence group allowed him to apply his methods in Algeria. In 1956, Galula could finally implement his own thoughts on counterinsurgency in Algeria and realize the limits of transposing the methods used in the French-Indochina War to a new conflict. Like Lacheroy, he made his methods known to his superiors through reports, newspaper articles, by his writing in *Contacts*, or more confidential journals. Unlike Lacheroy, who had achieved a certain ce-lebrity, Galula would remain anonymous to the media, the obscure Cap-tain in Kabylia. *Le Monde* and *Humanité,* although critical of his methods, never mentioned him by name. The support of chief of the general staff of the armed forces was essential for Lacheroy to reach a position of re-sponsibility matching his ambitions. Galula's rise owed to the same con-ditions. Just as the support of Guillaume had been essential to Lacheroy, Ely's had been fundamental to Galula. In both cases, the support of Gen-eral Bourgès-Maunoury was essential in promoting these two theorists of psychological warfare. This minister named Lacheroy to the head of a psychological warfare service and was also the recipient of Galula's re-port on operations at Djebel Aïssa Mimoun. In 1958, Galula was named to the Division of Information with responsibilities in Algeria, Africa, and in parts of France. During the same time, Lacheroy was assigned by Salan to do psychological warfare in the Government General of Algeria. He controlled all information in Algeria and worked to influence public opin-ion and journalists by the seizure of newspapers criticizing the army. The circumstances in the midst of the war and the political crisis of the Fourth French Republic accelerated the careers of both officers.

Galula and Lacheroy would eventually meet at a Division of Informa-tion meeting which Lacheroy attended in his capacity as Director of Psy-chological Warfare and Information. The meeting was to decide on the establishment of a "rapid response counter-psychological warfare group." This group included representatives from the ministries of Foreign Af-fairs, Information, Interior, a shortwave broadcast director from the RTF, a representative from the secret services (SDECE), and officers from the psychological warfare group. The psychological warfare group of national defense, of which Galula was a part "gave daily intelligence briefings on points for immediate response that the meeting was to clarify."[48] It was for the implementation of an informational response that Lacheroy was pres-ent for a meeting of the Radio Steering Committee, and it was to Galula to conduct counterpropaganda by means of French media. The meeting of September 2, 1958 took the decision of centralizing and selecting Arabic language programming, news from French and foreign news agencies and intelligence services, Ministries of the Interior, the SDECE, and Govern-ment General of Algeria into a bureau composed of a representative from the Ministry of Information, psychological warfare, and the SDECE for Arabic programming for the mainland, Algeria, Tunisia, Morocco, and the Middle East. Information destined for Muslim audiences was to be con-trolled tightly by the authorities.

Lacheroy spoke twice during this meeting to explain that FLN attacks in mainland France had a negative effect on the mindset of Muslims, as they demonstrated the FLN's strength. He warned that the revolutionary tax levied by the FLN in France accounted for half of its total budget and concluded, "part of the Algerian War will be won in France." He set out the FLN's strategy to counter the referendum on the Fifth Republic, which he summarized in four points: not registering to vote, abstaining, voting no, and terrorizing Muslims.

The meeting establishes that Galula met the founder of the French school of revolutionary warfare at least once and that he was familiar with his thinking and methods of operation. It seems difficult to imagine that these two specialists of psychological operations in Algeria, both recognized by their superiors, at the same meeting tables, did not compare notes. The conversation, whether verbal or in correspondence, must have been animated between two such different thinkers. One can only be surprised at the difference in notoriety between Galula, known by his operations and thinking to a reserved circle of superior officers and by a few American journalists, whereas Lacheroy was publicized, attended hundreds of conferences, and led a psychological warfare service created by and for him. What must have Lacheroy, originator of the psychological warfare group in Algeria, thought of Galula? Here was a young major claiming that the application of Lacheroy's Indochina theories were inadequate in Algeria, and moreover that, based on his personal experience as a subdistrict commander, they simply didn't work. How might have Lacheroy responded to a young officer telling him that he had learned more about revolutionary warfare based on four years of observations of a successful guerilla war in China and by reading the essential writings of Mao translated into English? What might Lacheroy have said, covered in his experience from the French-Indochina War, to Galula's thinking based on his observations and operations with counterinsurgencies in Indochina, Malaysia, the Philippines, of guerilla combat in China and Greece, as well as his own methodological experiments in Algeria? Lacheroy was at the peak of his fame from 1957 to 1958. No senior officer questioned the worth of his theories to the staff or ministry. How could he have received even a well-founded criticism from an obscure major from the colonial infantry? Lacheroy must have noticed the value of Galula's insights and experiences, yet was unable to accept criticism or challenge just at the moment he had reached the pinnacle of his career.

Lacheroy might have been a powerful supporter of Galula by making his insights known in initial training, applied schools, the war collage, or at the general staff or even disseminated them across echelons through the psychological warfare group. He could have put Galula before the French media and revealed a 20th-century Clausewitz to the public. If none of this came to pass, Lacheroy must have become aware, upon analyzing Galula's arguments, that he had more to lose than to gain by supporting Galula. If he had highlighted Galula in military and journalistic circles, he would have quickly realized the limits in his thinking and predicted the failure of his psychological warfare approach. Galula would have arisen as an adversary, or worse, a competitor. How to explain this Galula's lack of currency with his promotion to an important, but anonymous posting

with respect to Lacheroy, who benefited from media celebrity and political notoriety, and who had been appointed as director of information and
psychological warfare in Algeria? Lacheroy's celebrity had gone so far
that a columnist for *Le Figaro,* wrote of him, "Now I know, one day, who
will be the great leader of the French army."

The disagreement between these two officers paradoxically transpired
in silence: they knew each other, they met, but they never mentioned each
other, though they worked in the same field. If their counterinsurgency
theories and tactics sometimes conflicted, their experience and insights
are sometimes complimentary, even similar. Galula never cited Lacheroy
in his writing or pronounced an opinion on the other's theory or tactics.
As for Lacheroy, it is very likely that he never mentioned Galula's name
during a conference, though it is hard to see why he would have, as Galula
was still unknown at the time.

But fame is fleeting, as Lacheroy would learn to his detriment. With
the departure of Salan, Lacheroy lost his position in Algeria. He was not
promoted to general, being given a symbolic teaching post instead. At
the same moment, Galula gave the Division of Information in Africa and
Europe his every effort. Lacheroy joined the coup of April 1961 led by
Generals Challe, Jouhaud, and Salan against the rule of de Gaulle. For
Galula, the departure of Ely marked the end of psychological warfare,
which lost its influence among the political and military hierarchy.

At the March 10, 1961,[49] meeting concerning broadcast problems in
Africa and in French speaking countries, Galula met a key figure in the
history of Africa. J. Jacques Foccart, founder of the Gaullist network of
African heads of state and organizer of dirty tricks, organizer of African
coups, founder of the protection service of the Gaullist party, the Civil Action Service, inspiration of the paramilitary group in Algeria, called "The
Spooks." According to interviews given to P. Gaillard, Foccart explained
that he began his career in the Free French secret services (BCRA, *Bureau
central du renseignment et de l'action*), then becoming party secretary general for the RPF (*Rassemblement pour la République*) and organizing local
committees across France. He organized de Gaulle's travels through the
AOF and AEF in 1953 and became the RPF's African specialist. He maintained contact with the French secret service, the SDECE (*Service de documentation extérieur et du contre-espionnage*), for whom he was a reserve
officer in the 11th shock parachute regiment (a military unit detailed to
the SDECE). He organized the propaganda effort for de Gaulle's return to
power in April–May 1958 with A. Astoux, future deputy director general
of the ORTF. He was responsible for relations between the president and
de Gaulle's RPF. In this capacity, he named Soustelle minister of information in 1958. He was also secretary general of the French Community and
special advisor on Africa to de Gaulle. According to his memoirs, he received more than 11 memos per day on Africa from the SDECE of which
he made a selection to show de Gaulle.[50]

P. Messmer, minister of the armed forces, prime minister to Georges Pompidou (de Gaulle's successor to the presidency) provided some sobering facts about Foccart. With the SDECE's help, Foccart tried to organize a coup against Touré in Guinea in 1959, running arms by way of an intermediary in Senegal to the Fulani ethnic group, who were hostile to the ruling government. The plot was uncovered by Touré and failed. Foccart supported the secession of Biafra, an oil-producing region in southern Nigeria populated by ethnic Christians in conflict with northern Muslims, by supplying arms to guerillas through the Côte d'Ivoire and Gabon from 1967 to 1969. Diori, one of his friends, was overthrown in a military coup provoked by dissatisfaction with the diversion of food aid to relive famine in the Sahel by Diori's wife. Acting president A. Poher (who replaced Pompidou after he died in office), Messmer, and the minister of defense opposed this initiative.[51]

Galula worked closely with this very influential person who had control over diplomatic policy in France and Africa. Control of information was a means of French influence in Algeria, which could not have escaped Foccart.

GALULA'S PSYCHOLOGICAL WARFARE RECORD AT THE DIVISION OF INFORMATION

Galula's posting to the Division of Information was the culmination of his thinking on counterinsurgency in Asia and Greece and the application of his tactical thinking at Aïssa Mimoun, and his communication effort within the military hierarchy. If Guillermaz's support was essential to his career in the intelligence section in China, Ely's was essential for his transfer to Division of Information, psychological warfare section. Galula exchanged a very local application of psychological operations, for a national, even continental, theatre. He contributed to the organization of radio jamming efforts and improvement of African and Algerian radio infrastructure. He worked with decision makers and leading specialists in intelligence, signals, defense, law enforcement, and diplomacy to find solutions to propaganda and counterpropaganda challenges. If the military hierarchy refused to detach Galula to study in the United States in 1962, it probably wasn't due to a lack of confidence in his ability but from a fear that he would tell of his experiences organizing radio broadcasts at the highest levels of the French state.

What were the results? If radio jamming was successful: "Owing to the progress in the systematic jamming of The Voice of the Algerian Resistance and The Arab Voice are almost inaudible in Algeria," explained the former director of RFI, Benhalla.[52] The technological delays, obsolescent infrastructure, and financial cost of new equipment, were real obstacles to the counterpropaganda effort in which Galula played a part. The propaganda impact on listeners could be measured by the audience for RTF, particularly during news broadcasts. C. Méadel studied the audiences of the three main French stations: RTF (the public station), Radio Luxembourg, and Radio Europe (the two major private French stations). In May 1958, for the evening news program RTF logged 26 percent of the listening audience, Radio Luxembourg 24 percent, and Radio Europe 14 percent. In April 1959, RTF fell to 19 percent of the listening audience, Radio Luxembourg went to 28 percent, and Radio Europe was at 11 percent. RTF's audience reached 20 percent fewer listeners and found itself outpaced by Radio Luxembourg, known for its independence. In January 1960, a listenership poll was conducted over a week for each broadcast slot at 8:00 A.M., 1:00 P.M., and 8:00 P.M. Though RTF was dominant in terms of audience for the evening news, Radio Luxembourg reached a third of listeners between 1:00 P.M. to 8:00 P.M. Radio Luxembourg dominated for the rest of the broadcast day, also broadcasting news programs every hour between 8:00 A.M. and 2:00 P.M.[53] RTF's credibility and objectivity was widely questioned, as indicated by the listenership for RTF which only reached 15 percent to 24 percent of the audience during the main news hour at 7:30 P.M.

How did Galula evaluate his own actions? Allusions to his past at the Division of Information and his experience with high-level psychological operations can be found in *Counterinsurgency Warfare*. "The counterinsurgent is tied to his responsibilities and to his past, and for him, facts speak louder than words. If he lies, cheats, and does not prove, he may achieve some temporary successes, but at the price of being discredited for good. . . . For him, propaganda can be no more than a secondary weapon."[54] Galula showed that propaganda must be backed by, and can only compliment, action. If propaganda issues from lies, action is forever compromised. Galula belonged to a service definitively concerned with propaganda or broadcast counterpropaganda; by stating in his book that it can be used only occasionally, he called into question the effectiveness of some of his own work. Galula spoke of the role of propaganda with great wariness: "its use requires prudence, a solid sense of reality, and proper preparation." Propaganda was a weapon that could be turned against its wielder. Its use had to be well informed and the consequences well measured. "If the target is a rural population, propaganda is most effective when based on local events, issues on which citizens are confronted with on a daily basis and conducted through individual contacts . . . rather than toward the population as a whole." The concern here was to ensure the sector commander understood that he would have to attend personally to propaganda—the commentary was rather harsh for propaganda efforts coming from higher, even national echelons with respect to the rural population. Such was the case in Algeria, where the majority of Muslims lived in the countryside. Galula summed up his opinion succinctly: "It is hardly possible to 'precook' this sort of propaganda at a high level." Perhaps this was also a way of putting the impact of his work and service at the Division of Information into perspective, or even of criticizing it. Higher echelons, according to him, had a modest role. "How can he [the local commander] fulfill his role if the higher echelons do not come to his aid in developing strategic propaganda, updating the language elements depending on the situation on the ground, training specialists in psychological warfare and sowing discord among the enemy?"[55]

The archival records for 1958 to 1960 were opened to research this book, however those from 1961 to 1962 were excluded from the exemption. In March 1961, Ely was relieved of his duties as the Chief of Staff of National Defense. Galula, who shared the thinking of his superiors on psychological warfare, could only have been disillusioned by its declining influence with the new political and military authorities. Furthermore, with the policy of self determination in Algeria, the fight against the FLN lessened in urgency. According to Galula's widow, Galula thought de Gaulle's new policy toward Algerian independence "was not the right thing to do but it was the necessary thing."[56] We can only speculate about the role Galula played in his department, whose name was changed in 1961 (and certainly the missions performed) to *Centre opérationnel de la Défense*. Propaganda and broadcast counterpropaganda had been used to influence or support new, independent African states or to destabilize them when they turned against France. In Algeria, the RTF encouraged voting for various independence referendums for Algeria or to combat propaganda from the *Organisation de l'armée secrète* (OAS). The OAS was a clandestine organization made up of officers who had deserted and European Algerians who employed terrorism against de Gaulle's independence policy. The OAS set up pirate broadcasts beginning in January 1961.[57] Transcripts of OAS broadcasts can be found in the service's archives, which show that it had been involved in the fight against the OAS. Three months after a revolt by Europeans in Algiers (Week of the Barricades, January 1960), Radio Algiers was taken back and J. Oudinot was named director. Oudinot sent three journalists to propose reforms for the constitution of the Fifth Republic.[58] Radio Algiers was quickly seen as the OAS's adversary. OAS activists besieged the station and injured its director.[59] If the new direction of the Division of Information and its declining influence only could have displeased Galula, his position allowed him to rub shoulders with the highest French military and political leaders. The poise he developed would later serve him when dealing with experts and military officials in the United States. The experience also familiarized him with the problems of radio and electronics, enabling him to begin a second, short career at the French electronics company, Thomson.

It would be easy in hindsight to deride the broadcasting efforts at the end of the 1950s and the beginning of the 1960s. Yet it was the major vehicle of information for African populations which were often illiterate. In his memoirs, Ely, Galula's direct superior, wrote, "modern broadcast means, like radio and television, have transformed the assumptions about our problems overseas."[60] Radio of the time is as important as the Internet is to ours. Certainly, information was broadcast under the exclusive control of the state and not by private companies. The government could not afford to neglect information warfare and it became a major concern at higher and higher levels of state among political and military authorities. In May of 1968, six years after the end of the Algerian War, the journalists, producers, and technicians of ORTF (*Office de la radio télévision française*), symbol of censorship and control, demanded freedom of information and programming autonomy with respect to political power.[61] Only Radio Europe 1 and Radio Luxembourg (RTL), the secondary private stations, were able to maintain their independence from political power.

Conclusion

Taking stock of the counterinsurgency procedure outlined by Galula shows mixed results. The first step concerning the concentration of troops was a decision made by higher command. As luck would have it, Galula commanded in an area set aside for experimentation in counterinsurgency methodology. He had instructions for applying these methods in his subdistrict (arming the population, CHPT propaganda) which failed due to the OPA or the inadaptability of the methods to the cultural environment. Although critical of them, he would see his own counterinsurgency methods upset by the OPA.

The second step involved the necessary allocation of sufficient troops to prevent the resurgence of rebels and deployment of units to each village. Galula had little autonomy in deciding the deployment of his platoons in his *sous-quartier*. He persuaded his superiors of the value of dispersing his company. The ALN forces in the area numbered less than a platoon so Galula's company would have numerical superiority if they came in contact. He experimented with the ink spot strategy (pacifying one village after another and occupying them with his platoons). But this strategy had its limits: carrying it out required additional manpower which he was not granted. With the expansion of his subdistrict, Galula was given responsibility for two further villages. He had neither the men, nor the time to operate in depth in these two villages. He had to draw from his platoons to occupy even one of them. He gives only four pages to describing operations in these two villages, which essentially consisted of dismantling the OPA, choosing a mayor, and setting up a school in under a month.[1] Throughout his subdistrict, Galula occupied most of the villages, but the presence of a platoon in a village should not be linked with effective control of the population, an assumption Galula automatically makes. A platoon's presence contributed to improved security for villagers but did not stop the OPA from operating within the population. Therefore, this step was never achieved.

The third step was building relations with the population, controlling it, and preventing all contact with the rebels. Inspired by Servan Schreiber, Galula instructed his men on how to reassure the population while remaining suspicious of it. Galula benefited from SAS reports while improving the SAS's effectiveness by deploying his platoons to the villages. This synergy was a success: Galula's actions were appreciated greatly at Djebel Aïssa Mimoun, as SAS reports show: "Captain Galula's subdistrict devoted himself to his task in an admirable way" (January 31, 1957) or on the 45th BIC commander's evaluation report of July 1957: "Completely succeeded in his mission, firmly applying original methods to bring a majority from a hostile position to one favorable to our objectives."[2] At Djebel Aïssa Mimoun, there was at the same time, a meeting of minds with the SAS officer regarding the work to undertake among the population and the operational complementarity between the SAS and Galula's subdistrict. The attitude of a portion of the population toward the army seemed to have changed due to the implementation of economic and social aid. This is especially worth noting, as in 1956–57 too few units made any effort toward the population and very few had a good record[3] against the OPA or in rallying the population. It is true that Galula enjoyed a more favorable security environment upon arriving in his subdistrict: the relative weakness of the ALN was balanced by the activism of the OPA. Such conditions allowed Galula's company to devote its efforts to the population. But Galula exaggerated his operations in giving a quantitative account in terms of populations and numbers of people treated by the AMG. While the numbers of schoolchildren enrolled are correct, he omitted mentioning that thanks to this strategy, the FLN was able to ask that parents send their children to school en masse to sabotage his school policy. If Galula's subdistrict benefitted the SAS's initiative, it also suffered from negative impact when the SAS came upon financial and administrative difficulty. If the census allowed him to be informed about the people living in his area, he avoids talking about cultural problems it posed. As for controlling the population's movement, it was insufficient to monitor comings and goings or the marketplace. Galula's control of the population also raised the question of the legality of his penal code. The types and severity of sanctions were invented in the absence of any law enforcement or judicial authority. Having no precise instructions, Galula seized the opportunity to become policeman and judge. It could be seen, after a fashion, as the early assumption of civil powers that would be granted to the military in March 1956. But in Algeria, in the absence of any law enforcement or judiciary, these two functions theoretically fell to SAS officers but not

at the subdistrict level. These special powers also raised problems about
the legitimate level of control of a civilian population threatened by violent clandestine organizations and their use by totalitarian states who
restrain the freedom of information and violate individual freedoms. Galula doesn't explicitly mention these moral issues although *Le Monde,* via
Adour, explicated the drawbacks of this system and the moral hazard they
represented to a democratic society. The third step was successful: Galula
seems to have succeeded in reassuring the population. His company took
advantage of the aid and support of the SAS to help the population. Control of the population was managed in the villages; however, it failed to
control the movements of this same population.

The fourth step, destroying the OPA, was an initial, short-term success
but failed over the long term. Galula was able to decapitate the first generation of the OPA already implanted before his arrival in each village he
controlled (November–December 1956). He partially destroyed the less-
active, embryonic leadership of the second generation (January–February
1957). But Galula was dead wrong in thinking that he decisively defeated
the OPA, which instead adapted and took advantage of the 45th BIC's re-
deployment to show its power to cause harm and regain its influence, as
Adour warned in *Le Monde.* Taking a pacification operation in another
region and a later period (1959–61) as an example, over three years the
SAS commander at Catinat in Constantine destroyed the leadership of six
different OPA cells within a resettlement camp. He shared with his fellow
SAS officers that he had to "kill four OPA before he could say that the
camp had been cleaned up."[4] As Galula remained for a much shorter
time at Djebel Aïssa Mimoun, a little more than a year, his results against
the OPA should be considered more modest. Operations supporting the
population obscure the clash between Galula and the OPA's effort to impose its influence on the population. Every action supporting the population was an opportunity for Galula to spot the OPA's response, to learn
about the measures they put in place, and then neutralize them. The OPA,
in turn, used every means at its disposal to counteract Galula's and the
SAS's efforts: propaganda, symbolic action, calls to boycott initiatives or
else flood them with demand, infiltration of municipal government, *harka*
militias, targeted assassinations, intelligence on the soldiers' habits. "It is
easy, as *Le Monde* did, to evoke the myth of Sisyphus when speaking of the
destruction of rebel cells. On the contrary, if the operation is properly conducted, it is irreversible," wrote Galula in *Lettre d'informations.*[5] Galula's
underestimation of the OPA's capacity to rebuild itself was a serious error.
If Galula doesn't accept the comparison between the myth of Sisyphus
and the fight against the OPA, with the king of Thessaly eternally sen-
tenced by Zeus to push a boulder up a mountainside, an SAS officer also
in Kabylia can't resist reference to the Greek myth of the Labors of Hercu-
les, comparing the OPA to the Hydra of Lerna, the nine-headed monster
who terrorized the population of Argos, who regrew two heads for each

one it lost.[6] Galula's thinking seems to have changed with hindsight, as shown in his theoretical work in 1965, wherein he indeed compares the OPA to the Hydra,[7] amounting to an admission that victory against the OPA could never be definitive and the fight would be continual. A situation close to fair comparison with Sisyphus! Galula nevertheless adds a bit of nuance to his remarks on the Hydra, adding, "the heads would grow back unless they were all cut off at the same moment." At Djebel Aïssa Mimoun, the OPA systematically grew back to counter the army and the SAS, as was seen in terms of community building. Galula, while he discusses his success against the general strike of January 1957, neglects to mention his failure at Bou Souar, where the delegates, infiltrated by the OPA, observed the boycott. Moreover, one might think that it was in the in light of this experience that he wrote in *Counterinsurgency*: "Nor can elections be staged when the insurgent cell still exists, for the elections would most likely bring forth the insurgent's stooges."[8] The resurgence of the OPA, whose leadership was never totally decapitated, largely explains the deterioration after Galula's departure and the reversal of progress made toward pacification.

The fifth step of designating new officials was clearly a failure, in spite of the efforts of the army, the SAS, and the *prefecture*. The archival record is unanimous in showing that the situation was not yet ripe for elections. Artificially drawn electorates, too many communities, incompetent candidates forced to stand, and the infiltration of municipalities contributed to this phase's failure. Galula bears his share of responsibility in choosing and encouraging candidates under the assumption that he had dismantled the OPA, which was eager to infiltrate the municipalities. Subordinates in direct contact with elected officials also shoulder their share of responsibility. Galula allowed them great freedom of action without sufficient oversight of their activity. The absence of subordinate oversight could be explained by the manifold tasks Galula had to perform during operations such as propaganda, writing reports, attending meetings at higher headquarters, with the SAS, government officials, and journalists.

The sixth step, testing the loyalty and efficiency of elected officials and involving the population in maintaining order, was a failure. The incompetent and FLN supporters among the elected officials were rooted out, but could not be replaced. The army and SAS had to resort to forced paternalism to avoid losing their credibility with the population. They agreed on the relevance of projects to recently-elected officials and suggested other projects. This policy came up against a lack of finances. Such municipal policy was completely artificial and could only be carried out with involvement of the SAS and Galula's company. Muslim involvement in law enforcement was ambiguous: the militias, or *harkas* were created to defend against ALN bands, outsiders in the region, as well as from death threats made against elected officials. Their presence was in no way a sign of loyalty to France. The *harkis* were selected but insufficiently vetted, as the year 1958 would reveal. The fact that certain *harkis* informed to the OPA.

Galula supported the seventh step of forming a national political movement locally. He promoted and organized a movement on the regional level. But due to incompetence, passivity, and infiltration of local officials, this movement was bound to fail in the long term with the departure of its founder and due to the failure of the previous step.

The eighth step was to neutralize any remaining insurgents. The success of operations was due more to luck and in reaction to the ALN's local successes than tactics implemented by Galula. The passing of ALN bands from outside the region, unknown to the population and who terrorized them, tipped the scales for France, a pattern which would be seen in other parts of Algeria.[9] Finally, SAS commander Pfirrmann, from the point of view of his extensive military experience, was not always satisfied with the 45th BIC's operations against the ALN. This step was a short-term success but a long-term failure, as shown by the deterioration of the situation after Galula's departure with the return of the ALN.

Of the eight steps of counterinsurgency advocated by Galula and applied at Djebel Aïssa Mimoun: one step was an undeniable success (the third step: reassure, support, and control the population); three other steps were short-term successes and long-term failures (the second, fourth, and eighth steps, one unit in each village, the fight against the OPA and ALN); two steps were failures (the fifth and sixth: choosing officials and testing their reliability and efficiency); and, two steps did not fall within Galula's jurisdiction and had not proved effective (the first and seventh steps: concentrating troops and organizing a national political movement).

How can such a contrast in the assessment of pacification in Djebel Aïssa Mimoun be explained? The results are certainly interesting, but not as exceptional as a simple reading of *Pacification in Algeria* or some of Galula's more optimistic thoughts might suggest. "I set out to prove a theory of counterinsurgency warfare, and I am satisfied that it worked in my small area. What I achieved in my first six or eight months in Djebel Aïssa Mimoun was not due to magic and could have been applied much earlier throughout Algeria."[10] In reality, Galula's activities at Djebel Aïssa Mimoun lasted a short time, just 14 months, from August 1956 to October 1957. Over this period, a month was taken up in policing Tizi Ouzou, where he was cited for having contributed to the arrest of 27 rebels.[11] The period was too short to reasonably expect the subdistrict be pacified. Lasting pacification necessarily requires time; three years seems to be the right amount. One can imagine that the dispersion of Galula's activities did not make substantive work at Djebel Aïssa Mimoun any easier. Added to this dispersion was the expansion of Galula's subdistrict (without a corresponding increase in manpower), and the necessity of delegating responsibility to subordinates. Do Galula's modest results at pacifying Djebel Aïssa Mimoun over 1956–57 call into question the methods he developed in 1963? Galula responded clearly: "Like every similar concept, this one may be sound in theory but dangerous when applied rigidly to a specific case. It is difficult, however, to deny its logic because the laws . . . on which it is based can be easily recognized . . . in every recent revolutionary war."[12]

The main criticisms of Galula's tactics, having never been compared against the archival record and are more focused on the simplicity of its methods with respect to other, more elaborate French counterinsurgency doctrine thinkers. What some might see as a weakness is actually a doctrinal asset. The French army in Algeria did not lack for counterinsurgency theories, in the words of a too-indulgent Galula, but rather had an impressive number of revolutionary warfare theories and doctrine. These theories were all long on conceptualizations, but their two main disadvantages were the lack of tactical doctrine and an oversimplification of such doctrine, rendering the concepts ineffective. For example, Nemo a brilliant revolutionary warfare theoretician, distributed his "Reflections on Subversive Warfare."[13] The antisubversive methods he treats in the third part are very vague (techniques of influence, broadcasting, and action) and need to be interpreted to be correctly applied, at the risk of distorting them. As well, how many theoreticians of revolutionary warfare were asked to personally implement their thinking in Algeria? The answer was very few.[14] Major Prestat, a theoretician of the French school of revolutionary warfare, admitted in 1960 to a disconnection between psychological warfare with respect to what was going on the ground: "Psychological guidelines have little to do with reality."[15] Galula had indeed witnessed the methodological failure of three theoreticians of revolutionary warfare, such as the establishment of parallel hierarchies, the arming of the population, and CIMIC-based psychological operations.[16] Galula and his counterpart Trinquier stand out from other thinkers by their strategic vision of counterinsurgency in simple terms and the development of tactics that they applied personally in the field with relative success. These three factors obliged them to make a real effort to teach their methods to subordinates. They then spread their doctrine throughout military and opinion-making circles. Was not the best evidence of the effectiveness of Galula's theory that, in a completely different area of Algeria, commanders recognized its validity and, even in other operational contexts, the U.S. Army[17] recognized its relevance?

The apparent simplicity of Galula's counterinsurgency doctrine actually issues from the lack of bibliographical references to the works of other thinkers. In *Counterinsurgency* he cites only four books on Asia and made use of Chassin's work. Moreover, he deliberately avoids citing a number of references such as British general R. Thompson, the architect of the antiguerilla war in Malaysia (1948–60) employing strategic hamlets, even though he mentions Malaysia three times in his book. Similarly, Landsdale, who led the fight against the communists in the Philippines since 1950, is never cited, although Galula twice moved to the Philippines to study how the counterinsurgency fight was developing. Landsdale's operations were nevertheless popularized in two books, whose publication Galula could not have ignored.[18] Finally, when referring to strategic hamlet in Indochina, Trinquier's[19] name is not cited, as his translator de Montenon noted, nor were others, like Marshall Foch, or Clausewitz, yet he cites their words. In *Pacification*, Galula cites only one author who studied the general situation in Algeria. M. Clark author of *Algeria in Turmoil* (1959), which seems a bit light, given the abundance of works published during this period. He does also make an incomplete reference to H. Baldwin, whom he cites in order to challenge. Baldwin argued that France had lost the war in Algeria against the guerillas, unlike the British who had defeated the guerillas in Malaysia. Baldwin[20] edited military titles for the *New York Times* and authored a number of military and political history books. While he might have been known to American readers at the time, Galula failed to mention the article or book from which he extracted Baldwin's analysis. Moreover, we find the same inaccuracies in references to articles in *Le Monde* that called him into question.

This absence of sources and references to contemporary counterinsurgency thinkers might be surprising, especially as Galula was as researcher at the Center for International Affairs at Harvard from 1962 to 1963, during which time he published his two books, especially as compiling a bibliography would have been among his duties as a university researcher. This has made studying Galula's work more difficult with respect to others thinkers. This does not mean that Galula's thought is based solely on his own observations and experiences, as he says all too easily. Clearly, he was fueled by the study of guerilla theorists (T. E. Lawrence and Mao), strategists of colonial warfare (Gallieni, Lyautey, and the ink spot strategy), theoreticians from the French school of revolutionary warfare (Chassin, Nemo, Lacheroy, and Argoud, who published in *Contacts*), but also by the methods of propaganda these theoreticians adopted (CHTP), even though they had been criticized. The study of concrete cases in Algeria, whether those of Servan Schreiber and Argoud or others, seem to have also figured in developing his theory.

Galula had always looked to disseminate thinking about counterinsurrection in an effort to modify military methods in Algeria and, one might think, in hopes of being named to a post with responsibilities equal to his experience. He maintained an intense communications campaign with his superiors, writing in a report on pacification in November 1956, and making a tape recording for Ely, which was later heard by Bourgès-Maunoury. In March 1957, he wrote a second report that was approved by Lacomme and Guérin, who passed on his theories to Dulac, the chief of staff for Salan.[21] In June 1957, he met with Maisonneuve, the first deputy to Lacoste for planning development but without results. His efforts were finally successful after he was promoted to the psychological operations office of the general staff of national defense in 1958.[22] But he did not seem to have further career prospects. Fluent in English, Galula had married an American named Ruth Morgan whom he had met during his time in China. Owing to his knowledge of English, he was asked to attend a series of conferences with American NATO officers present in France at Orléans, Poitiers, and Verdun. He received a letter of congratulations from Ely, chief of staff of the armed forces, citing his "knowledge of the language and the American mindset of foreign officers." Naturally, he was chosen to attend staff college at Norfolk from January to July 1960. Taking advantage of his presence in the United States, now Lieutenant Colonel Galula was asked, in April of 1960, to lecture at the Special Forces school at Fort Bragg. According to comments made by M. Robin, Colonel Jonnes, who held a degree in psychology, was looking to introduce instruction in psychological warfare in his school with the objective of inventing new operations. His French lecturers were experienced practicioners, like Aussaresses, the academic Bernard Fall,[23] and Galula. He received a letter of congratulations from Colonel G. M. Jonnes to thank him for his service: "everyone [staff, professors, trainees] was deeply impressed by your comments and I think everyone in attendance learned a great deal thanks to your talk. This was a signal event to have a chance to speak with an officer from an allied nation, particularly one as competent in the subject as you are." Jonnes finished with the hope that he and Galula would meet in the future.[24] In 1960, Galula was now known to Americans as a leader of quality, a counterinsurgency specialist with an excellent reputation as an English-speaking lecturer.

It seems, however, that during his stay in Hong Kong, he might have met General Westmoreland, whom he might have impressed with his views. It might have been on the initiative of Westmoreland that Galula was invited to the United States to participate in a RAND seminar on counterinsurgency.[25] The seminar was organized by two of RAND's members, S. T. Hosmer and S. O. Crane, in Washington, D.C., from April 16 to 20, 1962. The RAND Corporation is a private think tank working for the government, which was then charged with providing expertise on various aspects of the Vietnam conflict and to guide the actions of the U.S. government. RAND would later study the impact of strategic hamlets and on the state of mind of Vietcong prisoners for the Pentagon.[26] This RAND seminar was an assessment on counterinsurgency methods concerning nine different theatres of operation (Algeria, China, Greece, Kenya, Laos, Malaysia, Oman, South Vietnam, and the Philippines). The minutes of the seminar published by RAND[27] show that different themes were treated in debate form. In the document, each of the 12 participants was introduced with a biography. Galula was the sole French officer present, which seems surprising given France's counterinsurgency experience in Indochina and Algeria and the easy availability of numerous theorists. French lack of fluency in English and the fact that French theoreticians had been dispersed by the minister of defense, Messmer, hostile to their thinking,[28] could explain why French presence at the seminar was merely symbolic.

Only participants with concrete experience were present. There was the Australian, Colonel White, who fought the guerillas in Malaysia from 1957 to 1960. Three British officers were also there: Captain Jeapes (an officer from 22 SAS, who had fought in Malaysia and Oman), General Powell-Jones (Malaysia 1957–58) and the best known British expert, Lieutenant Colonel Kitson who managed the counterinsurgency fight against the Mau-Mau in Kenya from 1953 to 1955 with great success and went on to Malaysia in 1957. He wrote of his experience in a book published in 1960.[29] The American, Landsdale, who had lead the counterguerilla fight against the Huk in the Philippines, who participated with the Philippine officers, Lieutenant Colonel Bohannan (who had been in combat with communist guerillas) and General Valeriano[30] who fought as a guerilla against the Japanese in the Philippines, later becoming head of the Philippine armed forces and then leading the fight against communist guerillas there. Three other American officers were present: Colonel Shirley (a leader of the counterguerilla fight in Malaysia and Kenya), Colonel Fertig (who conducted guerilla operations against the Japanese in the Philippines, a professor of tactics, and head of psychological warfare), Lieutenant Colonel Wilson (expert in antiguerilla operations against the Japanese in Burma, specialist in World War II partisan operations in the USSR, an instructor at Fort Bragg, and counselor to the secretary of defense).

This seminar was a real brain dump of American, Australian, British, French, and Philippine methodology which would aid the Americans in Vietnam. In his 2006 preface to the seminar's proceedings, Hosmer takes up Kitson's opinion of the meeting and gives us an idea of the participants' mood: "Although we came from such wildly divergent backgrounds, it was as if we had all been brought up together from youth. We all spoke the same language. Probably all of us had worked out theories of counterinsurgency procedures at one time or another, which we thought were unique and original. But when we came to air them, all our ideas were essentially the same. We had another thing in common. Although we had no difficulty in making our views understood to each other, we had mostly been unable to get our respective armies to hoist in the message."[31]

How was Galula's contribution received by his fellow specialists? He developed his theories widely from the first day and made many clarifying remarks on his and others' ideas. He had an important advantage over the others as only he could speak of six different theatres of operation (China, Indochina, Malaysia, the Philippines, Greece, and Algeria) in strategic as well as tactical terms, while the others, at best, could only speak of one or two different theatres. Of these six, only Galula could speak of China, Greece, and Algeria. If we look at the total of the examples Galula developed at the seminar, half concerned Algeria, a fifth China, with one-third given to other theatres of operation (Indochina, Greece, Philippines,

Burma). The majority mentioned, also found in *Pacification in Algeria*, were unfamiliar to the 11 other participants.

Galula's reflections went unchallenged and were often praised by others. Valeriano agreed with Galula that, in the Philippines, his method of purging the villages had been employed and was also used by the Japanese, but ultimately failed as (departing from Galula's method) the Japanese employed terror. Galula's experience was confirmed by Landsdale's commentary on the importance of coordinating political and psychological action in fighting guerillas. Galula explained his methods in terms of the six steps tested at Djebel Aïssa Mimoun. His method was indirectly approved of by Landsdale in referring to Malaysia: "We must show that we are fighting for something and not simply against something negative, in a defensive battle."[32] During the seminar, Galula's thinking was confirmed or filled out by foreign experts and went unchallenged. We also have the testimony of R. Phillips, a deputy to Landsdale, on how Galula was received. Phillips had served Landsdale as an advisor to the South Vietnamese army. He then served in Laos (where since 1957 the American army had supported the government against the communist Pathet Lao) as an agent of the CIA conducting civil operations among the Lao population. In 1962, he served as an advisor on counterinsurgency in rural affairs. Phillips only arrived in the afternoon of the third day of the seminar to speak about civil operations in South Vietnam with Colonel White, who developed the example of Malaysia for him. Galula filled out the examples given by these two officers by describing his own record in Algeria in educational, municipal, and economic development. The proceedings of the seminar stress that during these presentations "Colonel Galula, using different approaches with his own unit and also in terms of results, confirmed the remarks of M. White and M. Phillips."[33] Phillips remembered Galula: "I did not participate in the first few symposium sessions, but heard from Landsdale that there was a very unusual French officer named David Galula present, who had a lot of good ideas that sounded very much like our own. As I got involved in discussions with Colonel Galula, I discovered he wasn't anything like the vast majority of the French officers I had tried to work with as part of a joint American-French military advisory mission . . . in the 1954–55 days in Vietnam. Most had a colonial attitude toward the Vietnamese and saw them as lesser beings. Colonel Galula, however, was different. He didn't maintain an attitude of superiority. Rather, his mission involved trying to help the local Algerian population as their friend, and he imbued his troops with that attitude."[34] Two American counterinsurgency operators judged Galula very positively, noting that his thinking and experience squared with their own.

Galula's participation in the seminar was a major influence in shaping his thinking one year before *Pacification* was published (1963) and two years before *Counterinsurgency* (1964), since therein he treats characteristics of guerrilla organization and counterinsurgency tactics, intelligence problems, problems of communications and equipment, psychological warfare and civil affairs, and the indicators defining the moment when the counterinsurgent has won against the guerilla. Indeed, the examples Galula used in his statements during the seminar would be treated again two years later in *Counterinsurgency*. The seminar's proceedings were published in November 1962 after the participants had reread them. It is surprising that Galula makes no mention of the seminar in *Counterinsurgency* nor any mention of his exchanges with Landsdale and Valeriano or the other participants, although his own thinking was validated by them.

His participation must have played and important part in his decision to request his detachment to Harvard in 1962. His career prospects in the French army at the beginning of the 1960s were indeed limited with the dissolution of the French colonial empire, the dismissal of revolutionary warfare ideologues, the cessation of thinking about counterinsurgency,[35] the development of nuclear deterrence, and the transformation of a colonial army specialized in small wars into a conventional army designed to fight the Warsaw Pact. Galula's experience wasn't useful to the French, while the Americans were looking for people with this sort experience for Vietnam. It was therefore logical that Galula would request his separation from the army to follow opportunities in the United States. Westmoreland found him work as a research associate at the Harvard Center for International Affairs, where he met Henry Kissinger, who was then head of the Defense Studies Program.[36] The same year Galula published *Pacification in Algeria* at the request of Hosmer[37] from RAND, the U.S. Army translated Trinquier's work, *Modern Warfare*.[38] At the time, the Americans were recruiting other foreign counterinsurgency experts, like the Briton R. Thompson, who had organized counterinsurgency in Malaysia by means of strategic hamlets, a strategy that was subsequently applied in Vietnam from 1962 to 1965.[39] Jeapes, another Briton and participant of the RAND seminar, expert in counterinsurgency operations in Malaysia and Oman, served as an instructor to Special Forces at Fort Bragg. Shirley, also present at the RAND seminar, expert in communications operations in Malaysia and Kenya, took American citizenship and became one of the directors of a business charged with developing electronic warfare and telecommunications for the American army. Another seminar participant, Valeriano lent his experience won in the Philippine insurrection to the American military mission to South Vietnam in 1954–66, later becoming the military attaché to Thailand, a country considered to be one of the dominos threatened by communist expansion in Asia. Landsdale, who had greatly appreciated Galula's original ideas, became an advisor to the prime minister of South Vietnam from 1954 to 1956[40] and, from 1961, an advisor to the Pentagon. Two years after the RAND seminar, Westmoreland was appointed deputy, later commander of the U.S. Military Assistance Command, Vietnam. From 1964 he fought the Vietcong guerillas before being named Army Chief of Staff in 1968.[41]

Galula's influence on the implementation of counterinsurgency in Vietnam seems to have been important. RAND analyst, R. Komer, also a member of the CIA, was named to CORDS (civil operation and revolutionary operations support) which he commanded from 1966 to 1967, implementing pacification methods. Komer coordinated social and economic initiatives in Vietnam allowing Americans a different way of addressing the Vietnamese population. According to E. Tenenbaum, who consulted the American archives, the concept of CORDS took inspiration from *Pacification in Algeria* which was included in the report "Counterinsurgency and Nation Building," of September 25, 1967.[42] In 1968, pacification operations focused on fighting the OPA with Open Arms and Phoenix programs that allowed the US to win over 17,000 Vietcong cadres and to eliminate 20,000[43] of them but also witnessed many abuses (torture, falsified statistics covering up civilian deaths reported as Vietcong).[44] According to Tenenbaum Nelson Brickham, one of the designers of Operation PHOENIX, was impressed with Galula's *Counterinsurgency*.[45]

Galula's books fit not only into French, British, and American counterinsurgency thinking in Algeria and Asia of the 1940s, 1950s, and the beginning of the 1960s but also into the employment of their lessons by the U.S. Army in the Vietnam War. R. Phillips confirms this analysis: "In Vietnam, I was able to put into practice many of the principles and ideas that I had learned under Landsdale, which were reinforced by the [RAND] symposium. Unfortunately, most of our senior leadership in Vietnam during my active days, 1962–63 and 1965–68, was wedded to very different and more conventional concepts of warfare coming out of World War II and Korea."[46] Galula has been one of the theoretical architects of pacification methods used by the American army in Vietnam; the recent rediscovery of his writing by Americans looking to make use of it for conducting conflicts in Iraq and Afghanistan should cause us to forget this little known aspect of the use of his counterinsurgency theories. Only two of his superiors at the ministry of defense, describing Galula as an officer of the future in 1958 and an officer "who, in the interest of the service, must be kept up with" (1962)[47] would have been prescient enough to foresee his return to grace[48] in the thinking of French and American tacticians at the beginning of the 21st century.

Maps

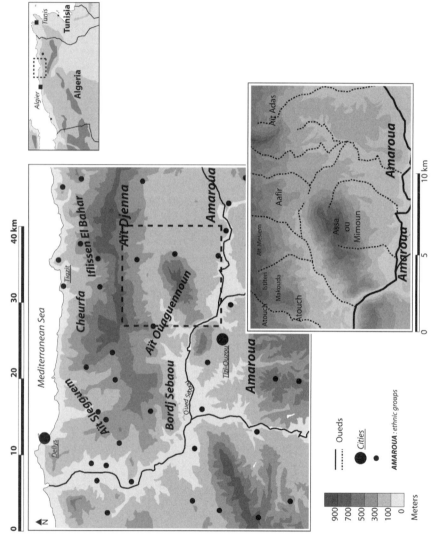

Localization of Djebel Aïsa Mimoun and Tribal Context. (Cartography by François Guiziou)

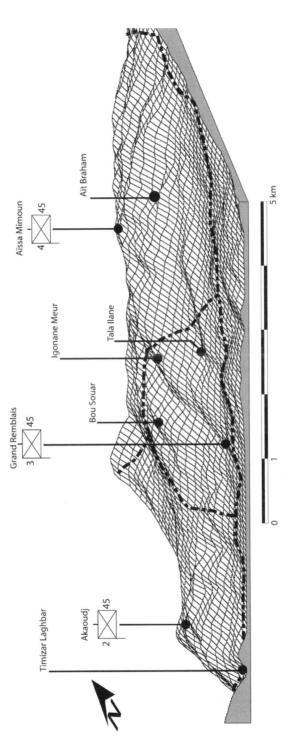

Initial deployment of 3/45th BIC. Approximately 2.3 square miles (6 km²). (Cartography by François Guiziou)

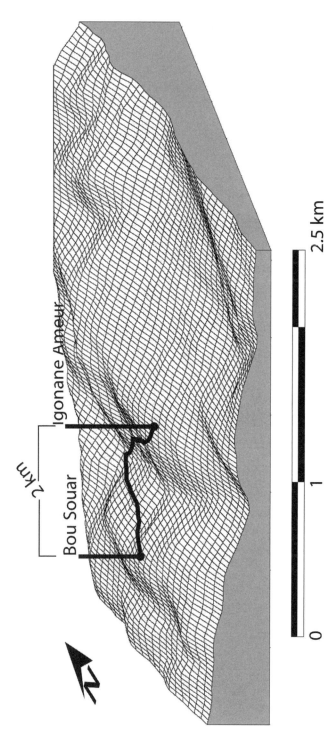

A path between Bou Souar and Igonane Ameur like the one Galula describes in *Pacification in Algeria* (p. 26). (Cartography by François Guiziou)

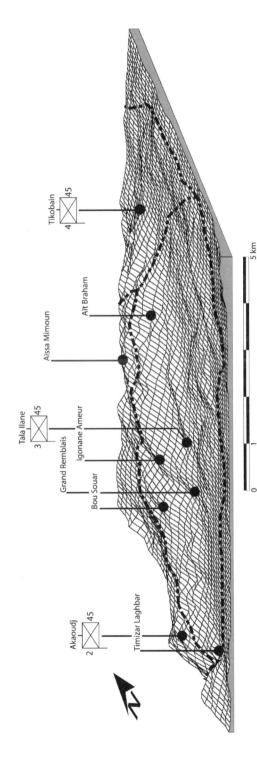

Final deployment of 3/45th BIC, 11.5 square miles (30 km²). Note incorporation of territory to the south along the tribal limit. (Cartography by François Guiziou)

Notes

PREFACE

1. General Stanley McChrystal, interview by Renaud Girard "Comment nous allons gagner en Afghanistan," *Le Figaro,* September 29, 2009.

2. Isabelle Lasserre, "La stratégie militaire française en Afghanistan," *Le Figaro,* December 31, 2008; The CDEF published a study of Galula. Bertrand Valeyre and Alexandre Guérin, "De Galula à Petraeus, l'héritage français dans la pensée américaine de la contre-insurrection," *Cahier de la recherche doctrinale* (June 2009). www.cdef.terre.defense.gouv.fr.

3. David Galula, *Pacification in Algeria 1956–1958* (Santa Monica: RAND Corporation, 1963; republished 2006).

4. A similar comparison between the account of counterinsurgency operations led by SAS Lieutenant Ontrup at Catinat in the Constantine from 1958 to 1960 and the archival record has already been undertaken by the author. Grégor Mathias, "La SAS de Catinat entre souvenirs d'un officier et écriture de l'histoire," in *La guerre d'Algérie au miroir des décolonisations françaises* (Paris: SFHOM, 2000), pp. 555–572.

5. Philippe de Montenon introduction "45 ans après, le couronnement de David Galula" to *Contre-insurrection, théorie et pratique,* by David Galula (New York: Praeger, 1964; Paris: Economica, 2008), pp. 15–27.

6. Adopting a thematic approach to Galula's operations, rather than a chronological one, it is difficult to avoid a certain amount of duplication.

CHAPTER 1

1. Lionel-Max Chassin, *La conquête de la Chine par Mao Tsé-Tung* (Paris: Payot, 1952; republished Livre de poche, 1963), p. 107.

2. Service historique des Armées (SHD), ESS.

3. Robert O. Paxton, *L'armée de Vichy, le corps des officiers français 1940–1944* (Paris: Tallandier, 2003), pp. 199–200. Only a few officers were exempt from this measure by special decree. Paxton cites the case of a general.

4. Ann Marlowe, "Forgotten Founder: The French colonel who wrote the book(s) on counterinsurgency," *Weekly Standard*, October 19, 2009.

5. Georges A. Groussard, *Service Secret 1940–1945* (Paris: Table ronde, 1964) p. 276, p. 339.

6. Ibid., pp. 66–72, p. 171.

7. General Groussard was a part of the pro-fascist, anti-German, Order of the Cowl, opposed to the Third Republic. Within the Vichy government he represented the anti-German faction. He called for the arrest of Pierre Laval, the pro-German prime minister under Pétain. Groussard would in turn be put under house arrest by Admiral Darlan. Groussard fled to Switzerland where he directed his resistance network.

8. Georges A. Groussard, *Service secret 1940–1945* (Paris: Table ronde, 1964), pp. 230–231, pp. 392–394.

9. Pierre Paillole, *Services spéciaux 1939–1945* (Paris: R. Laffont, 1975), p. 342.

10. Ibid., pp. 337–340, p. 390.

11. Seymour Topping, *The Peking Letter, a Novel of the Chinese Civil War* (New York: PublicAffairs, 1999), p. 33.

12. SHD, ESS. He was decorated at corps headquarters with the croix de guerre avec étoile de vermeil.

13. Jean de Lattre, *Histoire de la 1ère armée française* (Paris: Presse de la Cité, 1971), pp. 48–49.

14. Jean-Christophe Notin, *Les vaincus seront les vainqueurs. La France en Allemagne 1945* (Paris: Perrin, 2004), pp. 125–126, pp. 161–162.

15. Ibid., p. 174.

16. Jean de Lattre, *Histoire de la 1ère armée française* (Paris: Plon, 1949), pp. 533–548; Herremann Riedel, *Ausweg los . . . ! Letzer Akt des Krieg im Schwartzwald Ende April 1945* (Villingen-Schwenningen: A. Wetzel KG, 1974), pp. 23–29, p. 65; Bernd Serger, *Karin-Anne Böttcher, Gerd R. Ueberschär, Südbaden unter hakenkreuz und Trikolore* (Fribourg in Brisgau: Rombach Verlag, 2006), pp. 136–148. Accounts of the largely unsuccessful Werewolf operations.

17. SHD, ESS.

18. Jacques Guillermaz, *Une vie pour la Chine, mémoires 1937–1989* (Paris: R. Laffont, 1989), p. 116, p. 123, pp. 125–126.

19. Ibid., p. 129.

20. Biographical information provided by Galula himself in David Galula, *Pacification in Algeria 1956–1958* (Santa Monica: RAND Corporation, 1963; republished 2006), introduction, p. 1, p. 69, p. 100, p. 106. Appendix 2, p. 258, reproduced from the typescript of the journal *Contacts*, with reference to his experience in China and Greece. Stephen T. Hosmer and Sibylle O. Crane, *Counterinsurgency: A Symposium, April 16–20, 1962* (Santa Monica: RAND Corporation, November 1962; republished 2006), bibliography, pp. 19–20.

21. Jacques Guillermaz, *Une vie pour la Chine* (Paris: R. Laffont, 1989), pp. 157–158.

22. Ann Marlowe, "Forgotten Founder: The French colonel who wrote the book(s) on counterinsurgency," *Weekly Standard*, October 19, 2009.

23. Seymour Topping, *The Peking Letter, a Novel of the Chinese Civil War* (New York: Public Affairs, 1999), p. 32.

24. Ibid., pp. 30–31, p. 33.

25. David Galula, *Counterinsurgency Warfare: Theory and Practice* (New York: Praeger, 1964; Paris: Economica, 2008), p. 1.

26. Seymour Topping, *The Peking Letter, a Novel of the Chinese Civil War* (New York: Public Affairs, 1999), p. 71.

27. SHD, ESS.

28. David Galula, *Counterinsurgency Warfare: Theory and Practice* (New York: Praeger, 1964; Paris: Economica, 2008), p. 80. The anecdote is also found in Stephen T. Hosmer and Sibylle O. Crane, *Counterinsurgency: A Symposium, April 16–20, 1962* (Santa Monica: RAND Corporation, November 1962; republished 2006), bibliography, pp. 10–11; and also reported by Jacques Guillermaz, *Une vie pour la Chine* (Paris: R. Laffont, 1989), pp. 164–165; Galula's exact itinerary: Beijing-Tatung (first period of captivity by the communists)-Taiyüan (hosted by the military governor and warlord)-Houma (second two weeks of communist captivity), Sian-Nankin.

29. Lionel-Max Chassin, *La conquête de la Chine par Mao Tsé-Tung* (Paris: Payot, 1952; republished Livre de poche, 1963), pp. 106–107.

30. François Géré, *La guerre psychologique* (Paris: Economica, 1997), p. 153.

31. Revue militaire d'information, October 1954.

32. Revue de Défense nationale, May 1956.

33. Lionel-Max Chassin, *La conquête de la Chine par Mao Tsé-Tung* (Paris: Payot, 1952; republished Livre de poche, 1963), pp. 106–107.

34. David Galula, *Counterinsurgency Warfare: Theory and Practice* (New York: Praeger, 1964; Paris: Economica, 2008), pp. 80–81. The prisoner story is also found in Stephen T. Hosmer and Sibylle O. Crane, *Counterinsurgency: A Symposium, April 16–20, 1962* (Santa Monica: RAND Corporation, November 1962; republished 2006), p. 35.

35. Lionel-Max Chassin, *La conquête de la Chine par Mao Tsé-Tung* (Paris: Payot, 1952; republished Livre de poche, 1963), p. 107.

36. David Galula, *Counterinsurgency Warfare: Theory and Practice* (New York: Praeger, 1964; Paris: Economica, 2008), p. 81.

37. Lionel-Max Chassin, *La conquête de la Chine par Mao Tsé-Tung* (Paris: Payot, 1952; republished Livre de poche, 1963), p. 106.

38. David Galula, *Counterinsurgency Warfare: Theory and Practice* (New York: Praeger, 1964; Paris: Economica, 2008), p. 27, p. 123.

39. Lionel-Max Chassin, *La conquête de la Chine par Mao Tsé-Tung* (Paris: Payot, 1952; republished, Livre de poche, 1963), pp. 105–119, pp. 124–125.

40. David Galula, *Contre-insurrection* (New York: Praeger, 1964; Paris: Economica, 2008), p. 54; Lionel-Max Chassin, *La conquête de la Chine par Mao Tsé-Tung* (Paris: Payot, 1952; republished Livre de poche, 1963), p. 20.

41. Lionel-Max Chassin, *La conquête de la Chine par Mao Tsé-Tung* (Paris: Payot, 1952; republished, Livre de poche, 1963), p. 29; General Joseph. W. Stilwell, *The Stilwell Papers* (New York: White, 1948); Général J.W. Stilwell, *L'aventure chinoise (1941–1944)* (Paris: éd. de la Baconnère, 1949). Stilwell commanded three U.S. infantry divisions in China. He was relieved by General Wedemeyer for trying to arm the communists against the Japanese.

42. Galula cites J. Lossing Buck, *Land Utilization in China* (Oxford: Oxford University Press, 1937); C.K. Yang, *A Chinese Village in Early Communist Transition*

(Cambridge: MIT Press, 1959); Mao Tse Tung, *Stratégie de la guerre révolutionnaire chinoise* (Paris: éd. sociales, 1950). The two Chinese examples are taken from an article in the *New York Times* of July 4, 1949.

43. Lionel-Max Chassin, *La conquête de la Chine par Mao Tsé-Tung* (Paris: Payot, 1952; republished Livre de poche, 1963), pp. 135–141, pp. 217–229.

44. Ann Marlowe, "Forgotten Founder: The French colonel who wrote the book(s) on counterinsurgency," *Weekly Standard*, October 19, 2009.

45. Samuel B. Griffith, *On Guerrilla Warfare* (New York: Praeger, 1961); S. B. Griffith, *Peking and People's Wars* (New York: Praeger, 1966). Collected articles published in the *Marine Corps Journal*.

46. Samuel B. Griffith, introduction to *The Art of War*, by Sun Tzu (Oxford: Clarendon Press, 1963); S. B. Griffith Sun Tzu, *L'art de la guerre* (Paris: Flammarion, 1995), pp. 73–86. Griffith's analysis of the influence of Sun Tzu on Mao.

47. David Galula, *Counterinsurgency Warfare: Theory and Practice* (New York: Praeger, 1964; Paris: Economica, 2008), p. 5.

48. Mao Tse Tung, *La stratégie de la guerre révolutionnaire en Chine* (Paris: éd. sociales, 1950), p. 15.

49. Mao Tse Tung, "Questions de stratégie dans la guerre de partisans antijaponaise," *La guerre révolutionnaire* (Paris: éd. sociales, 1955), p. 168.

50. David Galula, *Counterinsurgency Warfare: Theory and Practice* (New York: Praeger, 1964; Paris: Economica, 2008), p. 77. The prisoner story is also found in Stephen T. Hosmer and Sibylle O. Crane, *Counterinsurgency: A Symposium, April 16–20, 1962* (Santa Monica: RAND Corporation, November 1962; republished 2006), p. 30.

51. Lionel-Max Chassin, *La conquête de la Chine par Mao Tsé-Tung* (Paris: Payot, 1952; republished Livre de poche, 1963), p. 51. The passage is found in Mao Tse Tung, *La stratégie de la guerre révolutionnaire en Chine* (Paris: éd. sociales, 1950), p. 43.

52. David Galula, *Contre-insurrection* (New York: Praeger, 1964; Paris: Economica, 2008), pp. 70–88, 5 steps of communist insurrection; Stephen T. Hosmer and Sibylle O. Crane, *Counterinsurgency: A Symposium, April 16–20, 1962* (Santa Monica: RAND Corporation, November 1962, republished 2006), the six steps of pacification, p. 83; David Galula, *Contre-insurrection* (New York: Praeger, 1964; Paris: Economica, 2008), pp. 159–199, 8 steps of counterinsurgency; Mao Tse Tung, *La stratégie de la guerre révolutionnaire* (Paris, éd. sociales, 1950), pp. 66–67, 6 conditions for the offensive; Mao Tse Tung, *La guerre révolutionnaire* (Paris: éd. sociales, 1955), p. 133, 6 practical questions about strategic against the Japanese.

53. David Galula, *Counterinsurgency Warfare: Theory and Practice* (New York: Praeger, 1964; Paris: Economica, 2008), pp. 155–163.

54. Jacques Guillermaz, *Une vie pour la Chine* (Paris: R. Laffont, 1989), pp. 163–171, pp. 195–197.

55. SHD, ESS.

56. Jacques Guillermaz, *Une vie pour la Chine, mémoires 1937–1989* (Paris: R. Laffont, 1989), p. 185.

57. Jean Dalègre, *La Grèce depuis 1940* (Paris: L'Harmattan, 2006), pp. 88–90.

58. David Galula, *Contre-insurrection* (New York: Praeger, 1964; Paris: Economica, 2008), p. 23 describes the organization of Greek communist guerilla in battalions, regiments, and divisions, one of the causes for its defeat; p. 32 Greek guerillas supported by neighboring communist states (Albania, Yugoslavia, and Bulgaria);

pp. 56–57, the guerillas took advantage of the mountainous region, but the compartmentalization of the terrain favored the army; pp. 63–64, because of the break between Tito and Stalin, the communist guerillas received no further weapons from Yugoslavia.

59. Stephen T. Hosmer and Sibylle O. Crane, *Counterinsurgency: A Symposium, April 16–20, 1962* (Santa Monica: RAND Corporation, November 1962; republished 2006), bibliography, p. 43.

60. Jacques Guillermaz, *Une vie pour la Chine* (Paris: R. Laffont, 1989), pp. 218–219.

61. Ibid., p. 264.

62. Jacques Guillermaz, *Histoire du parti communiste chinois* (Paris: Payot, 1968); Jacques Guillermaz, *Le parti communiste au pouvoir* (Paris: Payot, 1972), Henri Eyraud, "Le Général Jacques Guillermaz (1911–1998), Pionnier de la Chine contemporaine," *Revue Historique des Armées* 1 (2003): 63–64.

63. SHD, ESS, and David Galula, *Counterinsurgency Warfare: Theory and Practice* (New York: Praeger, 1964; Paris: Economica, 2008), p. 44–45. He recounts the story of a Chinese from Canton in 1954 [implicated in] a system of informers. He also reports information collected in Hong Kong in 1952 from "a European" expelled from the island of Hanan about the opinions of peasant militias toward the communist regime and their efforts to resist infiltration from Taiwanese nationalist agents; Stephen T. Hosmer and Sibylle O. Crane, *Counterinsurgency: A Symposium, April 16–20, 1962* (Santa Monica: RAND Corporation, November 1962, republished 2006), p. 27, p. 47, in truth the information came from two priests.

64. Jacques Guillermaz, *Une vie pour la Chine* (Paris: R. Laffont, 1989), p. 215; David Galula [Jean Caran, pseud.], *Les moustaches du tigre* (Paris: Flammarion, 1965).

65. Jacques Guillermaz, *Une vie pour la Chine* (Paris: R. Laffont, 1989), p. 217.

66. Seymour Topping, *The Peking Letter* (New York: PublicAffairs, 1999), p. 71. Also mentions H. Luce in Beijing.

67. Ann Marlowe, "Forgotten Founder: The French colonel who wrote the book(s) on counterinsurgency," *Weekly Standard*, October 19, 2009.

68. David Galula [Jean Caran, pseud.], *Les moustaches du tigre* (Paris: Flammarion, 61), p. 47, p. 61, p. 88, p. 166.

69. Roger Trinquier, *La Guerre moderne* (Paris: Table ronde, 1961), p. 122 after an article by Lieutenant Colonel John E. Beebe, "Beating the Guerilla," *Military Review*, 1955.

70. Michel David, *Les maquis autochtones face au Viêt-minh 1950–1955* (thesis, Montpellier III University, 2001), p. 580. Lieutenant Colonel David was director of the History Department at St. Cyr Military Academy at Coëtquidan and of the Memorial Museum. He is a Defense Ministry lecturer specialized in revolutionary warfare, counterguerilla warfare, and psyops.

71. David Galula, *Counterinsurgency Warfare: Theory and Practice* (New York: Praeger, 1964; Paris: Economica, 2008), p. 123.

72. Correspondence with Lieutenant Colonel Michel David, October 19, 2009.

73. Jacques Dalloz, *Dictionnaire de la guerre d'Indochine 1945–1954* (Paris: A. Colin, 2006), p. 21; Jacques Dalloz, *La guerre d'Indochine* (Paris: Seuil, 1986), pp. 218–219.

74. The place names used by Galula in David Galula, *Pacification in Algeria 1956–1958* (Santa Monica: RAND Corporation, 1963; republished 2006) were

retained. In official documents, however, Aïssa Mimoun is referred to as "Djebel Aïssa Mimoun," Igonane Ameur as "Igounane Ameur," and Khelouyene is called "Ikhelouene."

75. David Galula, *Pacification in Algeria 1956–1958* (Santa Monica: RAND Corporation, 1963; republished 2006), pp. 26–27, p. 40.

76. SHD 1. H. 1222 Monograph of mostly undeveloped photos of SAS from 1959, names of SAS commanders and dates from 1955 to 1957. Archives nationales d'Outre-mer (ANOM). 5.SAS.217. Q4 report, 1959 claiming 7,121 inhabitants for Djebel Aïssa Mimoun.

77. Centre d'histoire de sciences politiques (C.H.S.P), archives d'histoire contemporaine, Paris, fonds Gérard Bélorgey GB 1, réactions et reprises dans la presse, Lettre d'informations politiques et économiques n°574 (December 1957), "Monographie de la pacification."

78. David Galula, *Pacification in Algeria 1956–1958* (Santa Monica: RAND Corporation, 1963; republished 2006), p. 107.

79. Ibid., pp. 46–47.

80. Claude Pfirrmann, interview with Grégor Mathias, February 4, 2009.

81. Claude Pfirrmann set up, after serving with the SAS at Djebel Aïssa Mimoun, the first SAU (*Section administrative urbaine*) in the upper Casbah of Algiers, July 1957 to October 1958. He wrote an article on this period for a historical review: Claude Pfirrmann, "Premières SAU dans la Casbah," *Historia magazine—Guerre d'Algérie*, n°255 (1972), pp. 1596–1604.

82. ANOM, SAS du Djebel Aïssa Mimoun 5.SAS.217. All reports are taken from this carton unless cited otherwise.

83. Reports from December 1957 and February 1958 are missing.

84. J. Soustelle was a trained ethnologist, a specialist in the Aztecs. He ran de Gaulle's secret services in London (the BCRA). He was appointed Governor General of Algeria in 1955 and held the post until 1966. As a deputy, he changed his position to oppose de Gaulle on Algeria's independence. He would become one of the political leaders of the OAS.

85. David Galula, *Counterinsurgency Warfare: Theory and Practice* (New York: Praeger, 1964; Paris: Economica, 2008), p. 132.

86. David Galula, *Pacification in Algeria 1956–1958* (Santa Monica: RAND Corporation, 1963; republished 2006), pp. 67–68.

87. Grégor Mathias, *Les sections administratives spécialisées en Algérie, entre idéal et réalité* (Paris: l'Harmattan, 1998), pp. 145–148.

88. David Galula, *Pacification in Algeria 1956–1958* (Santa Monica: RAND Corporation, 1963; republished 2006), p. 24.

89. Ibid., p. 107.

90. Claude Pfirrmann, interview with Grégor Mathias, February 4, 2009.

91. Moula Bouaziz et Alain Mahé, "La grande Kabylie durant la guerre d'indépendance d'Algérie" pp. 227–265 in Mohamed Harbi, *La guerre d'Algérie, 1954–2004 la fin de l'amnésie* (Paris: R. Laffont, 2004), p. 782. The OPA, before it was dismantled and downsized, was composed of a village headman, a council secretary, a second deputy in charge of supply, security, the watch, and liaison with the NLA. The OPA numbered five for each village, responsible for taxes, family allowances, justice, civil administration, health, and security and recruitment.

92. David Galula, *Pacification in Algeria 1956–1958* (Santa Monica: RAND Corporation, 1963; republished 2006), pp. 43–47, p. 51.

93. CHSP, GB 2 David Galula "Observations sur la pacification en Grande Kabylie," *Contacts* (April 1957), p. 11–19; David Galula, *Pacification in Algeria 1956–1958* (Santa Monica: RAND Corporation, 1963; republished 2006), supplemental report 2, pp. 258–269. Unlike the French version, the latter begins with an initial paragraph emphasizing Galula's experience with the Chinese and Greek insurrections. The villages are named. This study was written in November 1956.

94. David Galula, *Pacification in Algeria 1956–1958* (Santa Monica: RAND Corporation, 1963; republished 2006), p. 43.

95. David Galula, *Counterinsurgency Warfare: Theory and Practice* (New York: Praeger, 1964; Paris: Economica, 2008), p. 90.

96. ANOM. SAS de Aïssa Mimoun 5.SAS.217. Generally, the French army distributed shotguns to a dozen members of village self-defense groups.

CHAPTER 2

1. David Galula, *Pacification in Algeria 1956–1958* (Santa Monica: RAND Corporation, 1963; republished 2006), pp. 64–68.

2. Antoine Argoud, *La décadence, l'imposture et la tragédie* (Paris: Fayard, 1974), pp. 130–133.

3. David Galula, *Contre-insurrection* (New York: Praeger, 1964; Paris: Economica, 2008), pp. 119–120; David Galula, *Pacification in Algeria 1956–1958* (Santa Monica: RAND Corporation, 1963; republished 2006), pp. 69–70.

4. David Galula, *Counterinsurgency Warfare: Theory and Practice* (New York: Praeger, 1964; Paris: Economica, 2008), pp. 75–76.

5. Ibid., p. 120.

6. CHSP. GB.2. D. Galula, "Observations sur la pacification en Grande Kabylie," *Contacts* (April 1957), pp. 11–19

7. Camille Lacoste-Dujardin, *Opération Oiseau bleu* (Paris: La découverte, 1997), p. 23.

8. Moula Bouaziz and Alain Mahé, "La grande Kabylie durant la guerre d'indépendance d'Algérie," pp. 227–265 in Mohamed Harbi, *La guerre d'Algérie, 1954–2004 la fin de l'amnésie* (Paris: R. Laffont, 2004).

9. David Galula, *Pacification in Algeria 1956–1958* (Santa Monica: RAND Corporation, 1963; republished 2006), pp. 92–94.

10. Henri Burthey, "Chef de SAS de Tirmitine, Grande Kabylie, Tizi-Ouzou, 1956–1958," La revue *Les SAS, Bulletin historique des anciens des Affaires algériennes* n°30 (October 2008).

11. Camille Lacoste-Dujardin, *Opération Oiseau bleu* (Paris: La découverte, 1997), pp. 49–51, pp. 58–59, pp. 67–68, pp. 76–77, pp. 266–267.

12. David Galula, *Pacification in Algeria 1956–1958* (Santa Monica: RAND Corporation, 1963; republished 2006), p. 97.

13. David Galula, *Contre-insurrection* (New York: Praeger, 1964; Paris: Economica, 2008), p. 164.

14. Jean-Jacques Servan Schreiber, *Lieutenant en Algérie* (Paris: Julliard, 1957), p. 127.

15. David Galula, *Pacification in Algeria 1956–1958* (Santa Monica: RAND Corporation, 1963; republished 2006), p. 179.

16. Ibid., p. 83, p. 90.

17. Ibid., p. 90, p. 121, p. 124.

18. ANOM. SAS du Djebel Aïssa Mimoun 5.SAS.217.

19. David Galula, *Pacification in Algeria 1956–1958* (Santa Monica: RAND Corporation, 1963; republished 2006), p. 125; David Galula "Observations sur la pacification en Grande Kabylie," *Contacts* (April 1957).

20. ANOM. SAS du Djebel Aïssa Mimoun 5.SAS.217.

21. David Galula, *Pacification in Algeria 1956–1958* (Santa Monica: RAND Corporation, 1963; republished 2006), pp. 129–131.

22. CHSP. GB.2. David Galula "Observations sur la pacification en Grande Kabylie," *Contacts* (April 1957), pp. 11–19; David Galula, *Pacification in Algeria 1956–1958* (Santa Monica: RAND Corporation, 1963; republished 2006), appendix 2, pp. 258–269.

23. David Galula, *Pacification in Algeria 1956–1958* (Santa Monica: RAND Corporation, 1963; republished 2006), p. 127.

24. Marie-Catherine Villatoux, *La défense en surface (1945–1962)*, Cahiers d'histoire militaire appliquée, SHD, 2009, pp. 59–60.

25. David Galula, *Pacification in Algeria 1956–1958* (Santa Monica: RAND Corporation, 1963; republished 2006), p. 134, p. 172, pp. 188–193.

26. Gérard Chaliand, *Le nouvel art de la guerre* (Paris: l'Archipel, 2008), pp. 81–92.

27. David Galula, *Pacification in Algeria 1956–1958* (Santa Monica: RAND Corporation, 1963; republished 2006), appendix 3, p. 274 point n°9; David Galula, *Contre-insurrection* (New York: Praeger, 1964; Paris: Economica, 2008), pp. 144–148, the exact expression is not used by the strategy as described; CHSP. GB.1.C Dossier Algérie réactions et reprises dans la presse, ouvrages ultérieurs, correspondances: *Lettre d'informations politiques et économiques* n°574 (December 1957), "Monographie de la pacification," pp. 2–4, written by David Galula, whose name is never cited save under the moniker *Capitaine de Kabylie*. The expression is used twice.

28. Marie-Catherine Villatoux, *La défense en surface (1945–1962)*, Cahiers d'histoire militaire appliquée, SHD, 2009, pp. 38–39 in Jean Nemo "L'infanterie dans la guerre de surface," *Revue des forces terrestres*, n°3 (January 1956).

29. Jean Nemo, "La Guerre dans la foule, *Revue de Défense nationale* (June 1956), pp. 721–734.

30. David Galula, *Contre-insurrection* (New York: Praeger, 1964; Paris: Economica, 2008), pp. 171–176.

31. David Galula, *Pacification in Algeria 1956–1958* (Santa Monica: RAND Corporation, 1963; republished 2006), p. 69.

32. Ibid., p. 38.

33. Ibid., pp. 71–72, repeated on p. 132, p. 168.

34. Jean-Jacques Servan Schreiber *Lieutenant en Algérie* (Paris: Julliard, 1957).

35. Ibid., p. 129.

36. David Galula, *Pacification in Algeria 1956–1958* (Santa Monica: RAND Corporation, 1963; republished 2006), his company's operations at Rivet mentioned twice, p. 57, p. 71.

37. Jean-Jacques Servan Schreiber, 1957, about Captain Marcus p. 67 with a reproduction of Marcus's report, pp. 70–72.

38. Grégor Mathias, "Vie et destins des supplétifs d'Hammam Melouane," *Revue française d'histoire d'Outre-mer* n°328–329 (Spring 2000), pp. 241–265 analysis of counterinsurgency methods used by SAS officers, G. and E. Morin, as well as by

the army (Third RCA and 117th RI) south of Blida, based on the commitment of the population in auxiliary units (community defense, *harkis*, and *moghaznis*).

39. Antoine Argoud, "la guerre psychologique," *Revue de défense nationale* (March and April 1948).

40. Antoine Argoud, *La décadence, l'imposture et la tragédie* (Paris: Fayard, 1974), pp. 176–180 Argoud would criticize the Challe plan to eliminate ALN units while neglecting the importance of the population. Subsequently Argoud participated in the coup against de Gaulle and became a leader of the OAS, who engaged in terrorism in the name of French Algeria.

41. Ibid., pp. 130–133.

42. David Galula, *Contre-insurrection* (New York: Praeger, 1964; Paris: Economica, 2008), p. 18.

43. ANOM. SAS du Djebel Aïssa Mimoun 5.SAS.217.

44. CHSP, archives d'histoire contemporaine, Paris, fonds Gérard Bélorgey GB 1, réactions et reprises dans la presse *Lettre d'informations politiques et économiques*, n°578 (December 1957), "Monographie de la pacification."

45. ANOM. SAS de Aïssa Mimoun 5.SAS.217.

46. David Galula, *Pacification in Algeria 1956–1958* (Santa Monica: RAND Corporation, 1963; republished 2006), p. 164.

47. CHSP, archives d'histoire contemporaine, Paris, fonds Gérard Bélorgey GB 1, réactions et reprises dans la presse la *Lettre d'informations politiques et économiques* n°578 (December 1957), "Monographie de la pacification." The number given in December 1957 is 468 boys and 368 girls enrolled.

48. David Galula, *Pacification in Algeria 1956–1958* (Santa Monica: RAND Corporation, 1963; republished 2006), pp. 63–64.

49. Ibid., p. 100; David Galula, *Contre-insurrection* (New York: Praeger, 1964; Paris: Economica, 2008), strategy pp. 140–141, tactics pp. 173–174.

50. Germaine Tillion, *Il était une fois l'ethnographie* (Paris: Seuil, 2000), pp. 141–184 describes Berber measures of time in Aurès.

51. Grégor Mathias, *Les sections administratives spécialisées en Algérie* (Paris: L' Harmattan, 1998), pp. 43–47.

52. David Galula, *Pacification in Algeria 1956–1958* (Santa Monica: RAND Corporation, 1963; republished 2006), p. 99.

53. SHD 7.U.2791, JMO de la 3/45ème BIC census of Igonane Ameur on August 22, 1956 with number of houses and establishment of family records with the names of each occupant for each house.

54. David Galula, *Pacification in Algeria 1956–1958* (Santa Monica: RAND Corporation, 1963; republished 2006), p. 100; David Galula, *Contre-insurrection* (New York: Praeger, 1964; Paris: Economica, 2008), pp. 174–175.

55. David Galula, *Pacification in Algeria 1956–1958* (Santa Monica: RAND Corporation, 1963; republished 2006), pp. 101–102.

56. CHSP. GB.2. David Galula "Observations sur la pacification en Grande Kabylie" *Contacts* (April 1957), pp. 11–19; and in English, David Galula, *Pacification in Algeria 1956–1958* (Santa Monica: RAND Corporation, 1963; republished 2006), appendix 2, pp. 258–269.

57. David Galula, *Counterinsurgency Warfare: Theory and Practice* (New York: Praeger, 1964; Paris: Economica, 2008), pp. 86–87.

58. David Galula, *Pacification in Algeria 1956–1958* (Santa Monica: RAND Corporation, 1963; republished 2006), p. 97.

59. ANOM. SAS du Djebel Aïssa Mimoun 5.SAS.217.

60. David Galula, *Pacification in Algeria 1956–1958* (Santa Monica: RAND Corporation, 1963; republished 2006), p. 105.

61. SHD 7.U.2791, JMO de la 3/45ème BIC.

62. SAS intelligence reports were rarely archived. For the SAS at Djebel Aïssa Mimoun, only two remain even though gathering intelligence was a crucial mission for the SAS. Usually, the SAS sent them on a daily basis, sometimes sending up to six per day owing to their excellent intelligence gathering ability.

63. Moula Bouaziz and Alain Mahé, "La grande Kabylie durant la guerre d'indépendance d'Algérie," pp. 227–265 in Mohamed Harbi, *La guerre d'Algérie, 1954–2004 la fin de l'amnésie* (Paris: R. Laffont, 2004), p. 782. The destruction of schools and their boycott was part of FLN strategy in Kabylia in 1956. In 1959, the FLN changed strategy and encouraged school attendance, saying "the Algerian Republic will need educated people." FLN strategy at Djebel Aïssa Mimoun was atypical and represented the future strategy adopted in 1959.

64. David Galula, *Pacification in Algeria 1956–1958* (Santa Monica: RAND Corporation, 1963; republished 2006), p. 114.

65. ANOM. SAS du Djebel Aïssa Mimoun 5.SAS.217.

66. SHD 7.U.2791, JMO de la 3/45ème BIC.

67. David Galula, *Pacification in Algeria 1956–1958* (Santa Monica: RAND Corporation, 1963; republished 2006), pp. 115–117.

68. Ibid., pp. 129–130, p. 132.

69. ANOM. SAS du Djebel Aïssa Mimoun 5.SAS.217.

70. Jean Nemo, "La Guerre dans la foule," *Revue de Défense Nationale* (June 1956), pp. 721–734.

71. CHSP. GB.2. David Galula "Observations sur la pacification en Grande Kabylie," *Contacts* (April 1957), pp. 11–19.

72. Marie-Catherine Villatoux: Deux théoriciens de la guerre révolutionnaire, *Revue historique des Armées*, n°232 (2003).Thinking and methods of psychological warfare were distributed by the *Centre militaire de spécialisation et d'information sur l'Outre-mer* (CMISOM) led by Colonel Lacheroy beginning in 1955. Captain Hogard was the doctrinal psychological warfare editor in 1957. Colonel J. Nemo published his thoughts on revolutionary warfare in *Revue de Défense nationale*. Marie-Catherine and Paul Villatoux, "Le 5e Bureau en Algérie," p. 399–419 in Jean-Charles Jauffret, *Militaires et guérilla dans la guerre d'Algérie* (Paris: éditions Complexe, 2001). Colonel Fossey-François, former psychological warfare group chief in the Far East, headed the regional psychological warfare group that managed the CHPT. General Ely described their use in *Notice provisoire d'emploi*, June 26, 1956. The review *Contacts* was one of the outlets for officers to publish their counterguerilla tactics.

73. David Galula, *Pacification in Algeria 1956–1958* (Santa Monica: RAND Corporation, 1963; republished 2006), pp. 95–96.

74. Ibid., pp. 52–54, pp. 66–67. He describes the failure to establish the parallel hierarchy advocated by Colonel Lacheroy, in a sector of Orléansville by Colonel Goussault, head of civil-military affairs in Algiers, whom he had warned.

75. Marie-Catherine Villatoux, "Deux théoriciens de la guerre révolutionnaire," *Revue historique des Armées*, n°232 (2003).

76. David Galula, *Counterinsurgency Warfare: Theory and Practice* (New York: Praeger, 1964; Paris: Economica, 2008), p. 5.

77. Ibid., p. 126.

78. David Galula, *Pacification in Algeria 1956–1958* (Santa Monica: RAND Corporation, 1963; republished 2006), p. 106.

79. CHSP. GB.2. David Galula, "Observations sur la pacification en Grande Kabylie," *Contacts* (April 1957), p. 11–19; David Galula, *Pacification in Algeria 1956–1958* (Santa Monica: RAND Corporation, 1963; republished 2006), pp. 100–101; David Galula, *Contre-insurrection* (New York: Praeger, 1964; Paris: Economica, 2008), pp. 180–183.

80. David Galula, *Pacification in Algeria 1956–1958* (Santa Monica: RAND Corporation, 1963; republished 2006), pp. 163–164.

81. Ibid., p. 136.

82. SHD 7.U.2791, JMO de la 3/45ème BIC, February 2 and 3, 1957.

83. CHSP, archives d'histoire contemporaine, Paris, fonds Gérard Bélorgey GB 1, réactions et reprises dans la presse la *Lettre d'informations politiques et économiques* n°574 (December 1957), "Monographie de la pacification."

84. David Galula, *Contre-insurrection* (New York: Praeger, 1964; Paris: Economica, 2008), p. 187.

85. David Galula, *Pacification in Algeria 1956–1958* (Santa Monica: RAND Corporation, 1963; republished 2006), p. 145.

86. Ibid., pp. 90–91.

87. SHD 7.U.2791, JMO de la 3/45ème BIC.

88. David Galula, *Pacification in Algeria 1956–1958* (Santa Monica: RAND Corporation, 1963; republished 2006), pp. 123–124.

89. The reason for shadow *moghaznis* was to allow the SAS commander to add one to five auxiliaries to their organization. This was easy to do as most *moghaznis* were illiterate and signed their names with a cross. In the best cases, the money destined for auxiliaries went to fund off-budget projects in the form of purchase of materials, paying workers hired in excess, or the salaries of elected officials.

90. David Galula, *Pacification in Algeria 1956–1958* (Santa Monica: RAND Corporation, 1963; republished 2006), pp. 166–167.

91. Claude Pfirrmann, interview by Grégor Mathias, July 3, 2009. Pfirrmann, a former Native Affairs officer, was obliged to spend two years as an SAS officer in Algerian Affairs. His Foreign Legion unit had no billet for a captain, so he did a stint in a training company of the Third Spahis in Germany. He returned to Algeria, charged with reconstituting the Fourth squadron of First REC (*régiment étranger de cavalerie*) from 1959 to 1962. Pfirrmann wrote articles in the journal *Historia* about the 4/1st REC. He was then posted to the First Hussards in Tarbes from 1962 to 1965.

92. David Galula, *Pacification in Algeria 1956–1958* (Santa Monica: RAND Corporation, 1963; republished 2006), p. 157.

93. CHSP, archives d'histoire contemporaine, Paris, fonds Gérard Bélorgey GB 1, réactions et reprises dans la presse, la *Lettre d'informations politiques et économiques* n°577 (December 1957), "Monographie de la pacification."

94. David Galula, *Pacification in Algeria 1956–1958* (Santa Monica: RAND Corporation, 1963; republished 2006), pp. 134–135.

95. David Galula, *Contre-insurrection* (New York: Praeger, 1964; Paris: Economica, 2008), pp. 190–191.

96. David Galula, *Pacification in Algeria 1956–1958* (Santa Monica: RAND Corporation, 1963; republished 2006), p. 158.

97. Thomas Edward Lawrence, "Twenty-Seven Articles," *The Arab Bulletin* (August 20, 1917). Article 15 drawn from F.M. 3–24.2 *Tactics in Counterinsurgency*, Department of the Army; April 2009), appendix D, pp. 267–268. In 1926, Lawrence also wrote in *The Seven Pillars of Wisdom* rules for guerilla warfare and of their implementation in Arabia and Syria against the Turks.

98. David Galula, *Contre-insurrection* (New York: Praeger, 1964; Paris: Economica, 2008), p. 192.

99. David Galula, *Pacification in Algeria 1956–1958* (Santa Monica: RAND Corporation, 1963; republished 2006), pp. 159–163.

100. Ibid., p. 168.

101. Ibid., pp. 169–173.

102. CHSP, archives d'histoire contemporaine, Paris, fonds Gérard Bélorgey GB 1, réactions et reprises dans la presse la *Lettre d'informations politiques et économiques* n°578 (December 1957), "Monographie de la pacification"; David Galula, *Pacification in Algeria 1956–1958* (Santa Monica: RAND Corporation, 1963; republished 2006), pp. 172 173. Of six or seven rebels, two were killed and their leader was wounded and captured.

103. David Galula, *Contre-insurrection* (New York: Praeger, 1964; Paris: Economica, 2008), p. 194.

104. Yves Courrière, *La guerre d'Algérie 1957–1962, L'heure des colonels et les feux du désespoir,* Volume 2 (Paris: Fayard, 2001), p. 15.

105. *Contacts,* July 1958 republished in Raul Girardet's, *l'idée coloniale en France* (Paris: Pluriel, 1972), p. 358.

106. Raoul Girardet, *l'idée coloniale en France* (Paris: Pluriel, 1972), p. 358.

107. David Galula, *Contre-insurrection* (New York: Praeger, 1964; Paris: Economica, 2008), p. 101.

108. Paul Villatoux, "Le colonel Lacheroy, théoricien de l'action psychologique," pp. 494–508, in Jean-Charles Jauffret, *Des hommes et des femmes en guerre d'Algérie* (Paris: Autrement, 2003).

109. David Galula, *Pacification in Algeria 1956–1958* (Santa Monica: RAND Corporation, 1963; republished 2006), pp. 234–235.

110. Georgette Elgey, *Histoire de la IVe République, la fin—La République des Tourmentes* (Paris: Fayard, 2008), p. 796.

111. David Galula, *Pacification in Algeria 1956–1958* (Santa Monica: RAND Corporation, 1963; republished 2006), pp. 236–239.

112. ANOM, 5.SAS.201 ELA de Tizi-Ouzou.

113. David Galula, *Contre-insurrection* (New York: Praeger, 1964; Paris: Economica, 2008), pp. 196–197.

114. David Galula, *Pacification in Algeria 1956–1958* (Santa Monica: RAND Corporation, 1963; republished 2006), pp. 74–81.

115. Ibid., p. 103, pp. 196–199.

116. Ibid., pp. 125–127.

117. CHSP, archives d'histoire contemporaine, Paris, fonds Gérard Bélorgey GB 1, réactions et reprises dans la presse la *Lettre d'informations politiques et économiques* n°574 (December 1957), "Monographie de la pacification."

118. Antoine Argoud, *La décadence, l'imposture et la tragédie* (Paris: Fayard, 1974), pp. 128–129.

119. David Galula, *Pacification in Algeria 1956–1958* (Santa Monica: RAND Corporation, 1963; republished 2006), p. 133.

120. CHSP, archives d'histoire contemporaine, Paris, fonds Gérard Bélorgey GB 1, réactions et reprises dans la presse *Lettre d'informations politiques et économiques* n°574 (December 1957), "Monographie de la pacification."

121. Ibid., pp. 202–204.

CHAPTER 3

1. CHSP. GB.2. David Galula, "Observations sur la pacification en Grande Kabylie," *Contacts,* April 1957, p. 2, pp. 11–19.

2. David Galula, *Pacification in Algeria 1956–1958* (Santa Monica: RAND Corporation, 1963; republished 2006), p. 12.

3. Bertrand Valeyre and Alexandre Guerin, "De Galula à Petraeus, l'héritage français dans la pensée américaine de la contre-insurrection," *Cahier de la recherche doctrinale*, June 2009, p. 18 www.cdef.terre.defense.gouv.fr.

4. ANOM. SAS de Aïssa Mimoun 5.SAS.217.

5. David Galula, *Pacification in Algeria1956–1958* (Santa Monica: RAND Corporation, 1963; republished 2006) p. 5, p. 132.

6. Ibid., p. 153.

7. Ibid., pp. 146–147.

8. Georgette Elgey, *Histoire de la IVe République, la fin—La République des Tourmentes* (Paris: Fayard, 2008), p. 161, pp. 279–281.

9. David Galula, *Pacification in Algeria 1956–1958* (Santa Monica: RAND Corporation, 1963; republished 2006), pp. 153–154.

10. Ibid, unexpurgated report, appendix 2, pp. 257–270.

11. CHSP. GB.2. D. Galula, "Observations sur la pacification en Grande Kabylie," *Contacts*, April 1957, pp. 11–19.

12. David Galula, *Pacification in Algeria 1956–1958* (Santa Monica: RAND Corporation, 1963; republished 2006), note 1, p. 150.

13. Blog entry by Gérard Bélorgey, aperçus d'histoire et de société contemporaines, www.ecritures-et-societé-com/catégorie-10194107.html and centre-histoire. sciences-po.fr/archives/fonds/gerard.belorgey.html. G. Bélorgey was chief of staff for Jacques Chirac at the State Secretariat for Employment (1967–69), technical adviser to Prime Minister Messmer (1969–74), secretary general of the Hachette Group and general manager of Broussac St. Frères (1980–85), delegate to the Secretariat for Employment at the side of M. Belebarre and P. Seguin (1985–88), and CEO of RFO (1994–97). Consultant to the federation of overseas companies, he currently serves on the editorial board and is a contributor to the *Revue Politique et Parlementaire.*

14. CHSP. GB.1.C Dossier Algérie réactions et reprises dans la presse, ouvrages ultérieurs, correspondances. Letter to Minister of Overseas Departments, G. Defferre, November 7, 1957.

15. CHSP. GB.1.C Dossier Algérie, typescript. *Contents*: 1. Logique des faits 2. L'ennemi et les populations 3. Les cadres de la pacification 4. Missions de secteur 5. Missions opérationnelles 6. Problèmes et conséquences de la recherche du renseignement 7. Ni monstres, ni saints 8. La guerre sociologique 9. Paternalisme, propagande et police 10. Dépassionner, démystifier et décoloniser.

16. Ibid, GB.1.C Dossier Algérie réactions et reprises dans la presse, ouvrages ultérieurs, correspondances

17. CHSP. GB.1.C Dossier Algérie, typescript. S. Adour's insights on sociological warfare are found in chapter 8: "The welcome this article has received by the
officers' corps of the French army is proof of its resonance."

18. *Le Monde*, November 1, 1957, II La pacification en marche, S. Adour refers
to "an almost absolute power given to colonels, majors, and captains in the *sous-
secteurs, quartiers,* and *sous-quariers* in their charge," a pointed reference to Galula
and his *sous-secteur* in Kabylia.

19. *Le Monde*, October 31, 1957, I Conception et méthodes de pacification,
S. Adour explains that sociological warfare (a term derived from Galula's article)
leads to "an odd trilogy of propaganda, torture, and candy."

20. CHSP. GB.1.C Dossier Algérie réactions et reprises dans la presse, ouvrages
ultérieurs, correspondances.

21. Galula picks up the phrase again, *Pacification in Algeria 1956–1958* (Santa
Monica: RAND Corporation, 1963; republished 2006), in note 2, p. 154.

22. CHSP. GB.1.C Dossier Algérie réactions et reprises dans la presse, ouvrages
ultérieurs, correspondances. Letter from J. Lanoire, February 4, 1958. Extracted
from the parliamentary debate between P. Cot (Communist Party) and J. Soustelle
(Gaullist, former minister and governor general of Algeria) undated; letter from
S. Adour of November 16, 1957, to J. Soustelle; letter from J. Soustelle to S. Adour,
December 16, 1957.

23. Jean Charles Jauffret, *Ces officiers qui ont dit non à la torture, Algérie
1954–1962* (Paris: Autrement, 2005), p. 173.

24. CHSP, archives d'histoire contemporaine, Paris, fonds Gérard
Bélorgey GB 1, réactions et reprises dans la presse, Lettre d'informations
politiques et économiques n°578 (December 1957), "Monographie de la pacification."

25. David Galula, *Pacification in Algeria 1956–1958* (Santa Monica: RAND Corporation, 1963; republished 2006), pp. 118–119.

26. Ibid, p. 184.

27. Yves Courrière, *La guerre d'Algérie 1957–1962, L'heure des colonels et les feux
du désespoir* (Paris: Fayard, 2001), pp. 431–433; R. Branche, *La torture et l'armée pendant la guerre d'Algérie* (Paris: Gallimard, 2001), pp. 362–374; F. Géré, *La guerre psychologique* (Paris: Economica, 1997), pp. 229–230.

28. Philippe de Montenon, préface couronnement de David Galula, p. 21.
David Galula, *Contre-insurrection* (New York: Praeger, 1964; Paris: Economica,
2008).

29. David Galula, *Pacification in Algeria 1956–1958* (Santa Monica: RAND Corporation, 1963; republished 2006), p. 103. A tax collector from Tala Ou Abba was
in custody when he asked to go to the toilet and was then killed while attempting to escape. The gendarmerie opened an investigation (p. 121). November 1956,
Oudiaï was surrounded at his house near Bou Souar and killed while attempting
to escape.

30. Ibid, p. 186.

31. SHD 7.U.2791, unit history of the 3/45ème BIC.

32. Claude Pfirrmann, interview by Grégor Mathias, July 3, 2009.

33. ANOM. SAS de Aïssa Mimoun 5.SAS.217. Report to SAS commander Pfirrmann, who hasn't enough men to guard them. A platoon from Galula's company
at Grand Remblai is ordered to guard the prisoners.

CHAPTER 4

1. SHD, 1H1222 Monograph of SAS Lieutenant Meneault, SAS commander in November 1957.

2. David Galula, *Pacification in Algeria 1956–1958* (Santa Monica: RAND Corporation, 1963; republished 2006), p. 135 about Captain Herrmann (pseudonym).

3. Ibid., p. 175.

4. Ibid., p. 208.

5. CHSP, archives d'histoire contemporaine, Paris, fonds Gérard Bélorgey GB 1, réactions et reprises dans la presse la Lettre d'informations politiques et économiques n°577 (December 1957), "Monographie de la pacification."

6. David Galula, *Pacification in Algeria 1956–1958* (Santa Monica: RAND Corporation, 1963; republished 2006), p. 208.

7. A study of Galula's counterinsurgency operations at Tizi-Ouzou, without reference to the Bordj Menaïel, which is found in David Galula, *Pacification in Algeria 1956–1958* (Santa Monica: RAND Corporation, 1963; republished 2006), pp. 148–156, pp. 213–240. A battalion staff officer, Galula no longer had the freedom of action that he enjoyed as a *sous-quartier* captain.

CHAPTER 5

1. David Galula, *Pacification in Algeria 1956–1958* (Santa Monica: RAND Corporation, 1963; republished 2006), preface, p. 9.

2. Philippe de Montenon introduction "45 ans après, le couronnement de David Galula" to *Contre-insurrection, théorie et pratique,* by David Galula (New York: Praeger, 1964; Paris: Economica, 2008), p. 20.

3. Ann Marlowe, "Forgotten Founder: The French Colonel Who Wrote the Book(s) on Counterinsurgency," *Weekly Standard,* September 10, 2009.

4. Correspondence with A. Marlowe, November 2009.

5. Pierre Messmer, *Après tant de batailles* (Paris: Albin Michel, 1992), p. 269; Marie-Catherine Villatoux, *Guerre et action psychologiques en Algérie,* Cahier d'histoire militaire appliquée, SHD, 2008, p. 53.

6. SHD, DPG and 5.Q.25. Service d'information générale et d'action psychologique. Etudes et travaux sur la radiodiffusion en Algérie, au Moyen-Orient et en Afrique noire.

7. Maurice Faivre, *Le général Ely et la politique de Défense (1956–1961)* (Paris: Economica, 1998), p. 140.

8. David Galula, *Pacification in Algeria 1956–1958* (Santa Monica: RAND Corporation, 1963; republished 2006), p. 178.

9. Ibid., p. 153.

10. CHSP. GB.2. David Galula, "Observations sur la pacification en Grande Kabylie," *Contacts* (April 1957), pp. 11–19.

11. David Galula, *Contre-insurrection* (New York: Praeger, 1964; Paris: Economica, 2008), 2008, p. 141.

12. Ibid., pp. 162–163, pp. 169–171, pp. 180–182. Propaganda accompanies the first three stages of counterinsurgency.

13. David Petraeus and John Nagl, Foreword to *Contre-insurrection, théorie et pratique,* by David Galula (New York: Praeger, 1964; Paris: Economica, 2008), p. 11.

14. Marc Martin, "La radio dans les crises françaises liées à la guerre d'Algérie" pp. 17–26, in Michèle de Bussière, Cécile Meadel, Caroline Ulmann-Mauriat, *Radios et télévision au temps "des événements d'Algérie"* (Paris: L'Harmattan, 1999).

15. Ibid., pp. 17–26.

16. Fouad Benhalla, *La guerre radiophonique* (Paris: PUF, 1983), p. 139.

17. Jacques Parrot, *La guerre des ondes, de Goebbels à Kadhafi* (Paris: Plon, 1987), pp. 232–233.

18. Marc Michel, "Action psychologique et propagande au Cameroun à la fin des années 50," pp. 361–370 *La guerre d'Algérie au miroir des décolonisations françaises,* SFHOM, 2000.

19. SHD, 5.Q.25.

20. SHD, 5.Q.24. Service d'information générale et d'action psychologique. Courrier et éléments de documentation sur le développement de la radiodiffusion en Afrique du Nord (dossier n1) et en Algérie (dossier n2).

21. Maurice Faivre, *Le général Ely et la politique de Défense (1956–1961)* (Paris: Economica, 1998) reproduced from SHD documents, 1.K.233/49.

22. SHD, archive boxes of *Service d'information générale et d'action psychologique* 5 Q 24, 5 Q 25, 5 Q 26, 5 Q 27/2.

23. SHD, 5.Q.24.

24. SHD, 5.Q.24.

25. Fouad Benhalla, *La guerre radiophonique* (Paris: PUF, 1983), p. 113, p. 145.

26. SHD, 5.Q.24.

27. Fouad Benhalla, *La guerre radiophonique* (Paris: PUF, 1983), p. 141.

28. SHD, 5.Q.24.

29. Pierre Messmer, *Les blancs s'en vont* (Paris: Albin Michel, 1998), pp. 108–109, pp. 116–126, p. 142.

30. Marc Michel, "Action psychologique et propagande au Cameroun à la fin des années 50," pp. 361–370 in *La guerre d'Algérie au miroir des décolonisations françaises,* SFHOM, 2000.

31. SHD, 5.Q.24.

32. Fouad Benhalla, *La guerre radiophonique* (Paris: PUF, 1983), p. 191.

33. SHD, 5.Q.24.

34. Fouad Benhalla, *La guerre radiophonique* (Paris: PUF, 1983), p. 147.

35. Marc Michel, "Action psychologique et propagande au Cameroun à la fin des années 50," pp. 361–370 in *La guerre d'Algérie au miroir des décolonisations françaises,* SFHOM, 2000.

36. Pierre Messmer, *Les blancs s'en vont* (Paris: Albin Michel, 1998), pp. 92–93.

37. Maurice Faivre, *Le général Ely et la politique de Défense (1956–1961)* (Paris: Economica, 1998), pp. 101–105.

38. Antoine Sabbagh, "La propagande à Radio Alger," pp. 27–40 in Michèle de Bussière, Cécile Meadel, Caroline Ulmann-Mauriat, *Radios et télévision au temps "des événements d'Algérie"* (Paris: L'Harmattan, 1999).

39. SHD, ESS.

40. SHD, 5.Q.26. Service d'information générale et d'action psychologique. Report on worldwide French broadcasting and in Arabic- and Berber-speaking countries with respect to psychological operations.

41. SHD, 5.Q.24.

42. The radio surveillance group of Mont Valérien was responsible for detecting subversive emissions and implementing countermeasures (jamming).

43. SHD, 5.Q.25.
44. SHD, 5.Q.25.
45. Marie-Catherine and Paul Villatoux, "Le 5ᵉ Bureau en Algérie," pp. 309–419 in Jean-Charles Jauffret, *Militaires et guérilla pendant la guerre d'Algérie* (Paris: Complexe, 2001).
46. A similar comparison of Galula's career and that of another revolutionary warfare theorist has already been done. Grégor Mathias "David Galula et Jean Nemo, deux visions différentes des méthodes de contre-insurrection en Algérie?" pp. 231–242 in Antoine Champeaux, *Les maquis de l'histoire. Guerre révolutionnaire, guerres irrégulières* (Paris: Lavauzelle, 2010).
47. Information about Lacheroy comes from Paul Villatoux, "Le colonel Lacheroy, théoricien de l'action psychologique," pp. 494–507, in Jean-Charles Jauffret, *Des hommes et des femmes en guerre d'Algérie* (Paris: Autrement, 2003); Marie-Catherine and Paul Villatoux, *La guerre et l'action psychologique en France (1945–1962)*, thesis (Paris I, 2002), pp. 405–416, pp. 496–509, pp. 562–570.
48. SHD, 5.Q.25.
49. SHD, 5.Q.24.
50. Philippe Gaillard, *J. Foccart parle, entretiens avec Philippe Gaillard* (Paris: Fayard-Jeune Afrique, 1995), p. 51, p. 87, p. 100, pp. 110–111, p. 130, p. 155, pp. 180–181, p. 182.
51. Pierre Messmer, *Les blancs s'en vont* (Paris: Albin Michel, 1998), pp. 94–95, p. 219, pp. 247–248.
52. Fouad Benhalla, *La guerre radiophonique* (Paris: PUF, 1983), p. 145.
53. Cécile Meadel "1954–1962: Quels programmes pour la radio?" in Michèle de Bussière, Cécile Meadel, Caroline Ulmann-Mauriat, *Radios et télévision au temps des événements d'Algérie* (Paris: L'Harmattan, 1999).
54. David Galula, *Contre-insurrection* (New York: Praeger, 1964; Paris: Economica, 2008), p. 26.
55. Ibid., pp. 181–182.
56. Ann Marlowe, "Forgotten Founder: The French Colonel Who Wrote the Book(s) on Counterinsurgency," *Weekly Standard*, September 10, 2009.
57. Louis Bitterlin, *Nous étions tous des terroristes, histoire des barbouzes* (Paris: éd. Témoignage chrétien, 1983), pp. 240–241.
58. Rémy de Guilhermier, "Louis Terrenoire, un ministre dans la guerre d'Algérie," pp. 59–76, in Michèle de Bussière, Cécile Meadel, Caroline Ulmann-Mauriat, *Radios et télévision au temps "des événements d'Algérie"* (Paris: L'Harmattan, 1999).
59. Jacques Parrot, *La guerre des ondes, de Goebbels à Kadhafi* (Paris: Plon, 1987), pp. 231–232.
60. Paul Ely, *Mémoires, Suez . . . 13 mai* (Paris: Plon, 1969), p. 463.
61. Jean-Pierre le Goff, *Mai 68, l'héritage impossible* (Paris: La découverte, 2002), p. 70, p. 72.

CONCLUSION

1. David Galula, *Pacification in Algeria 1956–1958* (Santa Monica: RAND Corporation, 1963; republished 2006), Timizar Laghbar and Tala Atmane pp. 188–193, map p. 189.

2. SHD, ESS.

3. The most publicized case: J. Y. Alquier, *Nous avons pacifié Tazalt,* (Paris: R. Laffont, 1957). A reserve officer, platoon leader, and SAS commander, he followed a pragmatic policy with respect to the population and did not refer to any revolutionary warfare doctrine.

4. Grégor Mathias "La SAS de Catinat entre souvenirs d'un officier et écriture de l'histoire," pp. 555–572, *La guerre d'Algérie au miroir des décolonisations françaises,* SFHOM, 2000, p. 683.

5. CHSP GB.1.C Dossier Algérie réactions et reprises dans la presse, ouvrages ultérieurs, correspondances.

6. Grégor Mathias, Les sections administratives spécialisées en Algérie, 1998, p. 119.

7. David Galula, *Contre-insurrection: théorie et pratique* (New York: Praeger, 1964; republished Paris: Economica, 2008), pp. 159–160.

8. Ibid., p. 120.

9. Grégor Mathias, "Vie et destins des supplétifs d'Hammam Mclouanc," Revue française d'histoire d'Outre-mer, n°328–329, Fall 2000 pp. 241–265.

10. David Galula, *Pacification in Algeria 1956–1958* (Santa Monica: RAND Corporation, 1963; republished 2006), p. 247.

11. SHD, ESS.

12. David Galula, *Contre-insurrection* (New York: Praeger, 1964; republished Paris: Economica, 2008), p. 120.

13. SHD, CMISOM, doc. n°9663, J. Nemo "Réflexions sur la guerre subversive," December 30, 1958.

14. Antoine Argoud, *La décadence, l'imposture et la tragédie* (Paris: Fayard, 1974), pp. 119–158, pp. 179–181; Jean Pouget, Bataillon RAS, 1981; republished 1983; France loisirs, pp. 140–151, Alain Leger, *Aux carrefours de la guerre* (Paris: Presse de la cité, 1983).

15. François Géré, *La guerre psychologique,* 1997, p. 298 citing Major Prestat's 1960 article. Prestat became one of the leaders of *La Fondation pour les Etudes de Défense Nationale* and the journal *Stratégiques.*

16. David Galula *Pacification in Algeria 1956–1958* (Santa Monica: RAND Corporation, 1963; republished 2006), pp. 52–54, pp. 95–96 on G5 and CHTP operations, pp. 66–67 on parallel hierarchies, pp. 92–94 on rallying the population and arming civil defense militias Christophe Delabroye, *Approche de l'univers mental d'une génération d'officiers 1954–1962: la guerre d'Algérie—enquête orale sur 19 officiers français, Mémoire de maîtrise d'histoire,* dir. R. Ilbert, université Aix-Marseille I, 1989, pp. 52–53. SAS operations were the most successful revolutionary warfare initiatives of those undertaken by the Cinquième Bureau, according to witnesses interviewed by C. Delabroye, including Major Morin, commander of First REP, who later served on the staff of the 10th DP.

17. The U.S. military, concerned with the tactical implementation of counterinsurgency strategy, included procedures in FM 3.24.2, published April 2009, consisting of appendices C and D "Twenty-Eight Articles: Fundamentals of Company-Level Counterinsurgency" by Australian Lieutenant Colonel David Kilcullen (first published in *Military Review,* May–June 2006), Twenty-Seven Articles of T. E. Lawrence (*Arab Review,* August 1917). If Galula's "eight steps" do not appear in the appendices with these authors, his book is listed among five others recommended to officers charged with carrying out counterinsurgency (appendix B), in addition to R. Trinquier's book. Similar strategies, those of R. Thomson (Malaysia),

are summarized in chapter 3 in five points, those of Galula "based on his experience in Indochina [*sic*] and Algeria in four points, and Callwell (Boer War) in four.

18. Graham Green, *Un Américain bien tranquille* (Paris: R. Laffont, 1956); Eugène Burdick and William Lederer, *The ugly american Le vilain américain* (Paris: R. Laffont, 1961), p. 288.

19. Roger Trinquier, *La Guerre moderne* (Paris: La Table ronde, 1961).

20. David Galula, *Pacification in Algeria 1956–1958* (Santa Monica: RAND Corporation, 1963; republished 2006), p. 244.

21. David Galula, *Pacification in Algeria 1956–1958* (Santa Monica: RAND Corporation, 1963; republished 2006), p. 178.

22. SHD, ESS and Marie-Catherine Villatoux, *Guerre et action psychologiques en Algérie*, SHD, p. 53. The intelligence and psychological warfare services allegedly had the mission of intercepting and jamming radio transmissions from Arab and communist countries destined for Algeria, then use them for psyops on the armed forces, press, and Arab and Berber populations in Algeria.

23. Marie-Monique Robin, *Escadrons de la mort, l'école française* (Paris: La découverte, 2004) pp. 245–253.

24. SHD, ESS.

25. Tunisian Internet site, harissa.com/people search led by Freddy Galula on Galula's California relations and Ann Marlowe, "Forgotten Founder: The French Colonel Who Wrote the Book(s) on Counterinsurgency," *Weekly Standard*, October 19, 2009.

26. Stanley Karnow, *Vietnam* (Paris: Presse de la Cité, 1984), p. 146–148, p. 278.

27. Stephen T. Hosmer and Sibylle O. Crane, *Counterinsurgency: A Symposium, April 16–20, 1962* (Washington D.C., November 1962; republished 2006, RAND), p. 182.

28. Pierre Messmer, *Les Blancs s'en vont* (Paris: A. Michel, 2000), pp. 166–168. P. Messmer criticizes theorists of neglecting nationalism and Islam of the FLN, giving priority only to communist ideology and conspiracy abroad (Nasser's Egypt or the USSR) and to criticize government policy.

29. Frank E. Kitson, *Gangs and Counter-gangs* (London: Barrie and Rockliff, 1960). Kitson would subsequently put his counterinsurgency experience in service of the struggle against the IRA in Northern Ireland. E. Tenenbaum: De l'IRA à Irak, Transferts d'expérience contre-insurrectionnelle dans l'armée britannique, Thématiques du C2SD, n°18 (January 2009), p. 54. www.cdef.terre.defense.gouv.fr.

30. Charles Bohannan and Napoleon Valeriano, *Counterguerilla Operations, Lessons from the Philippines* (New York: Praeger, 1962).

31. Stephen T. Hosmer and Sibylle O. Crane, *Counterinsurgency: A Symposium, April 16–20, 1962* (Washington D.C., November 1962; republished 2006, RAND), preface to the new edition p. 4 echoing F. E. Kitson, *Bunch of Five* (London: Faber and Faber, 1977), pp. 200–201.

32. Ibid., p. 19, p. 81, p. 166.

33. Ibid, p. 108.

34. American website, Small Wars Journal, http://council.smallwarsjournal.com/showthread.php?p=58315.

35. Rémy Martinot-Leroy, *La contestation de la dissuasion dans la l'armée de Terre. L'atome et la guerre subversive dans les travaux de l'Ecole supérieure de Guerre 1962–1975,* thesis director J. Klein (Paris I, 2006) ; Gabriel Péries, *De l'action militaire à l'action politique: impulsion, codification et application de la guerre révolutionnaire au sein de l'armée française,* thesis director J. Lagroye (Paris I, 1995).

36. Ann Marlowe, "Forgotten Founder: The French Colonel Who Wrote the Book(s) on Counterinsurgency," *Weekly Standard*, October 19, 2009.

37. S. Hosmer wrote numerous books on the war in South Vietnam, aviation and bombardment, insurrection and counterinsurgency, the Kosovo War, and war in Iraq. He continues to work for RAND.

38. Roger Trinquier *Modern Warfare, a French View of Counterinsurgency* (Leavenworth: Combat Studies Institute, 1963).

39. Robert Thompson, *Defeating Communist Insurgency Experience from Malaya and Vietnam* (London: Chatto and Windus, 1966); S. Karnow, *Vietnam* (Paris: Presse de la Cité, 1984), pp. 147–149; R. Thompson criticized the hurried adoption of strategic hamlets. A deputy to the South Vietnamese colonel charged with strategic hamlets was a communist agent who had acted this way to alienate farmers and push them into the arms of the communists.

40. Stanley Karnow, *Vietnam* (Paris: Presse de la Cité, 1984), pp. 124–127, p. 214 on Lansdale's operations.

41. Ibid, p. 259, p. 263; General Westmoreland first attacked the Vietcong by conventional means: massive bombing of North Vietnam and a war of attrition, targeting Vietcong units in South Vietnam with search and destroy operations. Pacification was secondary.

42. Ann Marlowe, *David Galula: His Life and Intellectual Context*, SSI Monograph (août 2010), p. 15 citant Elie Tenenbaum, *L'influence française de la stratégie américaine de la contre-insurrection 1945–1972*, Master II de l'Institut d'études politiques de Paris, juin 2009, p. 157.

43. François Géré, *La guerre psychologique* (Paris: Economica, 1997), pp. 342–347; Maurice Prestat, "De la guerre psychologique à la guerre médiatique," pp. 25–85 in Gérard Chaliand, *La persuasion de masse, guerre psychologique et guerre médiatique* (Paris: R. Laffont, 1992).

44. Stanley Karnow, *Vietnam* (Paris: Presse de la Cité, 1984), pp. 372–373.

45. Ann Marlowe, *David Galula: His Life and Intellectual Context*, SSI Monograph (août 2010), p. 15 citant Elie Tenenbaum, *L'influence française de la stratégie américaine de la contre-insurrection 1945–1972*, Master II de l'Institut d'études politiques de Paris, juin 2009, p. 168–169.

46. American website, Small Wars Journal, http://council.smallwarsjournal.com/showthread.php?p=58315; Rufus Phillips, *Why Vietnam Matters*, Hardcover, 2008.

47. SHD, ESS.

48. A. Marlowe, "Forgotten Founder: The French Colonel Who Wrote the Book(s) on Counterinsurgency," *Weekly Standard*, October 19, 2009. According to Marlow, Galula had to leave Harvard in November 1963 due to the hostility of R. Bowie, head of the Department of International Affairs, toward Galula. Between 1964 and 1966, Galula worked for the French company Thomson in London which was then involved in the design of a new radar for NATO. He died at the American Hospital in Paris, May 11, 1967, aged 48 years. Between 1963 and 1967, Galula published three books. In 1963 Rand published *Pacification in Algeria*. In 1964, Praeger published *Counterinsurgency Warfare: Theory and Practice*. In 1965 Flammarion published Galula's novel, *Les Moustaches du Tigre*, under the pseudonym J. Caran. It would not be until 2008 that *Counterinsurgency Warfare* would be translated into French. *Pacification in Algeria* has yet to be translated to French.

Bibliography

WORKS BY DAVID GALULA

On the Chinese Civil War

Report reproduced in L.-M. Chassin, *La conquête de la Chine par Mao Tse-Tung*. Paris: Payot, 1952; republished Paris: Livre de poche, 1963, pp. 106–107.

Galula, D. "Subversion and Insurgency in Asia." *China and the Peace of Asia* edited by A. Buchan, pp. 175–184. New-York: Praeger, Studies in International Security, n°9, 1965.

On Hong Kong

Caran, J. (alias D. Galula). *Les moustaches du tigre.* Paris: Flammarion, 1965 (roman).

On Alger1ia

Galula, D. *Pacification in Algeria 1956–1958.* Washington, D.C.: RAND Corporation, 1963; republished 2006.

Galula, D. "Observations sur la pacification en Grande Kabylie." *Contacts*, April 1957, pp. 11–19.

"Monographie de la pacification." *Lettre d'informations politiques et économiques* n°574 to n°578. November–December 1957.

On Counterinsurgency

Galula, D. *Contre-insurrection: théorie et pratique.* New York: Praeger, 1964; republished Paris: Economica, 2008.

Hosmer, S.T., and S.O. Crane. *Counterinsurgency: A Symposium, April 16–20, 1962,* November 1962, Washington, D.C.; republished RAND, 2006.

ARCHIVAL SOURCES ON GALULA

Service Historique de la Défense (SHD) de Vincennes

1.H.1222 Monographie de la SAS du Djebel Aïssa Mimoun.
7.U.2791, JMO de la 3/45ème BIC. ESS: état signalétique des services (D. Galula's military personnel file)
5.Q.24 Service d'information générale et d'action psychologique. Courrier et éléments de documentation sur le développement de la radiodiffusion en Afrique du Nord (dossier n°1) et en Algérie (dossier n°2).
5.Q.25 Service d'information générale et d'action psychologique. Etudes et travaux sur la radiodiffusion en Algérie, au Moyen-Orient et en Afrique noire.
5.Q.26 Service d'information générale et d'action psychologique. Rapport sur la situation de la radiodiffusion française dans le monde et surtout dans les pays de langue arabe et berbère en vue de l'action psychologique.

ANOM: Archives nationales d'Outre-mer d'Aix-en-Provence, Center for Overseas Archives

5.SAS.217. Rapports de la SAS de Djebel Aïssa Mimoun.
5.SAS.201. ELA de Tizi-Ouzou.

Centre d'histoire de Sciences Politiques (CHSP), Archives d'histoire Contemporaine, Paris

Bélorgey, G. Fonds. GB.1.C Dossier *Algérie réactions et reprises dans la presse, ouvrages ultérieurs, correspondances*, typescript of S. Adour to *Le Monde, Lettre d'informations politiques et économiques* n°574, December 1957, "Monographie de la pacification."
Bélorgey, G. Fonds. GB 2 D. Galula "Observations sur la pacification en Grande Kabylie." *Contacts*, April 1957, pp. 11–19.

ARTICLES AND WORKS REFERRING TO GALULA

Adour, S. (alias G. Bélorgey). "En Algérie : de l'utopie au totalitarisme," *Le Monde* from October 31, 1957 to November 6, 1957, pp. 3–4.
Chassin, L.-M. *La conquête de la Chine par Mao Tsé-Tung*. Paris: Payot, 1952; republished Paris: Livre de poche, 1963.
Guillermaz, J. *Une vie pour la Chine, mémoires 1937–1989*. Paris: R. Laffont, 1989.
"Un sous-lieutenant témoigne." *L'Humanité*. November 5, 1957, p. 3.
Topping, S. *The Peking letter, a Novel of the Chinese Civil War*. New York: Public Affairs, 1999.

RECENT ARTICLES ON GALULA

Marlowe, A. '"Forgotten Founder: The French Colonel Who Wrote the Book(s) on Counterinsurgency." *Weekly Standard*, October 19, 2009. http://www.

theweklystandard.com:Utilities/printer_preview.asp?idArtcile=17054&
    R=1638335DEB.
Mathias, G. "David Galula et Jean Nemo, deux visions différentes des méthodes
    de contre-insurrection en Algérie?" *Les maquis de l'histoire, guerre révolution-
    naire, guerres irrégulières. Mélanges offerts au lieutenant-colonel Michel David.*
    Paris: Lavauzelle, 2010.
Tenenbaum, E. *L'influence française sur la stratégie américaine de la contre-insurrection
    1945–1972,* Master II, IEP Paris, juin 2009.
Tenenbaum, E. "Pour une généalogie atlantique de la contre-insurrection." In
    Faut-il brûler la contre-insurrection?, edited by G.-H. Bricet des Vallons,
    pp. 23–62. Paris: Choiseul, 2010.
Valeyre, B. and A. Guerin. "De Galula à Petraeus, l'héritage français dans la pen-
    sée américaine de la contre-insurrection." *Cahier de la recherche doctrinale*
    (June 2009), 70 p., www.cdef.terre.defense.gouv.fr.

ON WORLD WAR II

Groussard, Georges A. *Service secret 1940–1945.* Paris: Table ronde, 1964.
de Lattre, J., *Histoire de la 1ère armée française.* Paris: Plon, 1949.
Notin, J.-C. *Les vaincus seront les vainqueurs. La France en Allemagne 1945.* Paris:
    Perrin, 2004.
Paillole, P. *Services spéciaux 1939–1945.* Paris: R. Laffont, 1975.
Paxton, R. O. *L'armée de Vichy, le corps des officiers français 1940–1944.* Paris:
    Tallandier, 2003.
Riedel, H. *Ausweg los . . . ! Letzer Akt des Krieg im Schwartzwald Ende April 1945.*
    Villingen-Schwenningen: A. Wetzel KG, 1976.
Serger, B., K.-A. Bottcher, and G. Ueberschar *Südbaden unter hakenkreuz und Triko-
    lore.* Freiburg: Rombach verlag, 2006.

ON THE CHINESE CIVIL WAR

Griffith, S. B. *On Guerrilla Warfare.* New York: Praeger 1961.
Griffith, S. B. *Sun Tzu, The Art of War.* Oxford: Clarendon Press, 1963; *Sun Tzu, l'art
    de la guerre.* Paris: Flammarion, 1995.
Griffith, S. B. *Peking and People's Wars.* New York: Praeger, 1966.
Guillermaz, J. *Histoire du parti communiste chinois.* Paris: Payot, 1968.
Guillermaz, J. *Le parti communiste au pouvoir.* Paris: Payot, 1972.
Mao Tse Tung. *La stratégie de la guerre révolutionnaire en Chine.* Paris: éd. sociales, 1950.
Mao Tse Tung. *La guerre révolutionnaire.* Paris: éd. sociales, 1955.
Stilwell, J. W. *L'aventure chinoise (1941–1944).* Paris: éd. de la Baconnère, 1949.
Stilwell, J. W. *The Stilwell Papers.* New York: éd. White, 1948.

ON THE GREEK CIVIL WAR

Dalegre, J. *La Grèce depuis 1940.* Paris: L'Harmattan, 2006.

ON THE INDOCHINA WAR

Dalloz, J. *Dictionnaire de la guerre d'Indochine 1945–1954.* Paris: A. Colin, 2006.
Dalloz, J. *La guerre d'Indochine.* Paris: Seuil, 1986.

David, M. *Les maquis autochtones face au Viêt-minh 1950–1955.* thesis director
D. Domergue-Clorec, université de Montpellier III, 2001.

Grintchentko, M. *Atlante-Aréthuse, une opération de pacification en Indochine.* Paris:
Economica, 2001.

ON THE WAR IN ALGERIA

Bouaziz, M., and A. Mahe. "La grande Kabylie durant la guerre d'indépendance
d'Algérie." In *La guerre d'Algérie, 1954–2004 la fin de l'amnésie,* edited by
M. Harbi, pp. 227–265. Paris: R. Laffont, 2004.

Branche, R. *La torture et l'armée pendant la guerre d'Algérie.* Paris: Gallimard, 2001.

Branche, R. *L'embuscade de Palestro.* Paris: A. Colin, 2010.

Courriere, Y. *La guerre d'Algérie 1957–1962, L'heure des colonels et les feux du désespoir.*
Paris: Fayard, 2001.

Elgey, G. *Histoire de la IVe République, la fin—La République des Tourmentes.* Paris:
Fayard, 2008.

Girardet, R. *l'idée coloniale en France.* Paris: Pluriel, 1972.

Jauffret, J.C. *Ces officiers qui ont dit non à la torture, Algérie 1954–1962.* Paris: Autrement, 2005.

Messmer, P. *Les Blancs s'en vont.* Paris: Albin Michel, 2000.

Planchais, J. "Du technique à la politique: à la rubrique 'défense' du journal
Le Monde (1945–1965)." *Militaires en République 1870–1962—Les officiers,
le pouvoir et la vie politique en France,* edited by O. Forcade, E. Duhamel, and
P. Vial, pp. 529–545. Paris: Publications de la Sorbonne, 1999.

Thenault, S. *Une drôle de justice. Les magistrats pendant la guerre d'Algérie.* Paris:
La découverte, 2001.

Tillion, G. *Il était une fois l'ethnographie.* Paris: Seuil, 2000.

OTHER WORKS ON COUNTERINSURGENCY
OR PSYCHOLOGICAL WARFARE DURING
THE ALGERIAN WAR

Alquier, J. Y. *Nous avons pacifié Tazalt.* Paris: R. Laffont, 1957.

Argoud, A. *La décadence, l'imposture et la tragédie.* Paris: Fayard, 1974.

Burthey, H. "Chef de SAS de Tirmitine, Grande Kabylie, Tizi-Ouzou, 1956–1958."
Les SAS, Bulletin historique des anciens des Affaires algériennes, n°30, October 2008, p. 6.

Delabroye, C. *Approche de l'univers mental d'une génération d'officiers 1954–1962:
la guerre d'Algérie—enquête orale sur 19 officiers français.* Mémoire de maîtrise
d'histoire, dir. R. Ilbert, université Aix-Marseille I, 1989.

Géré, F. *La guerre psychologique.* Paris: Economica, 1997.

Kayanakis, N. *Algérie 1960: la victoire trahie, guerre psychologique en Algérie.* Fried-
berg: Editions Atlantis, 2000.

Lacoste-Dujardin, C. *Opération Oiseau bleu.* Paris: La découverte, 1997.

Léger, A. *Aux carrefours de la guerre.* Paris: Presse de la cité, 1983.

Martinot-Leroy, R. *La contestation de la dissuasion dans la l'armée de Terre. L'atome et
la guerre subversive dans les travaux de l'Ecole supérieure de Guerre 1962–1975.*
thesis director J. Klein, Paris I, 2006.

Mathias, G. *Les sections administratives spécialisées en Algérie, entre idéal et réalité.* Paris: l'Harmattan, 1998.

Mathias, G. "La SAS de Catinat entre souvenirs d'un officier et écriture de l'histoire." In *La guerre d'Algérie au miroir des décolonisations françaises,* pp. 555–572. Paris: SFHOM, 2000.

Mathias, G. "Vie et destins des supplétifs d'Hammam Melouane." *Revue française d'histoire d'Outre-mer,* n°328–329, Spring 2000, pp. 241–265.

Nemo, J. "L'infanterie dans la guerre de surface." *Revue des forces terrestres,* n 3, January 1956, pp. 65–89.

Nemo, J. "La guerre dans la foule." *Revue de Défense Nationale,* June 1956, pp. 721–734.

Nemo, J. "Réflexions sur la guerre subversive." CMISOM Conference. SHD archives, doc. n 9663, December 30, 1958.

Peries, G. *De l'action militaire à l'action politique: impulsion, codification et application de "la guerre révolutionnaire" au sein de l'armée française.* Thesis director J. Lagroye, Paris I, 1995.

Pouget, J. *Bataillon RAS.* 1981; republished Paris: France loisirs, 1983.

Prestat, M. "De la guerre psychologique à la guerre médiatique." In *La persuasion de masse, guerre psychologique et guerre médiatique,* edited by G. Chaliand, pp. 25–85. Paris: R. Laffont, 1992.

Servan Schreiber, J. *Lieutenant en Algérie.* Paris: Julliard, 1957.

Trinquier, R. *La Guerre moderne.* Paris: Table ronde, 1961; republished Paris: Economica, 2007.

Trinquier, R. *Guerre, subversion, révolution.* Paris: R. Laffont, 1968.

Villatoux, M.C. "Deux théoriciens de la guerre révolutionnaire (J. Hogard et J. Nemo)." *Revue historique des Armées,* n°232 (2003): pp. 8–11.

Villatoux, M.C. *Guerre et action psychologiques en Algérie,* Cahiers d'histoire militaire appliquée, SHD, 2008.

Villatoux, M.C. *La défense en surface (1945–1962).* Cahiers d'histoire militaire appliquée, SHD, 2009.

ON BROADCAST WARFARE

Benhalla, F. *La guerre radiophonique.* Paris: PUF, 1983.

Bitterlin, L. *Nous étions tous des terroristes, histoire des barbouzes.* Paris: éd. Témoignage chrétien, 1983.

Bussière, M., C. Méadel, and C. Ulmann-Mauriat. *Radios et télévision au temps "des événements d'Algérie.* Paris: L'Harmattan, 1999.

Ely, P. *Mémoires, Suez . . . 13 mai.* Paris: Plon, 1969.

Faivre, M. *Le général Ely et la politique de Défense (1956–1961).* Paris: Economica, 1998.

le Goff, J.-P. *Mai 68, l'héritage impossible.* Paris: La découverte, 2002.

Gaillard, P. *J. Foccart parle, entretiens avec P. Gaillard.* Paris: Fayard-Jeune Afrique, 1995.

Jauffret, J.-C. *Ces officiers qui ont dit non à la torture, Algérie 1954–1962.* Paris: Autrement, 2005.

Messmer, P. *Après tant de batailles.* Paris: A. Michel, 1992.

Messmer, P. *Les blancs s'en vont.* Paris: A. Michel, 1998.

Michel, M. "Action psychologique et propagande au Cameroun à la fin des an-
    nées 50." In *La guerre d'Algérie au miroir des décolonisations françaises*, edited
    by C.-R. Ageron, pp. 361–370. Paris: SFHOM, 2000.
Parrot, J. *La guerre des ondes, de Goebbels à Kadhafi*. Paris: Plon, 1987.
Villatoux, P. "Le colonel Lacheroy, théoricien de l'action psychologique." In *Des
    hommes et des femmes en guerre d'Algérie*, edited by J.C. Jauffret, pp. 494–508.
    Paris: Autrement, 2003.
Villatoux, M.C., and P. Villatoux. "Le 5e Bureau en Algérie." In *Militaires et guérilla
    dans la guerre d'Algérie*, edited by J.-C. Jauffret, pp. 399–419. Paris: éditions
    Complexe, 2001.

ON THE VIETNAM WAR

Burdick, E., and W. Lederer. *The Ugly American*. Paris: R. Laffont, 1961.
Goya, M. "La guerre vraiment au milieu des populations, l'expérience du Com-
    bined action program au Sud Vietnam." In *Les maquis de l'histoire, guerre
    révolutionnaire, guerres irrégulières Mélanges offerts au lieutenant-colonel
    Michel David*, edited by A. Champeaux, pp. 251–258. Panazol: Lavauzelle,
    2010.
Green, G. *The Quiet American*. Paris: R. Laffont, 1956.
Karnow, S. *Vietnam*. Paris: Presse de la Cité, 1984.
Thompson, R. *Defeating Communist Insurgency Experience from Malaya and Vietnam*.
    London: Chatto and Windus, 1966.

ON COUNTRIES WHERE COUNTERINSURGENCY WAS IMPLIMENTED

Bohannan, R., and N. Valeriano. *Counterguerilla Operations, Lessons from the Philip-
    pines*. New York: Praeger, 1962.
Courcelle-Labrousse, V., and N. Marmie. *La guerre du Rif (Maroc 1921–1926)*. Paris:
    Tallandier, 2008.
Kitson, F. E. *Gangs and Counter-gangs*. London: Barrie and Rockliff, 1960.
Kitson, F. E. *Bunch of Five*. London: Faber and Faber, 1977.
Lawrence, T. E. *Seven Pillars of Wisdom*, Paris: Payot, 1992.
Robin, M.-M., *Escadrons de la mort, l'école française*. Paris: La découverte, 2004.
Tenenbaum, E. "De l'IRA à Irak, Transferts d'expérience contre-insurrectionnelle
    dans l'armée britannique." *Thématiques du C2SD*, n 18, January 2009, 54 p.
    www.cdef.terre.defense.gouv.fr; www.cdef.terre.defense.gouv.fr.

COUNTERINSURGENCY THEORY

Beaufre, A. *La guerre révolutionnaire, les formes nouvelles de la guerre*. Paris: Fayard,
    1972.
Bricet des Vallons, G.-H. *Faut-il brûler la contre-insurrection ?* Paris: Choiseul,
    2010.
Chaliand, G. *Le nouvel art de la guerre*. Paris: l'Archipel, 2008.
Desportes, V. *La guerre probable*. Paris: Economica, 2008.
F.M. 3–24.2 *Tactics in Counterinsurgency*, U.S. Army, April 2009.

Gentile, G.P. "Les mythes de la contre-insurrection et leurs dangers: une vision critique de l'US Army." *Sécurité globale,* revue de la Fondation de la Recherche Stratégique et de l'Institut Choiseul (Winter 2009–2010): pp. 21–34.

Goya, M. *Irak, les armes du chaos.* Paris: Economica, 2008.

Goya, M. "Impressions de Kaboul." Lettre de l'Institut de recherche supérieur de l'Ecole militaire (IRSEM), Ministère de la Défense, November 12, 2009.

Goya, M. "L'expérience militaire britannique dans la province afghane du Helmand (2006–2009)." *Sécurité globale,* revue de la Fondation de la Recherche Stratégique et de l'Institut Choiseul (Winter 2009–2010): pp. 55–64.

Haeri, P., and L. Fromaget. "Stabiliser autrement, les PRT en Afghanistan." *Focus stratégique* n°4, IFRI (January 2004): 37 p.

Olsson, C. "Guerre totale et/ou force minimale? Histoire et paradoxes des cœurs et des esprits." *Cultures et conflits,* n°67(Autumn 2007): pp. 35–62.

Olsson, C. "Contre-insurrection et 'responsabilité de protéger': panacée ou supercherie?" *Sécurité globale,* revue de la Fondation de la Recherche Stratégique et de l'Institut Choiseul (Winter 2009–2010): pp. 65–74.

Potier, E. "Imaginaire du contrôle des foules dans l'armée de terre française." *Cultures et conflits,* n°56 (Winter 2004): pp. 35–49.

Schmitt, C. *La notion de politique. Théorie du partisan.* Paris: Flammarion, Champs classique, 2009.

Smith, R. *Utility of Force, the Art of War in the Modern World.* London: Alan Lane, 2005; republished as *Utilité de la force.* Paris: Economica, 2007.

Ucko, D.H. "Les dilemmes de la doctrine de contre-insurrection américaine: répétition, pertinence et effet." *Sécurité globale,* revue de la Fondation de la Recherche Stratégique et de l'Institut Choiseul (Winter 2009–2010): pp. 55–64.

Index

Abdesselam, Robert, 51
Afghanistan, 103
Algerian War, 82, 84
Alsop, Joseph, 9
Arab Voice (Cairo), 77, 88
Arendt, Hannah, 57
Argoud, Antoine: on absence of counterinsurgency doctrine in Algeria, 18; memoirs of, 26
Assign and install sufficient troops (step 2), 21–24, 92–93; concentration of manpower, 21; controlling population, 22; ink-spot strategy, 23, 92, 98; special operations troops, 23
Audiovisual technology, 71

Banditry, itinerant, 7
Battle of the airwaves (1958–1962), 70–91; Arab Voice (Cairo), 77, 88; audiovisual technology, 71; BBC, 72; Broadcast Radio Steering Committee, 71, 76–77, 78; broadcast warfare, 73; censorship and freedom of information, 91; control of information and public opinion, 71; counterpropaganda, 73–74, 79; Dakar memo (Galula), 81; French interests worldwide, 77–78; Galula's contribution, 76–82; information warfare, 91; infrastructure (radio equipment), 74–75, 80, 88; jamming, 73, 74, 75, 77, 78, 79, 80, 81–82, 88; mimeograph (antecedent of photocopier), 71; Muslims, 72, 77, 79, 89; Operation SOPHIE, 78; pacification techniques, 71; propaganda objectives, 71, 88, 89, 90; propaganda of hostile states, 73; Radio Algiers, 72, 90; radio as "newspaper of the illiterate," 73; Radio Brazzaville, 72; Radio Conakry, 81; Radio France, 74; Radio Free Europe, 73, 74, 79; Radio Mali, 81; Radio Maroc (Voice of the Sahara), 81; Radio Moscow, 73–74, 80; radio on the African continent, 72–75, 79–80; Radio Tangier, 74; transistor radios, 72–73; Voice of America, 74, 80; Voice of France, 80. See also Division of Information (psychological warfare group)

About the Author

GRÉGOR MATHIAS works for the *Service Historique de la Defense* as a researcher specializing in the Algerian War and a professor of history and geography at the College Foch a Haguenau, Bas-Rhin, France. He taught International Relations at the ENSOA (*Ecole nationale des sous-officiers d'active*) and he was a lecturer at the St. Cyr military academy treating the role of the French army in the Algerian War. He is author of the *Sections Administratives Spécialisées en Algerie, Entre Ideal et Réalité 1955–62*, the definitive study of the SAS, the French military-civilian pacification program during the Algerian War published by L'Harmattan. As a researcher Mathias has collected extensive oral histories of *harkis*, the Muslim Algerians who served as irregular local auxiliaries of the French Army during the Algerian War. Recently, he has been studying little-known aspects of the Algerian War, publishing the first study on the blood donations forced upon Europeans by the FLN uncovered while researching his book on Galula's pacification operations. He is currently a doctoral candidate at the University of Toulouse le Mirail, where he works on pacification policy carried out by the SAS in Algeria.